# Women and Feminism
# in American History

## AMERICAN GOVERNMENT AND HISTORY INFORMATION GUIDE SERIES

Series Editor: Harold Shill, Chief Circulation Librarian, Adjunct Assistant Professor of Political Science, West Virginia University, Morgantown

*Also in this series:*

AMERICAN EDUCATIONAL HISTORY—*Edited by Michael W. Sedlak and Timothy Walch*

AMERICA'S MILITARY PAST—*Edited by Jack C. Lane*

IMMIGRATION AND ETHNICITY—*Edited by John D. Buenker and Nicholas C. Burckel*

PROGRESSIVE REFORM—*Edited by John D. Buenker and Nicholas C. Burckel*

PUBLIC ADMINISTRATION IN AMERICAN SOCIETY—*Edited by John E. Rouse, Jr.*

PUBLIC POLICY—*Edited by William J. Murin, Gerald Michael Greenfield, and John D. Buenker*

SOCIAL HISTORY OF THE UNITED STATES—*Edited by Donald F. Tingley*

U.S. CONSTITUTION—*Edited by Earlean McCarrick*

U.S. CULTURAL HISTORY—*Edited by Philip I. Mitterling*

U.S. FOREIGN RELATIONS—*Edited by Elmer Plischke*

U.S. POLITICS AND ELECTIONS—*Edited by David J. Maurer*

URBAN HISTORY—*Edited by John D. Buenker, Gerald Michael Greenfield, and William J. Murin*

---

The above series is part of the
## GALE INFORMATION GUIDE LIBRARY

The Library consists of a number of separate series of guides covering major areas in the social sciences, humanities, and current affairs.

General Editor: Paul Wasserman, Professor and former Dean, School of Library and Information Services, University of Maryland

Managing Editor: Denise Allard Adzigian, Gale Research Company

# Women and Feminism in American History

## A GUIDE TO INFORMATION SOURCES

*Volume 12 in the American Government and History Information Guide Series*

### Elizabeth Tingley

*Child Care Center*
*Harvard University Law School*
*Cambridge*

### Donald F. Tingley

*Professor of History*
*Eastern Illinois University*
*Charleston*

*Gale Research Company*
*Book Tower, Detroit, Michigan 48226*

**Library of Congress Cataloging in Publication Data**

Tingley, Elizabeth.
　　Women and feminism in American history.

　　(American Government and history information guide
series ; v. 12) (Gale information guide library)
　　Includes indexes.
　　1. Women—United States—History—Bibliography.
2. Feminism—United States—History—Bibliography.
I. Tingley, Donald Fred, 1922-　joint author.
II. Title. III. Series.
Z7964.U49T52　[HQ1410]　016.3054'0973　80-19793
ISBN 0-8103-1477-0

# VITAE

Elizabeth Tingley is a teacher in the Child Care Center of the Harvard University Law School in Cambridge, Massachusetts. She holds the B.A. in English from Oberlin College and the M.S. degree in the program in infant and parent development from Bank Street College of Education in New York. She has been active in the feminist movement.

Donald F. Tingley is professor of history at Eastern Illinois University in Charleston, Illinois. He received his B.S. from Eastern Illinois University and his M.A. and Ph.D. in history from the University of Illinois.

Donald Tingley is the editor and coauthor of ESSAYS IN ILLINOIS HISTORY IN HONOR OF GLENN HURON SEYMOUR (Southern Illinois University Press, 1968), THE EMERGING UNIVERSITY: A HISTORY OF EASTERN ILLINOIS UNIVERSITY (Eastern Illinois University, 1974), SOCIAL HISTORY OF THE UNITED STATES: A GUIDE TO INFORMATION SOURCES (Gale Research Co., 1979), and THE STRUCTURING OF A STATE: THE HISTORY OF ILLINOIS, 1899-1928 (University of Illinois Press, 1980). He has published a number of articles and reviews in scholarly journals.

# CONTENTS

Preface .......................................... ix

Chapter 1.  Bibliographies ............................. 1
Chapter 2.  Manuscript Collections...................... 13
Chapter 3.  Biographical Directories ..................... 19
Chapter 4.  Periodicals of the Women's Movement............. 23
Chapter 5.  General Works ............................ 29
Chapter 6.  Women in the Colonial and Revolutionary Eras ........ 39
Chapter 7.  Strong-Minded Women:  The Romantic Age, 1800-1860 .. 49
Chapter 8.  The Woman Question:  Women in the Victorian Era .... 61
Chapter 9.  Women Achieve the Right to Vote:  The Progressive
            Era...................................... 77
Chapter 10. From the 19th Amendment to 1963 ................ 89
Chapter 11. 1963 to Present............................ 97
Chapter 12. Contemporary Feminist Thought and Analysis ......... 101
Chapter 13. Contemporary Socialist Feminism .................. 107
Chapter 14. Women, Law, and Politics ..................... 111
Chapter 15. Women in Science and Medicine .................. 119
Chapter 16. Women and the Arts ......................... 125
Chapter 17. Women in the Performing Arts .................... 137
Chapter 18. Women in Sports ............................ 145
Chapter 19. Women and Education ........................ 149
Chapter 20. Women in Business and the Professions ............. 155
Chapter 21. Women in the Labor Force ..................... 161
Chapter 22. Ethnic and Minority Women .................... 167
Chapter 23. Women and Crime ........................... 177
Chapter 24. Violence against Women ...................... 181
Chapter 25. Prostitution ............................... 185
Chapter 26. The Psychology of Women ..................... 189
Chapter 27. Sexuality and Sexual Orientation ................. 195
Chapter 28. Abortion, Birth Control, and Related Health Issues ..... 203
Chapter 29. Married and Unmarried Women .................. 213
Chapter 30. Motherhood ............................... 221
Chapter 31. Child-Care Programs and Politics ................. 225
Chapter 32. Men and Feminism .......................... 229
Chapter 33. Antifeminist Writing since 1940 ................. 231

# Contents

Addendum .......................................... 235

Author Index ....................................... 245
Title Index ........................................ 261
Subject Index ...................................... 281

# PREFACE

The demand for information about women historically and in contemporary life has increased dramatically over the past decade. As women have moved toward a position of equality, one criticism frequently heard from participants of that movement is that women are invisible in history textbooks and courses of study. Indeed, it is true that the female half of the citizenry has been neglected and ignored in traditional scholarship. As the voices of protest have spread, they have begun to be recognized. Scholars are beginning to respond and include women in their work. As they move to remedy this issue of the invisibility of women, scholars encounter some difficulties. In those times that women were less than full citizens, the amount and quality of primary documentation reflects this lower status of women. Women were not as important, so, to some degree, fewer records were kept about them. Sometimes the only way to glimpse the nature of women's lives in the past is through contemporary male descriptions of their mothers, wives, and daughters. This is not to say, however, that material does not exist; in fact, there is an abundance of information which is beginning to be ferretted out and assembled. More and more documentation is becoming available. Too much of the printed material yet is anthologized collections of a small bit of this author and that suffragist, but more is produced each year. It is certainly true that a large amount of material on contemporary women is being compiled and published. As information surfaces, it is necessary that it becomes easily accessible to students of history and American culture and society. It is hoped that the role of women in our past and present will become as much a part of our mainstream historical knowledge as the Pilgrims and Plymouth Rock. This volume, WOMEN AND FEMINISM IN AMERICAN HISTORY, is an effort to make information on women's history and condition, and their struggle to change that condition now and in the past, more readily available.

As we undertook the task of assembling the guide, the main issue which presented itself was, in fact, the great mass of work on women and feminism in existence and how to select the most important and relevant material. Given the focus of the project, it quickly became apparent that in no way would one short volume be a comprehensive index of women and the women's movement from the colonial period through the present. Instead, we had to sift through large quantities of material and find for the reader the primary and most important resources on women in history, women today, and the feminist struggle.

Some depth, of course, is possible even in this limited space, and we believe that the entries which follow give the reader a good introduction to the basic and most interesting work done on the history of women and feminism. in America.

Some mention of the question of definition must be made. Feminism in the contemporary women's movement has come to mean a very specialized viewpoint. To participants in the women's struggle, feminism is a very specific body of ideas which suggest that the world will be better for or is in need of a distinctly women's point of view, and that women as women have much in common, which needs to be expressed through a woman's culture and ideology. It can be juxtaposed to the women's liberationist point of view which says that the women's struggle lies in obtaining equal rights and opportunities and in eliminating discrimination between the sexes. However, in this volume we are using feminism in the broader, general sense. We include suffragism, equal rights, and all similar perspectives within the term feminism. It includes all efforts and sets of beliefs that have proposed bettering the condition of women in any way. Any activity or analysis which concerns itself with women and the action necessary for women to obtain their rightful status as full human beings, including, but not limited to, the creation of a women's culture, we have generally accepted as feminism.

This book is essentially organized in three parts. It begins with sections on general resources such as manuscript collections, biographical directories, and periodicals. This is followed by chapters which are divided by historical period. We have tried to base the divisions on events relevant to women and women's history rather than the standard demarcation of time. Much of the historical material is located in these period chapters, with some exceptions. The last chapter devoted to an era, 1961 to the present, includes only those works which generally describe the contemporary status of women or the story of the growth and consequences of the women's movement in the 1960s and 1970s. Separated from this factual aspect of the contemporary movement is a section which contains the thought and analysis of contemporary feminism, the ideology of the wide ranging and divergent women's struggle. This is followed by another chapter of ideology--socialist feminism. Currently much has been written about the relationship of Marx, historical materialism, and women's issues. All the entries in this chapter are not socialist, but rather concern themselves with issues of socialism and feminism. Next is a series of topical chapters intended to document women's status in many aspects of society--the arts, the sciences, in sports, women's education, and so on. These contain mostly contemporary references, but in places where context or continuum seemed important, historical entries are included. The sections on women in the arts, prostitution, and ethnic and minority women, for example, combine past and present listings. If a reader is looking for historical information on a topic, she/he would do well to look in the topic chapters and the period chapters. The next to last grouping of chapters is devoted to the issues or concerns addressed by the women's movement--abortion rights, day care, and other topics. The final chapter is on antifeminism as it, too, must be documented.

In the preparation of this manuscript, many people and institutes gave us invaluable assistance. We would particularly like to thank the staff at the Schlesinger Library of Radcliffe College, where we spent several pleasant and productive days. Likewise, valuable information came from the Sophia Smith Collection of Smith College, the University of Illinois Library, and Eastern Illinois University. We would also like to thank Professor Robert Hennings, chairman of the department of history at Eastern Illinois University, for making available the services of John Eichacher, graduate assistant in the department of history, who provided yeoman service in tracking down details for us. The project was partially financed by a grant from the Faculty Research Council of Eastern Illinois University. Special thanks go to Mary Craft Pearson for typing the manuscript, Professor Harold Shill, series editor, and the editors at Gale Research Co., who have provided invaluable help.

Inevitably it will happen that we have omitted somebody's favorite book. For this we take full responsibility because such judgments are ours alone and hopefully all will realize that not everything could be included.

Elizabeth Tingley
Donald F. Tingley

# Chapter 1

# BIBLIOGRAPHIES

ARTHUR AND ELIZABETH SCHLESINGER LIBRARY ON THE HISTORY OF
WOMEN IN AMERICA: THE MANUSCRIPT INVENTORIES AND THE CATA-
LOGS OF MANUSCRIPTS, BOOKS AND PICTURES. 3 vols. Boston: G.K.
Hall, 1973.

Volumes 1 and 2 contain facsimiles of the card catalog of books in
the library; volume 2 has a list of periodicals--listed by card; and
volume 3 is a facsimile list of manuscripts.

Ash, Lee, comp. SUBJECT COLLECTIONS: A GUIDE TO SPECIAL BOOK
COLLECTIONS SUBJECT EMPHASIS AS REPORTED BY UNIVERSITY, COLLEGE,
PUBLIC AND SPECIAL LIBRARIES IN THE UNITED STATES AND CANADA.
5th ed. New York: R.R. Bowker, 1978. 1,221 p.

This volume consists of a listing by subject collections held in
libraries across the country.

Astin, Helen S., et al., eds. SEX ROLES: A RESEARCH BIBLIOGRAPHY.
Rockville, Md.: National Institutes of Mental Health, 1975. ix, 362 p.

This bibliography is international but contains much on the United
States. The entries are annotated.

_____. WOMEN: A BIBLIOGRAPHY ON THEIR EDUCATION AND CAREERS.
Washington, D.C.: Human Service Press, 1971. v, 243 p.

The editors give excellent annotations for each entry. The selections are divided into sections: determinants of career choice,
marital status, women at work, history of women at work, education of women. There is an author and subject index. The authors
focus on role stereotyping and discrimination, and find female com-
petence so well established that discrimination under any circum-
stances is wrong.

Barlow, Marjorie Dana, comp. NOTES ON WOMEN PRINTERS IN COLONIAL
AMERICA AND THE UNITED STATES, 1639-1675. Charlottesville: University
of Virginia Press, 1977. 89 p.

Beginning with Elizabeth Harris Glover who in 1639 owned the first printing press in colonial America, this bibliographical account deals with the role of women in the printer's trade by periods of American history.

Bernays, Edward L., ed. SELECTED BIBLIOGRAPHY OF WOMEN'S ACTIVI-TIES. New York: McCall's Magazine, 1946. 82 p.

A listing of 155 books, arranged topically, concerning women and women's activities.

Bullough, Vern, et al., eds. A BIBLIOGRAPHY OF PROSTITUTION. New York: Garland Publishing Co., 1977. x, 419 p.

The editors divide their lists by topics, chronology, and geographic area. The scope is international, but much material on the United States is included.

Cabello-Argaudona, Roberto, et al., eds. THE CHICANA: A COMPREHEN-SIVE BIBLIOGRAPHIC STUDY. Los Angeles, Calif.: Chicano Studies Center, University of California, 1975. xiii, 308 p.

The editors include films, articles and government publications as well as books and monographs. The unannotated entries deal with Spanish-speaking women and the feminist movement, sex roles, discrimination in employment, health, family, and marriage.

Cantor, Aviva, comp. BIBLIOGRAPHY ON THE JEWISH WOMAN. Fresh Meadows, N.Y.: Biblio Press, 1979. 228 p.

This annotated bibliography lists books about Jewish women published during the period from 1960 to 1978. The works are arranged in alphabetical order by topics. One section is called "In United States and Canada."

CATALOG OF THE SOPHIA SMITH COLLECTION, WOMEN'S HISTORY AR-CHIVE: SMITH COLLEGE, NORTHAMPTON, MASSACHUSETTS. 7 vols. Boston: G.K. Hall, 1975.

Volumes 1 and 2 contain author catalogs and volumes 3, 4, and 5 a subject catalog. Volumes 6 and 7 relate to manuscript collections and 7 deals with photographs.

Chaff, Sandra L., et al., eds. WOMEN IN MEDICINE: A BIBLIOGRAPHY OF THE LITERATURE ON WOMEN PHYSICIANS. Metuchen, N.J.: Scarecrow Press, 1977. xi, 1,124 p.

The editors divide this volume into history, biography, recruitment, medical education, specialities, missionary activity, psychosocial factors, and medical societies. A section on fiction is included. Entries are annotated.

Common Women Collective. WOMEN IN U.S. HISTORY: AN ANNOTATED BIBLIOGRAPHY. Cambridge, Mass.: Common Women Collective, 1976. 114 p.

The compilers, in an attempt to place the history of women in the context of female culture, divide the selected works into twenty-six sections in a roughly chronological fashion. Entries are annotated.

Davis, Audrey B., ed. BIBLIOGRAPHY ON WOMEN: WITH SPECIAL EMPHASIS ON THEIR ROLES IN SCIENCE AND SOCIETY. New York: Science History Publications, 1974. 80 p.

This alphabetical list is not annotated; it includes entries from scholarly journals and books on women in science.

Davis, Lenwood G., ed. BLACK WOMEN IN AMERICAN SOCIETY: A SELECTION. Boston: G.K. Hall, 1975. ix, 159 p.

Davis lists books, articles, general reference works, reports, and pamphlets. There is a list of major black history collections, national organizations of black women, black female newspaper publishers and editors and elected officials. A statistical study is included.

Diner, Hasia R., ed. WOMEN AND URBAN SOCIETY: A GUIDE TO INFORMATION SOURCES. Urban Studies Information Guide Series, vol. 7. Detroit: Gale Research Co., 1979. 138 p.

This bibliography provides information concerning the impact of urbanization on women throughout the world. The citations deal with migration of women and their adaptation to the urban environment, women and the urban family, fertility patterns, employment and the sociological and psychological implications for women.

Dollen, Charles, comp. ABORTION IN CONTEXT: A SELECT BIBLIOGRAPHY. Metuchen, N.J.: Scarecrow Press, 1970. vii, 150 p.

Dollen concentrates on books and articles published around 1967-69. He includes all readily available materials. He sees the questions of population control and the legalization of homosexuality as related questions. He believes the question of abortion may destroy any chance of Catholic-Protestant unity.

Eichler, Margrit, comp. AN ANNOTATED SELECTED BIBLIOGRAPHY OF BIBLIOGRAPHIES ON WOMEN. Pittsburgh: KNOW, 1976. 35 p.

Eichler has compiled a list of over ninety bibliographies on many aspects of women in history and on the contemporary scene.

Feminist Theory Collective. AMERICAN WOMEN: OUR LIVES AND LABOR. AN ANNOTATED BIBLIOGRAPHY ON WOMEN AND WORK IN THE UNITED STATES, 1900-1975. Eugene, Oreg.: Amazon Reality, 1976. 36 p.

# Bibliographies

This bibliography, developed by a Marxist-feminist group, is organized by period, starting with the nineteenth century and ending in 1975. Each listing has a paragraph of description.

FILMS BY AND/OR ABOUT WOMEN, 1972: DIRECTORY OF FILMMAKERS, FILMS, AND DISTRIBUTORS, INTERNATIONALLY, PAST AND PRESENT. Berkeley, Calif.: Women's History Research Center, 1972. iv, 72 p.

The directory is divided into sections on films, female filmmakers, and items of further interest.

Franklin, Margaret Ladd, ed. THE CASE FOR WOMEN SUFFRAGE: A BIBLIOG-RAPHY. New York: National College Equal Suffrage League, 1913. Reprint. Washington, D.C.: Zenger Publishing Co., 1975. ii, 315 p.

This is a chronological listing of books, congressional documents, leaflets, plays, and periodical articles as well as the current suffrage journals. It is very useful on history of women for any given period prior to 1913.

Freedman, Carol Edry, and Goulet, Ginnie, eds. WOMEN'S YELLOW PAGES: THE ORIGINAL SOURCE BOOK. Boston: Boston Women's Collective, 1974. 160 p.

This is a resource manual for women in the Boston area. It lists organizations and their leadership.

Friedman, Barbara, et al., eds. WOMEN'S WORK AND WOMEN'S STUDIES/ 1973-1974. New York: Barnard College Women's Center, 1975. 370 p.

Divided topically, this bibliography is international in scope but should be consulted for material relating to women in the United States.

Friedman, Leslie J., ed. SEX ROLE STEREOTYPING IN THE MASS MEDIA: AN ANNOTATED BIBLIOGRAPHY. New York: Garland Publishing, 1977. xvii, 319 p.

This annotated bibliography contains a list of articles dealing with the subject, divided by media in general, advertising, television, radio, film, print and popular culture, with special sections on minority women and the children's media.

Garoogian, Andrew, and Garoogian, Rhoda, eds. CHILD CARE ISSUES FOR PARENTS AND SOCIETY: A GUIDE TO INFORMATION SOURCES. Social Issues and Social Problems Information Guide Series, vol. 2. Detroit: Gale Research Co., 1977. xiv, 367 p.

The editors include sections on the development of sex roles in children, day care, working mothers, single parents, and other topics of importance to the history of women.

# Bibliographies

THE GERRITSEN COLLECTION OF WOMEN'S HISTORY: A SHORT TITLE LIST. Glen Rock, N.J.: Microfilming Corp. of America, 1976. xii, 143 p.

This is a bibliography of the international Gerritsen Collection of Women's History in the Kenneth Spencer Research Library of the University of Kansas. It lists monographs and pamphlets as well as serials and periodicals.

Greenwood, Hazel, ed. THE EQUAL RIGHTS AMENDMENT: A BIBLIOGRAPHIC STUDY. Westport, Conn.: Greenwood Press, 1976. xxvii, 367 p.

The book has an author and organization index. The bulk of the material is pro-ERA, but anti-ERA writings are included.

Haber, Barbara, ed. WOMEN IN AMERICA: A GUIDE TO BOOKS, 1963-1975. Boston: G.K. Hall, 1978. 230 p.

Haber describes 450 significant books which have appeared since 1963, the date usually assigned as the starting point of the current feminist movement. The bibliography is arranged in sixteen chapters. Haber deals with topics relating to the experiences of women, such as, abortion, health, marriage, and work. Each entry is lavishly annotated.

Harrison, Cynthia E., ed. WOMEN IN AMERICAN HISTORY. Santa Barbara, Calif.: American Bibliographical Center, Clio Press, 1979. 428 p.

The editor has compiled 3,500 entries from 650 key journals in the period from 1963 to 1976. All deal with the literature on women in the United States and Canada. The entries are arranged by chronological periods, which are subdivided topically.

_____. WOMEN'S MOVEMENT MEDIA: A SOURCE GUIDE. New York: R.R. Bowker, 1975. 269 p.

Harrison offers a compendium of 550 sources of information on organizations which supply books, periodicals, films, tapes, and records for or about women. The entries are arranged by function and type.

Hinding, Andrea, and Richardson, Rosemary, comps. ARCHIVAL AND MANU-SCRIPT RESOURCES FOR THE STUDY OF WOMENS HISTORY: A BEGINNING. St. Paul: University of Minnesota Libraries, 1972. 42 p.

Arranged geographically, the list has a brief description of manuscript holdings of various depositories. There is no index.

Hughes, Marija Matich, ed. THE SEXUAL BARRIER: LEGAL, MEDICAL, ECO-NOMIC AND SOCIAL ASPECTS OF SEX DISCRIMINATION. Washington, D.C.: Hughes Press, 1977. xxi, 843 p.

Hughes divides the book into seventeen chapters arranged alphabetically. The book includes English-language books, articles, pamphlets, and government publications from the period 1960 to 1975.

Israel, Stan, comp. and ed. A BIBLIOGRAPHY ON DIVORCE. New York: Bloch Publishing, 1974. xiv, 300 p.

Israel divides the subject into categories: legal aspects, religious aspects, and sociological aspects. Most of his entries are from the late 1960s. His main entries are extensively annotated, and he includes an unannotated list of earlier publications.

Jacobs, Sue Ellen, ed. WOMEN IN PERSPECTIVE: A GUIDE TO CROSS-CULTURAL STUDIES. Urbana: University of Illinois Press, 1973. xvi, 299 p.

This book is international in scope with a section devoted to the United States. The second half of the book is divided topically into sections such as sex and sexuality, women in prison, modern feminism, and women in history. There is an author index. Entries are not annotated.

Kelly, Joan, ed. BIBLIOGRAPHY IN THE HISTORY OF EUROPEAN WOMEN. Bronxville, N.Y.: Sarah Lawrence College, Women's Study Publications, 1976. 132 p.

This bibliography is useful as background study of the history of women in the United States. The arrangement is roughly chronological. Entries are not annotated.

King, Judith D., ed. WOMEN: A SELECT BIBLIOGRAPHY OF BOOKS. Allendale, Mich.: Grand Valley State Colleges Library, 1974. 52 p.

The editor alphabetically lists books by topics, such as abortion, and the women's liberation movement.

Klotman, Phyllis Rauch, and Baatz, Wilmer H., comps. THE BLACK FAMILY AND THE BLACK WOMAN: A BIBLIOGRAPHY. New York: Arno Press, 1978. x, 231 p.

Two-thirds of the book is devoted to black women. Included are biographies and autobiographies, books on equal rights and status of women, books and articles on psychology and sociology of women, literary works, black women in literature, fine arts, the professions, sports, and the general labor force.

Krichmar, Albert, ed. THE WOMEN'S MOVEMENT IN THE SEVENTIES. Metuchen, N.J.: Scarecrow Press, 1977. xvi, 875 p.

This is an extensive listing of publications from 1970 to 1976 relating to women's issues. It includes items on the international scene as well as the United States. It is primarily a reference to periodicals.

_____. THE WOMEN'S RIGHTS MOVEMENT IN THE UNITED STATES 1848-1970. Metuchen, N.J.: Scarecrow Press, 1972. ix, 436 p.

This is a very complete bibliography divided into sections on legal and political status, economic status, education, religion, and biography. There is a section on manuscript sources, as well as a highly useful section on the periodicals of the women's liberation movement after 1968. Another checklist deals with earlier publications which promoted the cause of women.

Leonard, Eugenie Andruss, et al., eds. THE AMERICAN WOMAN IN COLONIAL AND REVOLUTIONARY TIMES 1565-1800. Philadelphia: University of Pennsylvania Press, 1962. 169 p.

This volume contains a syllabus on nearly every aspect of the life and status of colonial women. There is also a section listing 104 outstanding women of the period with minimum data about each and keyed to bibliographical references which note their accomplishments. Further, there is an extensive bibliography listed alphabetically by author.

Lerner, Gerda, ed. BIBLIOGRAPHY IN THE HISTORY OF AMERICAN WOMEN. Bronxville, N.Y.: Sarah Lawrence College, 1978. 79 p.

Lerner first collected this unannotated bibliography for her classes at Sarah Lawrence. She has avoided anthologies and collections in favor of historical works. Organization is both historical and topical.

Lillard, Richard G., ed. AMERICAN LIVE IN AUTOBIOGRAPHY: A DESCRIPTIVE GUIDE. Stanford, Calif.: Stanford University Press, ca. 1956. vi, 140 p.

This is a listing of autobiographies of prominent Americans by category or special interest, for instance, artists, lawyers, writers, and social leaders. There is an alphabetical listing and a separate breakdown of those that fit into minority groups of immigrants, Indians, Jews, and Negroes. There is a description of each entry. The list is not complete by any means but represents a good selection.

McKee, Kathleen Burke, ed. WOMEN'S STUDIES: A GUIDE TO REFERENCE SOURCES. Storrs: University of Connecticut Library, 1977. 112 p.

The editor lists guides, handbooks, library catalogs, directories, and various topical aspects of women's activities. A useful list of women's periodicals is appended.

McKenney, Mary, ed. DIVORCE: A SELECTED ANNOTATED BIBLIOGRAPHY. Metuchen, N.J.: Scarecrow Press, 1975. vi, 157 p.

The editor divides the book into sections on general historical works, legal aspects, financial considerations. She appends a section on divorce laws by states.

# Bibliographies

Mason, Elizabeth B., and Starr, Louise M., eds. THE ORAL HISTORY COL-
LECTION OF COLUMBIA UNIVERSITY. New York: Oral History Research
Office, 1979. xxvii, 305 p.

The Columbia Oral History Collection is a pioneer effort. Although
relatively few women have been interviewed on their own account,
many are included as part of one collection or another. For example, any study of women in politics would need to look at the
women interviewed in the Adlai Stevenson project.

MEN'S STUDIES BIBLIOGRAPHY. Cambridge: MIT, 1975. 58 p.

Doubtless intended as a counterbalance to feminism, this bibliography is divided into sections: masculinity, mental and physical
health, attitudes toward women, homosexuality, fatherhood and
family, employment, sexuality, power, violence, crime, military,
sports, history, literature, religion, and men's liberation. Entries
are not annotated. There is an author index.

Murdock, Mary Elizabeth, ed. CATALOG OF THE SOPHIA SMITH COLLEC-
TION: WOMEN'S HISTORY ARCHIVE. Northampton, Mass.: Smith College,
1976. 78 p.

This catalog lists the major collections of manuscripts and periodicals in the collection. There is an excellent cross reference system
by which the researcher can relate a subject to specific collections
or periodicals. A good index is provided.

O'Connor, Patricia, et al., eds. WOMEN: A SELECTED BIBLIOGRAPHY.
Springfield, Ohio: Wittenberg University, 1973. vi, 111 p.

This bibliography is divided by categories: anthropology and bi-
ology, psychology, economics, social condition and theory, law
and political science, history, biography, education, religion, and
literature. The entries are not annotated.

Parker, Franklin, and Parker, Betty June, eds. WOMEN'S EDUCATION--A
WORLD VIEW: ANNOTATED BIBLIOGRAPHY OF DOCTORAL DISSERTATIONS.
Westport, Conn.: Greenwood Press, 1979. 488 p.

The work focuses on worldwide education of girls and women. The
United States is included. It lists only works in English and contains a subject index.

Peterson, Deena, ed. A PRACTICAL GUIDE TO THE WOMEN'S MOVEMENT.
New York: Women's Action Committee, 1975. 213 p.

The editor provides an annotated list of women's periodicals, as
well as a directory of women's organizations.

Phelps, Ann T., et al., eds. NEW CAREER OPTIONS FOR WOMEN: A SELECTED

ANNOTATED BIBLIOGRAPHY. New York: Human Sciences Press, 1976. 144 p.

> The editors have sections on the woman at work in the seventies, women's training and education opportunities, sex differences, the working mother, career counseling, and legal issues.

PICTURE CATALOG OF THE SOPHIA SMITH COLLECTION. Northampton, Mass.: Smith College Collection, 1972. 127 p.

> This catalog presents reproductions of some of the hundreds of pictures in the Sophia Smith Collection relating to women in American history. The pictures are arranged by themes--abolition-slavery, arts and humanities, biography, countries, frontier, social reform, war, and women's rights.

Pool, Jeannie G., ed. WOMEN IN MUSIC HISTORY: A RESEARCH GUIDE. New York: 1977. iv, 42 p.

> Pool includes articles, books, records, periodicals, pamphlets and organizations which touch on women and music. Not all the information is specifically American, but nationality is noted so the reader may identify which sources are relevant to American women in history.

THE RAPE BIBLIOGRAPHY: A COLLECTION OF ABSTRACTS. St. Louis: St. Louis Feminist Research Project, 1976. 96 p.

> This lists primarily periodicals on rape from the academic fields of law, medicine, psychology, sociology, and the popular press. Selected items from the bibliographies are annotated.

Rosenberg, Marie Barovic, and Bergstrom, Len V., eds. WOMEN AND SOCIETY: A CRITICAL REVIEW OF THE LITERATURE WITH A SELECTED ANNOTATED BIBLIOGRAPHY. Beverly Hills, Calif.: Sage Publications, 1975. 375 p.

> The editors deal with history, politics, and work in brief bibliographic essays. Beyond this, material is divided into sections on political science, history, literature, biography, philosophy, economics, and general reference works.

Rowbotham, Sheila, ed. WOMEN'S LIBERATION AND REVOLUTION. Bristol, Engl.: Falling Wall Press, 1973. 24 p.

> Rowbotham has briefly annotated each listing. She includes entries under such general topics as "Women and the Puritan Revolution in England and America" and such issue topics as "Feminism and Socialist and Anarchist Movements."

Sell, Kenneth D., and Sell, Betty H., eds. DIVORCE IN THE UNITED STATES, CANADA, AND GREAT BRITAIN: A GUIDE TO INFORMATION

# Bibliographies

SOURCES. Social Issues and Social Problems Information Guide Series, vol. 1. Detroit: Gale Research Co., 1978. xvi, 298 p.

This volume has interest to the women's movement in terms of single-parent families, divorce statistics, and legal aspects of divorce. There is an interesting section on divorce in literature.

Soltow, Martha Jane, and Wery, Mary K., eds. AMERICAN WOMEN AND THE LABOR MOVEMENT, 1825-1974: AN ANNOTATED BIBLIOGRAPHY. Metuchen, N.J.: Scarecrow Press, 1976. 247 p.

Soltow and Wery include over seven hundred entries arranged alphabetically by topic, with short descriptive statements about each. The topics covered are employment, trade unions, working mothers, strikes, legislation, worker education, labor leaders, and supportive efforts.

Stanwick, Kathy, and Li, Christine, eds. THE POLITICAL PARTICIPATION OF WOMEN IN THE UNITED STATES: A SELECTED BIBLIOGRAPHY, 1950-1976. Metuchen, N.J.: Scarecrow Press, 1977. ix, 159 p.

The volume is divided by type of publication. Included are bibliographies, directories, periodicals, books, monographs, reports, articles, dissertations and theses, and papers given at professional meetings. There is an author and biography index.

Tingley, Donald F., ed. SOCIAL HISTORY OF THE UNITED STATES: A GUIDE TO INFORMATION SOURCES. American Government and History Information Guide Series, vol. 3. Detroit: Gale Research Co., 1979. 260 p.

This bibliography of sources in general social history contains many references of consequence to the history of women, particularly the chapters on women and feminism and marriage, divorce, family, and sexuality.

TUNING IN TO THE MOVEMENT: FEMINIST PERIODICALS. Pittsburgh: KNOW, 1974. 10 p.

This lists publications of the women's movement--newsletters, pamphlets, and newspapers--and women's presses and bookstores on the current scene in 1974.

Turner, Maryann, ed. BIBLIOTECA FEMINA: A HERSTORY OF BOOK COLLECTIONS CONCERNING WOMEN. New York: Tower Press, 1978. 118 p.

Turner has assembled a descriptive list of collections of books by and about women, primarily in the United States. She includes sections on women's organizations and professions, women's centers, microfilmed collections, oral collections, and archival activity. She also presents a proposal for compiling further collections.

Westervelt, Esther Manning, and Fisher, Deborah A., eds. WOMEN'S HIGHER AND
CONTINUING EDUCATION: AN ANNOTATED BIBLIOGRAPHY WITH SE-
LECTED REFERENCES ON RELATED ASPECTS OF WOMEN'S LIVES. New York:
College Entry Examination Board, 1971. 66 p.

> The authors organize their listings into categories. The two main
> areas covered are theories and research in women's capacities and
> the educational behavior and aspirations of women studies from
> high school to postgraduate school. Each entry has a substantial
> annotation.

Wheeler, Helen Rippier, ed. WOMANHOOD MEDIA: CURRENT RESOURCES
ABOUT WOMEN. Metuchen, N.J.: Scarecrow Press, 1972. 335 p.

> This volume deals with a basic book collection, nonbook resources
> of pamphlets, periodicals, and audiovisual materials. These are
> supplemented by a directory of sources, organizations, and speakers
> available to the feminist movement. Most of the entries are an-
> notated.

Williams, Ova, ed. AMERICAN BLACK WOMEN IN THE ARTS AND SOCIAL
SCIENCES: A BIBLIOGRAPHIC SURVEY. Metuchen, N.J.: Scarecrow Press,
1978. 197 p.

> Williams's unannotated entries are divided into two main sections,
> general and biography.

Winslow, Barbara, comp. WOMEN'S LIBERATION: BLACK WOMEN, WORK-
ING WOMEN, REVOLUTIONARY FEMINISM. Highland Park, Mich.: Sun
Press, 1976. 22 p.

> This unannotated bibliography lists works in three areas: black
> women, women in the work force, and women in revolution.

Womanpower Project. THE NEW YORK WOMEN'S DIRECTORY. New York:
Workman Publishing Co., 1973. 126 p.

> This is a directory of "where-to-find-it" in New York City, listing
> day care centers, abortion agencies, employment services, credit,
> self-defense, medical service, and feminist organizations.

WOMEN STUDIES ABSTRACTS. Rush, N.Y.: Women Studies Abstracts, 1972-- .
Quarterly.

> An attempt is made to abstract articles on women in more than two
> thousand periodicals concerning education, sex roles, characteristics
> and differences, employment, society and government, sexuality,
> family, women in history and literature, and the women's liberation
> movement. Most issues contain a bibliographical essay on some
> pertinent topic on women.

# Chapter 2

# MANUSCRIPT COLLECTIONS

With a few remarkable exceptions, libraries and archives have made little conscious effort to collect manuscripts pertinent to women's history. Indeed, most seem to have acquired the papers of women only as a part of a collection of family papers. In short, much has been preserved only by accident. In many instances these have remained hidden in the mass of papers relating to the achievement of male relatives. The only category of women who have been an exception are literary persons. Many libraries have collected the papers of women writers. Happily, many libraries at last are beginning to identify material relating to women in their collections and they are actively collecting such materials.

For detailed information and a listing of smaller holdings, the researcher should consult Hinding, Andrea, et al., eds. WOMEN'S HISTORY SOURCES: A GUIDE TO ARCHIVES AND MANUSCRIPTS IN THE UNITED STATES. 2 vols. New York: R.R. Bowker, 1979. This remarkable work lists eighteen thousand collections in twenty-four hundred depositories. For research in women's history, this replaces Hamer, Philip M., ed. A GUIDE TO ARCHIVES AND MANU-SCRIPTS IN THE UNITED STATES. New Haven, Conn.: Yale University Press, 1961.

It is impossible to list every library or archive which has a few items relating to women's history. Three major collections stand out in their richness: Schlesinger Library, Sophia Smith Collection, and the Library of Congress. These are discussed first. Other significant collections are listed geographically.

ARTHUR AND ELIZABETH SCHLESINGER LIBRARY ON THE HISTORY OF WOMEN IN AMERICA. RADCLIFFE COLLEGE. CAMBRIDGE, MASSACHUSETTS.

This collection began in 1943 with the Woman's Rights Collection donated by the late Maud Wood Park, a suffragist. Subsequently Arthur M. and Elizabeth Bancroft Schlesinger encouraged Radcliffe College to set up a separate library on women's history. Because of the Schlesinger's continued support, the library was named for them. Among the collections are the papers of women's rights advocates from Susan B. Anthony to Betty Freidan. There are papers of illustrious families such as the Blackwells, a family which included Elizabeth and

Emily, physicians; Anna, journalist; Ellen, artist; Samuel, husband of Antoinette Brown, first ordained clergywoman; and Henry, husband of Lucy Stone. The papers of the Hamilton family contain letters of Edith Hamilton, classicist; her sister Alice Hamilton, physician; and their sisters. There are also papers of female lawyers, philanthropists, political figures, educators, and settlement house workers. In addition to personal papers, the library has extensive holdings of papers of women's organizations, including recent ones such as Women's Equity Action League and the National Organization of Women as well as longer established groups such as the American Association of University Women and the League of Women Voters. The Schlesinger Library also operates the Black Woman Oral History Project. They interview black women over the age of seventy to document the life histories of these women and their contribution to improvement of life for black Americans. As of September 28, 1978, they had interviewed forty-nine women.

SOPHIA SMITH COLLECTION: WOMEN'S HISTORY ARCHIVE. SMITH COLLEGE. NORTHAMPTON, MASSACHUSETTS.

Named after the founder of Smith College, this international collection was begun in 1942. The manuscripts relate to women in nearly every kind of human endeavor. Among the collections dealing with women's rights, perhaps the most notable is that dealing with Margaret Sanger, which extends to 199 boxes of papers, 145 reels of microfilm, and 166 books. The Garrison family papers include materials on the many women involved in the abolitionist crusade. The library holds papers of the Peabody sisters, Elizabeth, Mary and Sophia, as well as Ida Tarbell, Carrie Chapman Catt, Jane Addams, Susan B. Anthony, Clara Barton, and Ellen Gates Starr. Of current interest are the papers of Congresswoman Patsy Mink and opera star Rise Stevens. The collection is especially rich in material relating to female physicians.

LIBRARY OF CONGRESS. WASHINGTON, D.C.

The Library of Congress has the papers of women engaged in many activities, including wives or official hostesses of various presidents. It holds the papers of Florence Jaffray Hamilton, peace advocate and diplomat; Evelyn Briggs Baldwin, arctic explorer; Harriet Mann Miller, ornithologist; Myrtilla Miner, founder of a school for black girls; Rebecca Gratz, philanthropist; and Mary Baker Eddy, founder of the Christian Science religion. They hold also the papers of many novelists, poets, and actresses. They have papers of feminists including Susan B. Anthony, Anna Elizabeth Dickinson, Ida Husted Harper, Margaret Sanger, Elizabeth Cady Stanton, and Julia Ward Howe. The Library of Congress is the depository for the papers of the League of Women Voters and its parent group, the National League of Women Voters, the National Woman's party, and the Women's Trade Union League of America as well as those of groups in which women played a large part, notably the American Antislavery Society and the American Peace Society. The library has oral history interviews with a number of former congresswomen.

New England: The Houghton Library of Harvard University, Cambridge, Massachusetts, holds papers largely concerning literary women, including Emily Dickinson, Amy Lowell, Louisa May Alcott, Sarah Orne Jewett, Kathleen Norris,
Margaret Fuller, and Julia Ward Howe. The American Jewish Historical Society in Waltham, Massachusetts, has papers relating to Jewish women, including Emma Lazarus, Molly Picon, and Rebecca Gratz. The Essex Institute in
Salem, Massachusetts, has manuscript diaries of some women of the colonial
and early national period. The John F. Kennedy Library, Waltham, Massachusetts, has the records of the President's Commission on the Status of Women,
1961-1964. The Connecticut College Library holds the papers of Frances Perkins, Secretary of Labor; Prudence Crandall Philleo, educator; and Belle Moskowitz, advisor to Governor Alfred E. Smith of New York.

Middle Atlantic States: The Franklin D. Roosevelt Library, Hyde Park, New
York, holds the papers of Eleanor Roosevelt and Anna Eleanor Roosevelt, as
well as Mary Williams Dewson and Lorana Hickok who were politically associated with the Roosevelt administration. The New York Public Library holds
the papers of a variety of literary figures, women associated with theater, and
a number of suffragists and reformers, including Lillian D. Wald of the Henry
Street Settlement House. Syracuse University Library has the Gerrit Smith Collection papers relating to women who were active in the abolitionist movement,
including Elizabeth Cady Stanton, Susan B. Anthony, Lucy Stone, Victoria
Woodhull, and Sojourner Truth. Vassar College, Poughkeepsie, New York,
has holdings that center on suffrage and the women's rights movement. Their
collections include papers of Maria Mitchell, Ruth Benedict, and Alma Lutz.
The Cornell University Library, Ithaca, New York, holds the papers of the
American Medical Women's Association. The Pennsylvania Historical Society,
Philadelphia, has papers of a number of authors and artists as well as organizations such as the Indigent Widows and Single Women's Society of Pennsylvania
and the Women's Dental Association of the United States. The Swarthmore College Library holds many items dealing with the peace and women's rights movements including papers of Jane Addams, Hannah J. Bailey, Belva Lockwood,
Lucretia Coffin Mott, Anne Garlin Spencer, and organizations such as the
Women's International League for Peace and Freedom. Princeton University holds
papers of Mary Livermore, feminist, and a few literary figures. The National
Archives for Black Women's History in Washington, D.C., contains records of
the National Council of Negro Women, correspondence of black leaders, and
photographs.

Midwest: In Ohio, the University of Akron holds the papers of a number of
early female psychologists in their archives in the history of american psychology. The Western Reserve Historical Society, Cleveland, has an impressive
collection of papers of women's organizations, including literary societies,
temperance and missionary groups, abolitionist societies, and charitable organizations as well as papers of individual women, mostly obscure. The Ohio Historical Society, Columbus, holds papers of women's clubs and has a few diaries.
In Illinois, the growing collection of the Midwest Women's Historical Collection
at the University of Illinois, Chicago Circle Campus, contains a massive holding of papers of Jane Addams and various residents of Hull House. They have
the papers of Rose Alschuler, promoter of the nursery school movement and pre-

school education, Esther Saperstein, Illinois legislator, and a wide variety
of social workers. They have the papers of many women's organizations such
as the Abortion Rights Association of Illinois, Chicago Women in Broadcasting,
the National Black Feminist Organization, and the Illinois Women's Political
Caucus. The Chicago Historical Society holds a wide variety of papers including labor leaders Lillian Herstein and Agnes Nestor. They include among their
holdings suffragists, social workers, and a few literary women. The Newberry
Library, Chicago, has papers of a number of literary figures, including Willa
Cather, Alice French, Eunice Tietjens, Edith Wyatt and Alice Gerstenberg,
pioneer in the little theatre movement. The University of Chicago has the
papers of Grace and Edith Abbott, social workers, and literary figures such as
Mary Aldis, Amy Bonner, Maurine Smith, and Harriet Monroe. The Northwestern University Library, Evanston, has a collection which focuses on the
liberation movement from 1961 to the present. The Minnesota Historical Society,
St. Paul, has papers of the Minnesota Woman Suffrage Association and the
Minnesota League of Women Voters. The University of Minnesota, Minneapolis,
has the records of the Association for Voluntary Sterilization, Association of
Junior Leagues of America, and the National Association of Social Workers,
as well as some collections of individual women. The University of Michigan,
in various of its libraries, holds papers of Elizabeth M. Chandler, abolitionist;
Bela Hubbard, geologist; Eliza Mosher, physician; Ellen Van Valkenberg, actress;
and Sarah and Angelina Grimke, abolitionists and feminists, as well as organi-
zations such as Daughters of the American Revolution, American Association of
University Women, and the Visiting Nurses Association. The State Historical
Society of Wisconsin, Madison, holds a massive collection of papers of Nancy
(Nettie) Fowler McCormick and Anita McCormick Blaine, both related to Cyrus Hall
McCormick, inventor of the reaper. It also holds papers of Sara Pryor, author; Zona
Gale, author; Ella Wheeler Wilcox, poet; and Ada L. James, suffragist. They also
hold records of the Women's Peace party, Daughters of the American Revolution, and
the Wisconsin Woman's Suffrage Association. The Harry S. Truman Library, Inde-
pendence, Missouri, contains papers of Bess Wallace Truman and Margaret
Truman Daniel.

The West: In California, the Stanford University Library has the papers of a
number of women writers as well as papers of Kate Douglas Wiggins, kinder-
garten movement, and Alice Park, birth control leader. The Bancroft Library
of the University of California, Berkeley, holds papers of women's rights leaders
Charlotte Perkins Gilman, Alice Paul, Carrie Chapman Catt, Mary Austin, Harriet Stanton Blatch, and Hester Harland. They have papers of scholars, such
as Mary Roberts Coolidge, sociologist, and Mary Ritter Beard, historian. They
have a collection of diaries of women in the Donner party as well as other
pioneers. Included also are papers related to Jessie Benton Fremont, Jeanette
Rankin, and Lou Henry Hoover, all political. Also of note are materials relating to literary figures, including Gertrude Stein and Alice B. Toklas, and
Millicent W. Shinn, editor of OVERLAND MONTHLY. The Bancroft Library
has instituted an oral history project on California women in politics from the
woman suffrage amendment to the current feminist movement. Women interviewed
represent every spectrum of political belief. Women who work in the two major
parties are excluded. The University of California at Los Angeles has a few
collections of suffragists and political figures including Helen Gahagan Douglas.
The Henry E. Huntington Library, San Marino, has the papers of a few women

writers and six major collections on woman's suffrage. The Ella Strong Denison Library of Scripps College, Claremont, holds the Ida Rust McPherson Collection on the humanistic accomplishment of women, suffrage, domestic economy, women in the westward movement, and the current women's movement. Also at Claremont, the graduate school has an oral history collection of women of prominence in the Claremont colleges, as well as interviews with nineteen women who served as missionaries in China. The University of Oregon Library, Eugene, holds manuscripts of many missionaries to China and Japan, literary figures, and scholars as well as papers of organizations, such as Women's Christian Temperance Union and Women's Republican Patriotic League. The University of Washington, Seattle, contains the papers of Anna Louise Strong, political figures such as Jeanette Rankin and Naomi Achenbach Benson, various suffragists, and authors. Washington State University holds papers of a number of suffragists and scholars as well as Catherine Dean Barnes May, former member of Congress. The Marriott Library of the University of Utah holds papers of the Utah Federation of Women's Republican Clubs and the Utah Society of the Daughters of the American Revolution. The University of Colorado Library holds papers of the Women's International League of Peace and Freedom.

The South: Atlanta University has materials relating to the history of black women including several organizations such as the Association of Southern Women for the Prevention of Lynching. The University of Virginia has the records of the League of Women Voters of Charlottesville, as well as papers of Dolley Madison and several female literary figures, including Ellen Glasgow. The University of North Carolina, Chapel Hill, holds the papers of a few southern women writers, including Caroline Lee Whiting Hentz, Grace Elizabeth King, Margaret Junkin, and Cornelia Phillips Spencer. Duke University, Durham, North Carolina, has the papers of a few southern literary women also. In Louisiana, both Louisiana State University and Tulane University holds a few collections of women writers' papers. The Mississippi Department of Archives and History, Jackson, has the records of the Daughters of Confederate Veterans and the United Daughters of the Confederacy.

# Chapter 3

# BIOGRAPHICAL DIRECTORIES

American Medical Association. DIRECTORY OF WOMAN PHYSICIANS IN THE U.S. Chicago: American Medical Association, 1973. xl, 432 p.

> In 1973 there were more than thirty thousand women physicians in the United States. The entries are alphabetical, as well as by state and city. Included are years of birth, education, license, specialties, and types of practice.

American Physical Society. WOMEN IN PHYSICS: A ROSTER. New York: American Institute of Physics, 1972. 85 p.

> This publication lists women in physics by areas of research interest, degrees, and employers.

Barrer, Myra E., ed. WOMEN'S ORGANIZATIONS AND LEADERS, 1975-1976. Washington, D.C.: Today Publishing and News Service, 1975. 230 p.

> This is a directory of more than eight thousand women's organizations and their leaders. Many individual leaders of the feminist movement are included.

Cameron, Mabel Ward, et al., eds. THE BIOGRAPHICAL CYCLOPEDIA OF AMERICAN WOMEN. 3 vols. New York: Halvord Publishing Co., 1924. Reprint. Detroit: Gale Research Co., 1975.

> These volumes are arranged alphabetically. The editors describe their time as the "age of women." Information includes that which might not be available otherwise. Selection tends to be skewed to the upper classes.

Center for the American Woman and Politics. WOMEN IN PUBLIC OFFICE: A BIOGRAPHICAL DIRECTORY AND STATISTICAL ANALYSIS. Metuchen, N.J.: Scarecrow Press, 1978. xix, 510 p.

> Women holding either elective or appointive posts in the state government, women mayors, and some other local officials are included. There is statistical report and profile of women holding office in 1977.

Daniel, Sadie Iola, ed. WOMEN BUILDERS. 1931. Washington, D.C.: Associated Publishers, 1970. 187 p.

> This volume contains biographical sketches of notable black women.

Dannett, Sylvia G.L., ed. PROFILES OF NEGRO WOMANHOOD. 2 vols. Chicago: Educational Heritage, 1964-66.

> This is a biographical dictionary dealing with prominent black women.

FILMS BY AND/OR ABOUT WOMEN, 1972: DIRECTORY OF FILMMAKERS, FILMS, AND DISTRIBUTORS, INTERNATIONALLY, PAST AND PRESENT. Berkeley, Calif.: Women's History Research Center, 1972. iv, 72 p.

> For annotation see page 4.

Gilman, Agnes Geneva, and Gilman, Gertrude Marcelle, eds. WHO'S WHO IN ILLINOIS: WOMEN-MAKERS OF HISTORY. Chicago: Eclectic Publishers, 1927. 265 p.

> The authors provide biographical sketches of 236 Illinois women of achievement. Most fit the goal, although a few are only society leaders and the achievements of some may seem slight by later standards.

Hale, Sarah Josepha, ed. WOMAN'S RECORD, OR, SKETCHES OF ALL DISTINGUISHED WOMEN FROM CREATION TO A.D. 1854. 1855. Reprint. New York: Source Book Press, 1970. 912 p.

> This directory is international in scope but contains material on American women.

Howes, Durward, ed. AMERICAN WOMEN: THE OFFICIAL WHO'S WHO AMONG THE WOMEN OF THE NATION. Los Angeles, Calif.: Richard Blank Publishing Co., 1935, 1937, 1939.

> This series was designed as a biennial volume. It survived for three years. Women are listed alphabetically. A list of women's organizations is appended to each volume. The list ranges from college sororities and Camp Fire Girls to serious organizations.

James, Edward T., et al., eds. NOTABLE AMERICAN WOMEN, 1607-1950: A BIOGRAPHICAL DICTIONARY. 3 vols. Cambridge, Mass.: Harvard University Press, 1971.

> These volumes contain more than thirteen hundred articles, some lengthy, about women who died between 1607 and 1950. For most of these women, their active careers were ended by 1920 and only a handful were born after 1900. Except for the wives of presidents, no subject was included because of her husband's status. Each had to stand on her own career.

Logan, Mary S. THE PART TAKEN BY WOMEN IN AMERICAN HISTORY. Wilmington, Del.: Perry-Nalle Publishing Co., 1912. Reprint. New York: Arno Press, 1972. 927 p.

> This is a biographical survey of both famous and obscure women. There are separate sections on Catholic and Jewish women.

Love, Barbara. FOREMOST WOMEN IN COMMUNICATIONS. New York: R.R. Bowker, 1970. 788 p.

> This is a biographical reference work covering women in broadcasting, publishing, advertising, and public relations.

Robinson, Wilhelmina S., ed. HISTORICAL NEGRO BIOGRAPHIES: INTERNATIONAL LIBRARY OF NEGRO LIFE AND HISTORY. New York: Publishers Co., 1968. 291 p.

> This is a recent biographical directory which is comprehensive. It includes black women.

Stern, Susan, ed. WOMEN COMPOSERS: A HANDBOOK. Metuchen, N.J.: Scarecrow Press, 1978. 191 p.

> Stern lists women composers of all periods and geographical areas. American women are included as is minimal biographical information. Bibliographies are listed.

Stuhler, Barbara, and Kreuter, Gretchen, eds. WOMEN OF MINNESOTA: SELECTED BIOGRAPHICAL ESSAYS. St. Paul: Minnesota Historical Society, 1977. 402 p.

> The editors have brought together sixteen biographical essays and more than one hundred sketches of women who contributed to the development of Minnesota.

Tolbert, Marguerite, et al., eds. SOUTH CAROLINA'S DISTINGUISHED WOMEN OF LAURENS COUNTY. Columbia, S.C.: R.L. Bryan Co., 1972. xviii, 273 p.

> The book consists of biographical sketches of thirty locally important women.

WHO'S WHO AMONG BLACK AMERICANS. Northbrook, Ill.: Who's Who Among Black Americans Publishing Co., 1978. xiii, 1,096 p.

> Arranged alphabetically, this work contains information about both men and women. Each entry contains vital statistics, education, marital status, present and previous positions, memberships, awards and honors, and military service.

WHO'S WHO OF AMERICAN WOMEN. Chicago: Marquis Who's Who, 1958--. Biennial.

> This volume is arranged alphabetically. Each entry contains vital statistics, education, marital status, career, political activities, military record, awards and honors, professional memberships, religion, clubs, publications. Only living women are included. Most are those who have achieved prominence in politics, business, the arts, science, entertainment or athletics.

WHO'S WHO OF THE COLORED RACE: A GENERAL BIOGRAPHICAL DIRECTORY OF MEN AND WOMEN OF AFRICAN DESCENT. Vol. 1. Edited by Frank Lincoln Mathers. Chicago: Privately printed, 1915. Reprint. Detroit: Gale Research Co., 1976. 961 p.

Willard, Frances E., and Livermore, Mary A., eds. AMERICAN WOMEN: FIFTEEN HUNDRED BIOGRAPHIES WITH OVER 1400 PORTRAITS: A COMPREHENSIVE ENCYCLOPEDIA OF THE LIVES AND ACHIEVEMENTS OF AMERICAN WOMEN DURING THE NINETEENTH CENTURY. 1897. Reprint. 2 vols. Detroit, Mich.: Gale Research Co., 1973.

> All of the familiar names of famous women of the nineteenth century may be found in these volumes, but most useful are references to lesser-known women who made contributions in their own day. The women listed are classified in an index by the nature of their contributions, for instance, actresses, authors, or temperance workers.

WOMEN'S WHO'S WHO OF AMERICA. A BIOGRAPHICAL DICTIONARY OF CONTEMPORARY WOMEN OF THE UNITED STATES AND CANADA, 1914-1915. Edited by John William Leonard. New York: American Commonwealth Co., 1915. Reprint. Detroit: Gale Research Co., 1976. 961 p.

# Chapter 4

# PERIODICALS OF THE WOMEN'S MOVEMENT

BIG MAMA RAG: A WOMAN'S JOURNAL. Denver: Big Mama Rag, Inc., 1972-- . Monthly.

> This news journal has a feminist point of view. It reports national and local events relevant to women. It conceives of itself as a forum for the development of the theory and practice of feminism. Each issue has a particular focus.

BIRTH CONTROL REVIEW. New York: American Birth Control League, 1917-38. Weekly.

> Driving forces behind this magazine were Margaret Sanger and Frederick A. Blossom, socialist, member of IWW, and former head of Cleveland Associated Charities.

BREAD AND ROSES: A MIDWESTERN WOMEN'S JOURNAL OF ISSUES AND THE ARTS. Madison, Wis.: Bread and Roses, Inc., 1977-- . Quarterly.

> This periodical proposes to establish "a midwest based journal to focus on cultural, political, and social concerns of American women . . . and to inspire and activate change."

CHRYSALIS: A MAGAZINE OF WOMEN'S CULTURE. Los Angeles: Chrysalis, Inc., 1979--. Quarterly.

> This periodical features poetry and fiction by women and essays on women's culture and feminist ideology.

THE CLUB WOMAN. Boston: General Federation of Women's Clubs, 1897-1904. Monthly.

> This journal reported on the activities of women's organizations like the General Federation of Women's Clubs and the State Federation of Women's Clubs around the turn of the century. The club's main areas of interest were social reform, general philanthropy, and education. Its views give a good indication of the thinking of politically moderate women of the period.

# Periodicals of the Women's Movement

THE COMING NATION. Chicago: Socialist Party, 1907-14. Weekly.

> This journal began as THE SOCIALIST WOMAN, changed its name
> in 1909 to THE PROGRESSIVE WOMAN, and in 1913 to THE
> COMING NATION. It was a forum for the socialist organization
> to examine the role of women in the socialist and labor movements.

COUNTRY WOMEN. Albion, Calif.: Country Women's Collective, 1972-- .
5 per year.

> This journal speaks for and about rural women, principally old-time
> country women and the newly returned back-to-the-land women.
> Each issue has a theme, such as animals, children's liberation, or
> humor. A portion of the magazine is devoted to practical matters
> of country life--gardening, machinery, animal husbandry, and so forth.

EQUAL RIGHTS: INDEPENDENT FEMINIST WEEKLY. Baltimore: National
Women's Party, 1935-36. Weekly.

> This publication aimed at contributing to the movement for equality
> between men and women, politically and personally. Each issue
> included a biography of a great woman, past or present; news on
> women's issues; and a calendar of meetings and conferences on
> women's rights. Among the editors were Zona Gale and Harriet
> Stanton Blatch.

FEMINIST STUDIES. Baltimore: University of Maryland, 1971-- . 3 per year.

> This scholarly journal focuses on European and American women
> in history.

FORERUNNER. New York: The Charlton Co., 1909-16. Monthly.

> Edited by Charlotte Perkins Gilman. This periodical was radical
> for its time. Its program included progress, social and intellectual
> equality for women, and nonviolent socialism. It included essays,
> fiction, and poetry.

FRONTIERS: A JOURNAL OF WOMEN'S STUDIES. Boulder, Colo.: Women's
Studies Program, University of Colorado, 1976-- . Triennial.

> This journal focuses each issue on a specific topic. Topics have
> included "Reproduction," "Who Speaks for the Women's Movement,"
> and "Fantasies and Futures."

HERESIES: A FEMINIST PUBLICATION ON ART AND POLITICS. New York:
Heresies Collective, 1977-- . Quarterly.

> This journal, produced collectively, consists of several articles on
> a particular topic. Topics to date have been "Feminism, Art and
> Politics"; "Patterns of Communication and Space Among Women";
> "Lesbian Art and Artists"; "Women's Traditional Arts/The Politics
> of Aesthetics"; "The Great Goddess"; "On Women and Violence";

"Working Together"; "Third World Women in the United States"; and "Women Organized/Women Divided: Power, Propaganda and Backlash."

THE KEYSTONE. Charleston: South Carolina Federation of Women's Clubs, 1899-1913. Monthly.

This publication was the official voice of the southern club woman --women's clubs and the United Daughters of the Confederacy. The journal discusses the activities of club women who were involved with philanthropy, civic affairs, horticulture, village improvement, libraries, and schools. These southern groups had some role in the early attempts for interracial cooperation in the Deep South.

THE LADDER. San Francisco: Daughters of Bilitis, 1956-72. Bimonthly.

This magazine was published by a lesbian activist group. It is a source of information about lesbian liberation.

THE LADIES GARMENT WORKER. New York: International Ladies Garment Worker's Union, 1910-18. Monthly.

This journal included sections written in Yiddish, Italian, and English. The conditions of women garment workers were graphically described. The journal aimed to be an organizing instrument for the union, and it touched on political issues, such as suffrage, other legislation. Some stories and poems written by women workers were published.

LADY'S FRIEND. Philadelphia: Deacon and Peterson, 1864-73. Monthly.

This journal was mainly concerned with fashion and literature. Women wrote most of the entries in the publication, centering on the traditional occupations of women--homemaking, fashion, food, handicrafts, and literature.

LESBIAN TIDE. Los Angeles: Tide Publishers, 1971-- . 6 per year.

This radical feminist magazine, in news format, covers events in the lesbian, gay, and feminist communities and contains other social change news as it affects lesbians. It is nationally distributed.

LIFE AND LABOR: Chicago: National Women's Trade Union League, 1911-21. Quarterly.

This journal discussed labor conditions nationally and internationally, but focused on the role of women. It was well illustrated by photographs of women workers, protesters, and organizers. Contributors included Alice Henry and Margaret Dreier Robbins.

MAJORITY REPORT. New York: Majority Report Co., 1969-- . Biweekly.

This newspaper presents women's news in New York City and to some degree, nationally. It has a liberal orientation, speaking primarily to mainstream feminists. It is one of the major feminist news sources on the contemporary scene.

MOM'S APPLE PIE. Seattle: Lesbian Mothers National Defense Fund, 1979-- . Bimonthly.

This newsletter reports on the struggles of lesbian mothers across the country.

MS. MAGAZINE. New York: Ms. Foundation for Education and Communication, 1970-- . Monthly.

This contemporary periodical is perhaps the most widely read national publication of the new feminist movement. It has a highly commercial and well-designed format. Each issue covers a wide range of subjects of current interest. It includes book and film reviews and news from women's communities across the country.

OFF OUR BACKS. Washington, D.C.: Off Our Backs, Inc., 1970-- . 11 per year.

This women's news journal is one of the major contemporary women's news sources for the feminist community.

PLEXUS: BAY AREA WOMEN'S NEWSPAPER. San Francisco: Feminist Publishing Alliance, 1974-- . Monthly.

This newspaper reports on national and international news of the women's struggle.

QUEST: A FEMINIST QUARTERLY. Washington, D.C.: Quest, 1975-- .

Each issue has a specific topic relating to the women's movement. In the past issues have covered such areas as leadership, organizations and strategies, money, fame and power, the sisterhood of women, women in their communities, and international feminism.

THE SECOND WAVE: A MAGAZINE OF THE NEW FEMINISM. New York: Female Liberation, Inc., 1971-- . Quarterly.

This periodical includes articles on the issues and culture generated in the contemporary women's movement.

THE SECOND WAVE: A MAGAZINE OF ONGOING FEMINISM. Cambridge, Mass.: Second Wave, 1973-- . Quarterly.

This periodical includes articles on issues of current interest to the women's community and on women's culture and art.

SIGNS: JOURNAL OF WOMEN IN CULTURE AND SOCIETY. Chicago:

University of Chicago, 1975-- . Quarterly.

> This academic publication has a multidisciplinary approach to women's issues with some anthropological emphasis. It covers international events and questions about women. Each journal has a topic, like incest, or power and powerlessness, and contains reviews of other works on women and essays on the new scholarship about women.

SOJOURNER: THE NEW ENGLAND WOMEN'S JOURNAL OF NEWS, OPINIONS AND THE ARTS. Cambridge, Mass.: Sojourner, Inc., 1975-- . Monthly.

> SOJOURNER reports local alternative news and provides space for women of various backgrounds to give their views. Special articles on the past have been on the equal rights amendment debate and feminism at the United Nations.

THE VANGUARD. Tacoma, Wash.: National Council of Women Voters, 1916-18. Monthly.

> This journal intended to educate newly franchised women voters as they achieved suffrage--first by state and later by constitutional amendment.

THE WOMAN PATRIOT. Washington, D.C.: Woman Patriot Publishing Co., 1919-32. Weekly.

> This antifeminist journal spoke in defense of womanhood, motherhood, the family, and the nation. It was opposed to suffragism, feminism, socialism, and the trade union movement.

WOMAN REBEL. New York: Margaret Sanger, 1914. Monthly.

> This magazine, edited by Margaret Sanger, was directed at working-class women. It took a radical stance urging contraception as a weapon against the capitalist class.

WOMAN'S COLUMN. Boston: American Woman Suffrage Association, 1892-1904. Weekly.

> This publication dealt with issues of women's suffrage, women and higher education, women in the church, the working woman, and the immigrant woman. Notable contributors were Alice Stone Blackwell, Henry B. Blackwell, Lucy Stone, and Florence M. Adkinson.

WOMEN: A JOURNAL OF LIBERATION. Baltimore: Women's Growth Center, 1971-- . Quarterly.

> This journal surveys a broad spectrum of issues for the women's liberationists, which have included conflict, feminist science, violence, and lesbians having children.

# Periodicals of the Women's Movement

WOMEN'S STUDIES NEWSLETTER. Old Westbury, N.Y.: Feminist Press's Clearinghouse on Women's Studies, 1973-- . Quarterly.

> This publication is for the National Women's Studies Association. It reports on feminist issues in the academic community and scholarly consensus related to women's history and studies.

WOMEN STUDIES ABSTRACTS. Rush, N.Y.: Women Studies Abstracts, 1972-- . Quarterly.

> For annotation see page 11.

THE WREE-VIEW. New York: Women's International Democratic Federation, 1975-- . Bimonthly.

> This bulletin reports on the conditions of U.S. women, working-class women, and the Third World struggle. The federation has a specific program advocated through the journal, especially an Economic Bill of Rights.

# Chapter 5

# GENERAL WORKS

Abbott, Edith. WOMEN IN INDUSTRY: A STUDY IN AMERICAN ECO-
NOMIC HISTORY. 1913. New York: D. Appleton and Co., 1928. xxii, 408 p.

This is a scholarly study of women factory workers from colonial
times to the early twentieth century by one of the Hull House
group. Abbott notes various problems, notably low wages.

Altbach, Edith Hoshino. WOMEN IN AMERICA. Lexington, Mass.: D.C.
Heath, 1974. x, 205 p.

Altbach explores the role of women in domestic life and in the
labor force from colonial times to the present. She also discusses
the women's movement in relation to "common" women.

Anticaglia, Elizabeth. TWELVE AMERICAN WOMEN. Chicago: Nelson-
Hall, 1975. xiv, 256 p.

This book consists of biographical sketches of Anne Hutchinson,
Mercy Otis Warren, Emma H. Willard, Margaret Fuller, Susan B.
Anthony, Dorothea L. Dix, Jane Addams, Ruth St. Denis, Mar-
garet Sanger, Eleanor Roosevelt, Rachel Carson, and Margaret
Mead. There is a useful bibliography appended.

Banner, Lois. WOMEN IN MODERN AMERICA: A BRIEF HISTORY. New
York: Harcourt Brace Jovanovich, 1974. xii, 276 p. Paper.

Banner begins with the status of women in 1890, legal, educational, sexual, and organizational. She observes the beginnings
of change but notes that until World War I there were two choices
for women, marriage or prostitution. She notes the new feminism
and the new attitudes of the twenties as well as the effects of the
Depression and war. She concludes with the new movements of the
1960s and 1970s and the gains made.

Baxter, Annette K. TO BE A WOMAN IN AMERICA, 1850-1930. New York:
Times Books, 1978. 240 p.

This is primarily a general pictorial history of women.

Beard, Mary Ritter. WOMEN AS A FORCE IN HISTORY: A STUDY IN TRA-
DITIONS AND REALITIES. New York: Macmillan, 1946. Reprint. New
York: Octagon Books, 1976. 382 p.

> Beard examines the tradition of subjugation of women in the light
> of historical reality and of the actual participation of women in
> almost every realm of human endeavor. She notes that women
> have done much more than just bear and raise children.

Berkin, Carol Ruth, and Norton, Mary Beth, eds. WOMEN OF AMERICA: A
HISTORY. Boston: Houghton Mifflin, 1979. xv, 442 p.

> This volume contains sections by fifteen scholars. The essays are
> wide-ranging, covering topics such as historiography, work,
> demography, business, education, religion, sexual stereotypes,
> Chinese women, birth control, and issues of the twentieth century.
> The sections are arranged in chronological fashion.

Bradford, Gamaliel. PORTRAITS OF AMERICAN WOMEN. New York: Houghton Mifflin, 1919. Reprint. Freeport, N.Y.: Books for Libraries Press, 1969.
x, 276 p.

> This book consists of biographical sketches of Abigail Adams,
> Sarah Alden Ripley, Mary Lyon, Harriet Beecher Stowe, Margaret
> Fuller, Louisa May Alcott, Frances Willard, and Emily Dickinson.
> All are from New England, except Frances Willard, so the title
> is misleading.

Brownlee, W. Elliott, and Brownlee, Mary M., eds. WOMEN IN THE AMERI-
CAN ECONOMY: A DOCUMENTARY HISTORY 1675-1929. New Haven,
Conn.: Yale University Press, 1976. viii, 350 p.

> The editors have selected accounts which deal with preindustrial
> women, farm and ranch women, the factories, domestic and secre-
> tarial services, and the professions. Other sections have to do
> with women as consumers and taxpayers.

Bullough, Vern L. THE SUBORDINATE SEX: A HISTORY OF ATTITUDES TO-
WARD WOMEN. Urbana: University of Illinois Press, 1973. viii, 375 p.

> Bullough traces attitudes toward women throughout Western civiliza-
> tion and describes the American pattern.

Calhoun, Arthur W. A SOCIAL HISTORY OF THE AMERICAN FAMILY. 3
vols. Cleveland: Arthur H. Clark Co., 1917-19.

> A detailed history to the end of World War I. Volume 1 deals
> with the colonial period, noting European customs and ideas
> brought to America and the position of women, courtship, marriage,
> sex, sin, and family life in the various colonies. Volume 2 deals
> with the period from Independence to the Civil War, covering
> marriage, sex, family, and the position of women and children in

various parts of the country as well as the sexual and family relationship of slaves in the South. Volume 3 covers the period
from the Civil War through World War I, including a lot of the
common ideas of the period about miscegenation, race sterility,
and race suicide.

Clark, Electa. LEADING LADIES: AN AFFECTIONATE LOOK AT AMERICAN
WOMEN OF THE TWENTIETH CENTURY. New York: Stein and Day, 1976.
252 p.

The author, in amusing fashion, looks at a wide variety of women,
feminists, artists, athletes, and business women. She ranges from
the submissive "dear little woman" of 1900 to the more aggressive
woman of the 1970s, predicting a much freer lot for women by
the year 2000.

Cooper, James L., and Cooper, Sheila McIsaac, eds. THE ROOTS OF AMERICAN
FEMINISM. Boston: Allyn and Bacon, 1973. 300 p.

The editors bring together key selections from Mary Wollstonecraft,
Sarah Grimke, Margaret Fuller, John Stewart Mill, Charlotte Gilman, Margaret Sanger, and Suzanne LaFollette on the rights and
status of women.

Cott, Nancy F., ed. ROOT OF BITTERNESS: DOCUMENTS OF THE SOCIAL
HISTORY OF AMERICAN WOMEN. New York: Dutton, 1972. 373 p.

Cott brings together fifty documents that illustrate the social history
of women from the colonial period to the twentieth century.

Dispenza, Joseph E. ADVERTISING THE AMERICAN WOMAN. Dayton, Ohio:
P. Flaurs, 1975. 181 p.

Dispenza presents a history of advertising that aims at showing how
advertising reflects traditional sex role stereotyping. The book
consists of reproductions of advertisements and short descriptive
and evaluative comments.

Douglas, Emily Taft. REMEMBER THE LADIES: THE STORY OF GREAT
WOMEN WHO HELPED SHAPE AMERICA. New York: G.P. Putnam's Sons, 1966.
254 p.

Taking her title from Abigail Adams, Douglas, herself a woman
who helped shape America, tells the story of creative women in
America from Anne Hutchinson to Eleanor Roosevelt. Noting that
"the dependency of wives sapped their initiative, she tells the
story of those who opened doors for us."

Filene, Peter Gabriel. HIM/HER/SELF: SEX ROLES IN MODERN AMERICA.
New York: Harcourt Brace Jovanovich, 1974. xiv, 351 p.

This is an essay on sex roles of middle-class men and women,

primarily in the twentieth century. The first part deals with the
period to 1919, including the end of Victorianism, the role
of women, men and manliness, and the impact of World War I.
The second part deals with the postwar generation, the period of
apathy (1930–60), and the upsurge of feminism in the 1960s. The
author tries to explain feminism or the lack of it in each period,
as well as its effect on men.

Flexner, Eleanor. CENTURY OF STRUGGLE: THE WOMEN'S RIGHTS MOVE-
MENT IN THE UNITED STATES. Cambridge, Mass.: Harvard University Press,
1959. 348 p.

   The book is divided into three parts, the first detailing the position of women in the colonial era, the first steps toward education,
   the beginnings of reform, and the Seneca Falls Convention of 1848.
   The second part details the intellectual progress of women, the suffrage movement, and women's organizations and their role in early
   labor unions. The third part is concerned with the period, 1900–
   20, including the successful end to the crusade for the right to
   vote.

Friedman, Jean E., and Shade, William G., eds. OUR AMERICAN SISTERS:
WOMEN IN AMERICAN LIFE AND THOUGHT. Boston: Allyn and Bacon,
1973. v, 354 p.

   This volume is composed of nineteen essays arranged in chronological sections. Each essay is written by a scholar who deals
   with attitudes toward women in the context of social history.

George, Carol V.R., ed. "REMEMBER THE LADIES": NEW PERSPECTIVES ON
WOMEN IN AMERICA. Syracuse, N.Y.: Syracuse University Press, 1975.
201 p.

   George provides essays in social history divided in rough chronological sections from 1600–1800, the nineteenth century, and recent issues of the twentieth century.

Goodsell, Willystine. A HISTORY OF MARRIAGE AND THE FAMILY. New
York: Macmillan, 1934. Reprint. New York: AMS Press, 1974. xiv,
590 p.

   A general history, but about half of the chapters refer to the
   United States.

Grabill, Wilson H., et al. THE FERTILITY OF AMERICAN WOMEN. New
York: John Wiley and Sons, 1958. xvi, 448 p.

   The authors survey fertility rates in the colonial era, the nineteenth,
   and twentieth century. They provide data by classifications of urban, rural, ethnic groups, educational level, occupational groups,
   and socioeconomic factors.

Graham, Abbie. LADIES IN REVOLT. New York: Woman's Press, 1934. 222 p.

> Graham describes the feminist movement in the nineteenth century. She includes breezy accounts of many of the feminists of the period including Susan B. Anthony, Amelia Bloomer, Elizabeth Cady Stanton, Frances Wright, Mary Wollstonecraft, Margaret Fuller, and Catherine Beecher. She includes a good bibliography of early writings.

Groves, Ernest Rutherford. THE AMERICAN WOMAN: THE FEMININE SIDE OF A MASCULINE SOCIETY. New York: Greenberg, 1944. Reprint. New York: Arno Press, 1972. vii, 465 p.

> Groves looks at the cultural origins of the status of women including the Judeo-Christian concept of the position of women. He traces the development of the status of women in the colonial period, on the frontier, and in various sections of the country and ends with the American woman in the twentieth century. He notes that, "rated by the scant attention she gets in American historical writing, (she) is the forgotten sex."

Hahn, Emily. ONCE UPON A PEDESTAL. New York: New American Library, 1974. 304 p.

> Hahn traces the revolt of women from Anne Hutchinson to the women's movement of the late twentieth century.

Hartman, Mary S., and Banner, Lois, eds. CLIO'S CONSCIOUSNESS RAISED: NEW PERSPECTIVES ON THE HISTORY OF WOMEN. New York: Harper and Row, 1974. Reprint. New York: Octagon Books, 1976. 253 p.

> This book consists of papers presented at the Berkshire Conference of Women Historians, held in 1973. The direction represented here is to avoid biography and uncritical flailing at male oppression. The essays deal with women as a group.

Henry, Alice. WOMEN AND THE LABOR MOVEMENT. New York: George H. Doran Co., 1923. xix, 241 p.

> This is a survey of the problems of women in industry from colonial times and the struggle for industrial legislation, including minimum wage, maximum hours, and the women's bureau, which in 1920 became a permanent agency of the Department of Labor. Its purpose was to protect women workers. The author also explores the role of women in World War I.

Hogeland, Ronald W. WOMEN AND WOMANHOOD IN AMERICA. Lexington, Mass.: D.C. Heath, 1973. xi, 183 p.

> Hogeland provides an anthology of writings which deal with historical method in studying women and traces the history of women with pro and con views in each period.

Humphrey, Grace. WOMEN IN AMERICAN HISTORY. Indianapolis, Ind.: Bobbs-Merrill, 1919. Reprint. Freeport, N.Y.: Books for Libraries Press, 1968. 223 p.

> The author provides short, popular sketches of Anne Hutchinson, Betsy Ross, Mary Lindley Murray, Molly Pitcher, Martha Washington, Jemima Johnson, Dolley Madison, Lucretia Mott, Harriet Beecher Stowe, Julia Ward Howe, Mary Livermore, Barbara Fritchie, and Clara Barton.

Irwin, Inez Haynes. ANGELS AND AMAZONS: A HUNDRED YEARS OF AMERICAN WOMEN. Garden City, N.Y.: Doubleday Doran, 1933. Reprint. New York: Arno Press, 1974. 531 p.

> The author describes the progress of the feminist movement and the successes of various elements of the crusade, including the right to vote. The appendix contains a useful list of organizations that promoted women's causes in 1933 along with their national officers, location, and purposes.

Kraditor, Aileen S., ed. UP FROM THE PEDESTAL: SELECTED WRITINGS IN THE HISTORY OF AMERICAN FEMINISM. Chicago: Quadrangle, 1968. 372 p.

> This anthology brings together documents from Anne Bradstreet to the National Organization of Women.

Lerner, Gerda. THE WOMEN IN AMERICAN HISTORY. Menlo Park, Calif.: Addison-Wesley, 1971. 207 p.

> Lerner divides the history of women in four chronological periods, analyzing their role in the home, as citizens, and as employed persons. She contends that despite discrimination women have been a major force in history.

Marlow, H. Carleton, and Davis, Harrison M. THE AMERICAN SEARCH FOR WOMEN. Santa Barbara, Calif.: American Biographical Center, Clio Press, 1976. 539 p.

> The authors historically survey American thought on the nature of women. Final chapters relate to the implications of the current women's movement.

Martin, Wendy. THE AMERICAN SISTERHOOD: WRITINGS OF THE FEMINIST MOVEMENT FROM COLONIAL TIMES TO THE PRESENT. New York: Harper and Row, 1972. 367 p.

> Martin includes forty-six selections that in some way bear on the feminist movement. Most of these are from the nineteenth and twentieth century. The only colonial selection is from the trial of Anne Hutchinson. Almost half deal with the movement since 1960.

Mead, Margaret. MALE AND FEMALE: A STUDY OF THE SEXES IN A CHANGING WORLD. New York: Morrow, 1949. Reprint. Westport, Conn.: Greenwood, 1977. xii, 477 p.

> Using the tools of anthropology, Mead demonstrates that sex roles are contrived, that either male or female may be stunted if reared to believe themselves somehow incomplete.

Nies, Judith. SEVEN WOMEN: PORTRAITS FROM THE AMERICAN RADICAL TRADITION. New York: Viking Press, 1977. xvi, 255 p.

> Leaving aside traditional definitions of radical, Nies writes that her subject is a "successful rebellion." She includes Sarah Grimke, Harriet Tubman, Elizabeth Cady Stanton, Mary "Mother" Jones, Charlotte Perkins Gilman, Anna Louise Strong, and Dorothy Day.

Olson, Vicky Burgess. SISTER SAINTS. Provo, Utah: Brigham Young University, 1978. xiv, 494 p.

> Olson writes accounts of twenty-four Mormon women from all periods.

O'Neill, William. EVERYONE WAS BRAVE: THE RISE AND FALL OF FEMINISM IN AMERICA. Chicago: Quadrangle, 1969. xi, 369 p.

> O'Neill traces feminism from the Seneca Falls Convention in 1848 to the militancy of the 1960s.

OUR FAMOUS WOMEN: AN AUTHORIZED RECORD OF THE LIVES AND DEEDS OF DISTINGUISHED WOMEN OF OUR TIMES. Hartford, Conn.: A.D. Worthington, 1886. Reprint. Freeport, N.Y.: Books for Libraries Press, 1975. xxvii, 715 p.

> This book consists of biographical sketches of thirty famous women of the nineteenth century. It is doubly interesting in that most of the subjects were still alive and many of them wrote sketches of other women. For example, Elizabeth Cady Stanton wrote the biography of Susan B. Anthony while Laura Curtis Bullard contributed a biography of Mrs. Stanton.

Parker, Gail, ed. THE OVEN BIRDS: AMERICAN WOMEN ON WOMANHOOD, 1820-1920. Garden City, N.Y.: Anchor Books, 1972. 387 p.

> This is an anthology of selections from Lydia Hunt Sigourney, Lydia Marie Child, Angelina Grimke, Catherine Beecher, Harriet Beecher Stowe, Sarah Orne Jewett, Elizabeth Cady Stanton, Jane Addams, and Charlotte Perkins Gilman. Short biographical sketches precede each selection.

Rosaldo, Michelle Zimbalest, and Lamphere, Louise, eds. WOMAN, CULTURE AND SOCIETY. Stanford, Calif.: Stanford University Press, 1974. vi, 352 p.

This is a body of work by several anthropologists that addresses women's issues from the anthropological perspective.

Rothman, Sheila. WOMAN'S PROPER PLACE: A HISTORY OF CHANGING IDEALS AND PRACTICES, 1870 TO THE PRESENT. New York: Basic Books, 1978. xiv, 322 p.

Rothman describes women by periods which she calls: "virtuous womanhood," "educated motherhood," "wife companion," and "woman as person."

Ryan, Mary P. WOMANHOOD IN AMERICA: FROM COLONIAL TIMES TO THE PRESENT. New York: New Viewpoints, 1975. 469 p.

Ryan describes the historical male-conceived view of women. She shifts the periodication of women's history into a feminist orientation. She believes that women in history must be studied from different concepts than the traditional male-dominated history.

Schneir, Miriam, ed. FEMINISM: THE ESSENTIAL HISTORICAL WRITINGS. New York: Random House, 1972. 360 p.

This anthology contains documents from the eighteenth century to the early years of the twentieth century. A few foreign writers are included.

Scott, Anne Firor. THE SOUTHERN LADY FROM PEDESTAL TO POLITICS 1830-1930. Chicago: University of Chicago Press, 1970. xv, 247 p.

Scott describes the stereotype of southern women as the submissive homemaker but asserts that the reality was quite different. She relates the changes brought by the Civil War and increasing education and notes the struggle for the right to vote and the changing image of the 1920s. The book contains an excellent bibliographical essay on sources.

_____, ed. THE AMERICAN WOMAN: WHO WAS SHE? Englewood Cliffs, N.J.: Prentice-Hall, 1971. viii, 182 p.

Scott has selected a wide-ranging group of essays, mostly from the twentieth century, on work, education, reform and the relationships of men and women.

Sinclair, Andrew. THE BETTER HALF. New York: Harper and Row, 1965. xxix, 401 p.

Sinclair traces the position of women in America to the ratification of the suffrage amendment. He deals with feminism, and social and economic position of women, as well as sexuality and contraception.

Smith, Page. DAUGHTERS OF THE PROMISED LAND: WOMEN IN AMERI-
CAN HISTORY. Boston: Little, Brown and Co., 1970. 392 p.

> Feminists find the interpretation in this book offensive although
> some of the information may prove useful.

Sochen, June. HERSTORY: A WOMAN'S VIEW OF AMERICAN HISTORY.
2 vols. New York: Knopf, 1974.

> Sochen has provided a feminist-humanist commentary on the history
> of the United States. She believes victims of progress have been
> ignored and regards women as among the victims. She includes
> attitudes about and from women, spanning time from discovery to
> the militant feminism of the 1960s.

_____. MOVERS AND SHAKERS: AMERICAN WOMEN THINKERS AND AC-
TIVISTS, 1900-1970. New York: Quadrangle, 1973. xix, 320 p.

> Sochen discusses thirty feminists, dividing them into general femi-
> nists, radical feminists, pragmatic writers, and feminist writers.

_____, ed. THE NEW FEMINISM IN TWENTIETH-CENTURY AMERICA.
Lexington, Mass.: D.C. Heath, 1971. 208 p.

> Sochen brings together feminist writings from the late nineteenth
> century to the recent writings of the 1960s.

Trabey, June. ON WOMEN AND POWER. New York: Avon Books, 1977.
xviii, 262 p.

> This is a popular advice book on how women can obtain greater
> control and power in their lives and work.

Truman, Margaret. WOMEN OF COURAGE FROM REVOLUTIONARY TIMES
TO THE PRESENT. New York: William Morrow and Co., 1976. 254 p.

> Truman chooses women whom she personally believes to have acted
> courageously and with spirit and dignity in American history. She
> tells the story of their actions informally and anecdotally. She
> selects figures such as Mother Jones, Susan B. Anthony, Dolley
> Madison, Margaret Chase Smith, Marian Anderson, and others.

Wald, Carol. MYTH AMERICA: PICTURING WOMEN 1845-1945. New York:
Pantheon Books, 1975. ix, 184 p.

> This is an arrangement of popular photographs of women. The ac-
> companying text points out the ongoing and yet changing stereo-
> types that existed.

Weibel, Kathryn. MIRROR, MIRROR: IMAGES OF WOMEN REFLECTED IN
POPULAR CULTURE. Garden City, N.Y.: Arbor Press, 1978. xxii, 256 p.

Weibel analyzes the changing portraits of women in advertising, magazines, fiction, television, films, and fashion.

Weitz, Shirley. SEX ROLES: BIOLOGICAL, PSYCHOLOGICAL, AND SOCIAL FOUNDATIONS. New York: Oxford University Press, 1977. 256 p.

Weitz studies sex roles in terms of psychology and economics as well as surveying the history and literature of the subject. Sex roles are compared to biological realities.

Welter, Barbara. DIMITY CONVICTIONS: THE AMERICAN WOMAN IN THE NINETEENTH CENTURY. Athens: Ohio University Press, 1976. 230 p.

Welter, in nine essays, defines feminism and describes women and the male attitude toward them in the nineteenth century. She deals with the problems of girls and the "cult of true womanhood," a term which has become commonplace since she resurrected it from nineteenth-century writers. She describes the antiintellectualism directed at women, the relationship of women to religion and literature, and poses Margaret Fuller as a transitional figure.

_____, ed. THE WOMAN QUESTION IN AMERICAN HISTORY. Hinsdale, Ill.: Dryden, 1973. 177 p.

Welter brings together essays from scholars who have worked with the sources.

Wheeler, Adade Mitchell, and Wortman, Marlene Stein. THE ROADS THEY MADE: WOMEN IN ILLINOIS HISTORY. Chicago: Kerr, 1977. 213 p.

The authors describe Illinois women in chronological fashion, beginning with Indian women and carrying the story to 1976.

# Chapter 6

# WOMEN IN THE COLONIAL AND
# REVOLUTIONARY ERAS

Adams, Abigail, and Adams, John. THE BOOK OF ABIGAIL AND JOHN:
SELECTED LETTERS OF THE ADAMS FAMILY 1762-1784. Edited by Lyman
Butterfield. Cambridge, Mass.: Harvard University Press, 1975. 411 p.

> This volume contains 216 letters between Abigail and John Adams.
> Mrs. Adams, in spite of her time, emerges as her own person.

Adams, Charles Francis. "Some Phases of Sexual Morality and Church Discipline in Colonial New England." PROCEEDINGS OF THE MASSACHUSETTS
HISTORICAL SOCIETY. 2d series, (1890-1891): 477-516.

> Adams views the frequent confessions of the sin of fornication in
> church records and believes they indicate the youth of the period
> did not have much of a reputation for sexual modesty. He believes
> that "though there was much incontinence, that incontinence was
> not promiscuous." He includes material on bundling. The work is
> important as an indication of female sexuality in the colonial period.

Alexander, William. THE HISTORY OF WOMEN FROM THE EARLIEST AN-
TIQUITY TO THE PRESENT TIME. 2 vols. Philadelphia: J.H. Dobelbower,
1796. Reprint. New York: AMS Press, 1976.

> Alexander belongs to the school of thought which believes women
> are innately evil. Among the evil characteristics which women
> possessed were pride, vanity, sexual passion, affection, fickleness,
> deceitfulness, hatefulness, and untruthfulness.

Anthony, Katharine. FIRST LADY OF THE REVOLUTION. Garden City, N.Y.:
Doubleday, 1958. 258 p.

> This is a biography of Mercy Otis Warren, sister of American revo-
> lutionary statesman James Otis. She was a playwright who wrote
> a history of the Revolution, which she had propagandized. She
> wrote in behalf of the Bill of Rights and for the Constitution. She
> did not fit the traditional pattern of women of the period.

Battis, Emery. SAINTS AND SECTARIANS: ANNE HUTCHINSON AND THE ANTINOMIAN CONTROVERSY IN THE MASSACHUSETTS BAY COLONY. Chapel Hill: University of North Carolina Press, 1935. xv, 379 p.

> This is the history of Anne Hutchinson's fight against the religious and civil establishment of Massachusetts Bay in theological dispute. Her determination led to her expulsion from the colony.

Benson, Mary Summer. WOMEN IN EIGHTEENTH CENTURY AMERICA: A STUDY OF OPINION AND SOCIAL USAGE. New York: Columbia University Press, 1935. 343 p.

> This is a study of attitudes toward women in the eighteenth century. The author goes into European ideas that influenced America in various periods and how these ideas moderated in the American environment. She looks at the position of women in the home and in education and the image projected in American fiction. A good bibliography is appended.

Blumenthal, Walter Hart. BRIDES FROM BRIDEWELL: FEMALE FELONS SENT TO COLONIAL AMERICA. Rutland, Vt.: C.E. Tuttle Co., 1962. 139 p.

> Blumenthal deals with English female felons sent to Virginia and Maryland and French female convicts who were sent to Louisiana.

_____. WOMEN CAMP FOLLOWERS OF THE AMERICAN REVOLUTION. Philadelphia: G.S. MacManus Co., 1952. 104 p.

> The author documents the presence of camp followers in both the British and American armies. Some of these were prostitutes and some were wives or legitimate servants who performed various tasks such as sewing and washing for the troops. Martha Washington and several wives of officers spent the winter at Valley Forge, for example. These women were an advantage in troop morale but created problems in troop movements and sometimes created disorder.

Booth, Sally Smith. THE WOMEN OF '76. New York: Hastings House, 1973. 329 p.

> This is a popular account of all sorts of women in the American Revolution. Some are familiar but many are more obscure. The author describes both the sacrifice and the contribution of women.

Boyer, Paul, and Nissenbaum, Stephen. SALEM POSSESSED: THE SOCIAL ORIGINS OF WITCHCRAFT. Cambridge, Mass.: Harvard University Press, 1974. xxi, 231 p.

> The authors attribute the Salem witchcraft episode to social maladjustment of the community, part of which was sexist in nature.

Branagan, Thomas. THE EXCELLENCY OF THE FEMALE CHARACTER VINDI-
CATED: BEING AN INVESTIGATION RELATIVE TO THE CAUSE AND EFFECTS
OF THE ENCROACHMENTS OF MEN UPON THE RIGHTS OF WOMEN, AND
THE TOO FREQUENT DEGRADATION AND CONSEQUENT MISFORTUNES OF
THE FAIR SEX. 1808. Reprint. New York: Arno Press, 1972. 322 p.

> This is an early example of male support of the concept of women's
> rights.

Brooks, Geraldine. DAMES AND DAUGHTERS OF COLONIAL DAYS. 1900.
Reprint. New York: Arno Press, 1977. 284 p.

> This volume contains biographical sketches of ten colonial women
> whom the author thought neglected by historians.

Brown, Alice. MERCY WARREN. 1896. Reprint. Spartanburg, S.C.: Reprint Co., 1968. xi, 316 p.

> Mercy Warren was unique in her generation. She wrote plays,
> history, constitutional analysis, and political commentary.

Byrd, William. ANOTHER SECRET DIARY OF WILLIAM BYRD OF WESTOVER
1739-1741. WITH LETTERS AND LITERARY EXERCISES 1696-1726. Edited by
Maude H. Woodfin. Translated and collated by Marion Tinling. Richmond,
Va.: Dietz Press, 1942. xiv, 490 p.

> This is an engaging account of the life of a colonial Virginia
> planter. Feminists will find evidence of the negative position of
> women in this society.

_____. PROSE WORKS; NARRATIVES OF A COLONIAL VIRGINIA. Edited
by Louis B. Wright. Cambridge, Mass.: Harvard University Press, 1966. viii,
488 p.

> This volume contains "Byrd's History of the Dividing Line," "Secret
> History of the Line," "A Progress to the Mines" and a "Journey to
> the Land of Eden." In each there is some insight into the life-
> styles of the women of Virginia as viewed by one of the upper class.

_____. THE SECRET DIARY OF WILLIAM BYRD OF WESTOVER, 1709-1712.
Edited by Louis B. Wright and Marian Tinling. Richmond, Va.: Dietz Press,
1941. xxviii, 622 p.

> One of the great plantation owners of Virginia, Byrd describes the
> operation of the plantation from his vantage point. For the most
> part, it is an upper-class view, but some insight into the lives of
> others, including women, can be gained from his description. It
> is an indispensible source of colonial history of women and the
> sexist attitude of the upper-class male.

Clark, David Lee. BROCKDEN BROWN AND THE RIGHTS OF WOMEN. Austin: University of Texas, 1922. 48 p.

> Brown was a novelist who promoted women's rights through novels such as ALCUIN (1798). His ideas were similar to Mary Wollstonecraft and William Godwin, English writers who are credited with providing much of the early stimulus for women's rights.

Cometti, Elizabeth. "Women in the American Revolution." NEW ENGLAND QUARTERLY 20 (1947): 329-46.

> Cometti describes the loneliness, sorrow, and hardships of the wives and widows of soldiers. Inadequately pensioned, they were hard pressed to make ends meet since so few job opportunities were available. She describes the role of women, which was largely limited to camp following as nurses. There was one female soldier.

Dexter, Elizabeth W. COLONIAL WOMEN OF AFFAIRS: A STUDY OF WOMEN IN BUSINESS AND THE PROFESSIONS IN AMERICA BEFORE 1776. Boston: Houghton Mifflin, 1924. vii, 204 p.

> Dexter describes the position of women who ran taverns, stores, and farms as well as females who functioned as craftsmen, teachers, and newspaper editors. She concludes that while these women were exceptional there was nothing in colonial society to preclude women earning a living if it was necessary.

Dow, George Francis. DOMESTIC LIFE IN NEW ENGLAND IN THE SEVENTEENTH CENTURY. Topsfield, Mass.: Privately printed, 1925. 48 p.

> This small volume is a lecture given at the opening of the American wing of the Metropolitan Museum of Art. It is an undocumented, anecdotal history. It has a useful appendix, being the account of supplies furnished to one household by the Massachusetts Bay Company, 1629-1634.

_____. EVERY DAY LIFE IN THE MASSACHUSETTS BAY COLONY. Boston: Society for the Preservation of New England Antiquities, 1935. Reprint. New York: Arno Press, 1977. 235 p.

> Dow covers home architecture, furnishings, clothing, medicine, games, and penology. In spite of the title, much of the work is representative of all of New England. Since female activities were largely confined to the home, insight is gained about the position of women.

Earle, Alice Morse. COLONIAL DAMES AND GOOD WIVES. Boston: Houghton Mifflin, 1895. Reprint. New York: Unger, 1962. 315 p.

> Earle gives a good account of the position of women in colonial America and their contributions to the Revolution and the economy

of the nation. She also writes of the manners and recreation of
the times.

_____. HOME LIFE IN COLONIAL DAYS. New York: Macmillan, 1898.
Reprint. Stockbridge, Mass.: Berkshire Traveller, 1975. xvi, 470 p.

Earle describes home life, food, clothing, and drink of the colonists. She notes also the home industries, gardens, and hospitality
of the times. It is slanted somewhat to the upper classes, although
in the early years there was not that much social class difference.
These activities were primarily those of women.

Eggleston, George Cary. LIFE IN THE EIGHTEENTH CENTURY. 1905. New
York: A.S. Barnes and Co., 1910. xiv, 264 p.

The author describes life in the early part of the eighteenth century and especially that in Georgia and the Carolinas. It is slanted
to the upper classes and to males, but much on women can be
found here also.

Ellet, Elizabeth F. THE WOMEN OF THE AMERICAN REVOLUTION. 3 vols.
New York: Baker and Scribner, 1848-50. Reprint. Brooklyn: Haskell House,
1969.

Ellet provides sketches of more than 160 women of the period of
the American Revolution. Although in popular anecdotal style,
the facts are carefully documented.

Engle, Paul. WOMEN IN THE AMERICAN REVOLUTION. Chicago: Follett
Publishing Co., 1976. xvii, 299 p.

Engle describes the part of women in the American Revolution with
considerable biographical data on individuals.

Evans, Elizabeth. WEATHERING THE STORM: WOMEN OF THE AMERICAN
REVOLUTION. New York: Scribner's, 1975. 372 p.

The author, working from letters and diaries, describes the lives of
women in the American Revolution.

Field, Vena B. CONSTANTIA. Orono: University of Maine Press, 1933.
118 p.

Constantia was the pen name of Judith Murray Sargent (1751-1820).
She wrote poems and plays, at least two of which were staged.
She also wrote a number of feminist pieces which particularly argued
for equality of intellectual ability of women and men and for equal
education for women.

Frost, J. William. THE QUAKER FAMILY IN COLONIAL AMERICA: A POR-
TRAIT OF THE SOCIETY OF FRIENDS. New York: St. Martin's Press, 1973.
vi, 248 p.

Frost describes the position of women as well as children and
youth in Quaker society. He takes note of education and the
courtship and marriage patterns of Quakers. He deals with the
life-style of the Quaker family and the function of women therein.

George, Margaret. ONE WOMAN'S "SITUATION." Urbana: University of
Illinois Press, 1970. 174 p.

George describes in detail the life of Mary Wollstonecraft, an
early feminist who wrote in the 1790s. George believes the history
of women is prehistory because women were passive and negative.
Wollstonecraft was widely read in the United States and influenced
liberal thought about women.

Holliday, Carl. WOMAN'S LIFE IN COLONIAL DAYS. Boston: Cornhill
Publishing Co., 1922. Reprint. Detroit: Gale Research Co., 1970. xvi,
319 p.

Jones, Mary Gwladys. HANNAH MORE. Cambridge, Engl.: Cambridge
University Press, 1952. Reprint. Westport, Conn.: Greenwood Press, 1978.
xi, 284 p.

This is a biography of Hannah More (1745-1843), who wrote about
women in the latter part of the colonial period using the theory
that women were weak and thus deserved special treatment by men.

Langdon, William Chauncy. EVERYDAY THINGS IN AMERICAN LIFE, 1607-
1776. 2 vols. New York: Scribner's, 1937.

Langdon describes the life-style of colonists with emphasis on housing but with accounts of furniture and utensils. Much of it deals
with upper-class women.

Leonard, Eugenie A. THE DEAR-BOUGHT HERITAGE. Philadelphia: University of Pennsylvania Press, 1965. 658 p.

The author studied colonial women to find out how they contributed
to life in the wilderness. She believes that next to childbearing,
their principal goal was improvement of the lot of their families.
She relates how colonial women did this.

More, Hannah. ESSAYS ON VARIOUS SUBJECTS, PRINCIPALLY DESIGNED
FOR YOUNG LADIES. Philadelphia: Young, Stewart and McCullock, 1786.
214 p.

More uses the "weaker vessel" argument that God created woman
from finer clay, thus exempting her from coarse and rough duties.
Men owe women lenient treatment because of this weakness.

Morgan, Edmund S. THE PURITAN FAMILY: ESSAYS ON RELIGION AND DOMESTIC RELATIONS IN SEVENTEENTH CENTURY NEW ENGLAND. Boston: Trustees of the Public Library, 1944. x, 196 p.

Morgan discusses the nature of love in the Puritan society and the considerations taken in marriage, the responsibility of parents for their children, their education, and the position of the family in society.

_____. VIRGINIANS AT HOME: FAMILY LIFE IN THE EIGHTEENTH CENTURY. Williamsburg, Va.: Colonial Williamsburg, 1952. 99 p.

Morgan describes the life-style of colonial Virginia, the process of growing up, marriage, and courtship. The tendency is to describe the customs of the upper classes and to present a somewhat idealized picture of marriage.

Nixon, Edna. MARY WOLLSTONECRAFT: HER LIFE AND TIMES. London: J.M. Deut and Sons, 1911. xii, 272 p.

Mary Wollstonecraft was an eighteenth-century Englishwoman who wrote VINDICATION OF THE RIGHTS OF WOMEN and other feminist essays. Putting her into a bibliography of Americans can be justified by the fact that her pioneering work had a profound influence on early American writers, for example, Margaret Fuller.

Powell, Chilton L. "Marriage in Early New England." NEW ENGLAND QUARTERLY 1 (1928): 323-34.

Powell describes the process by which marriage had become a civil ceremony in early New England. He finds that the concept dates back into sixteenth-century England. He also describes the development of common law marriages, the marriages made "under a hedge." The latter was common among all classes.

Ravenel, Harriet H. ELIZA PINCKNEY. 1896. Reprint. Spartanburg, S.C.: Reprint Co., 1967. xi, 331 p.

Eliza Pinckney (1722-1793) was a successful manager of an indigo plantation in South Carolina. She was the mother of two statesmen of the Revolution, C.C. and Thomas Pinckney.

"The 'Reforming Synod' of 1679 and 1680 and Its Confession of Faith." In THE CREEDS AND PLATFORMS OF CONGREGATIONALISM by Williston Walker, pp. 409-37. New York: Scribner's, 1893.

After a decade of bad fortune including King Philip's War, the General Court of Massachusetts Bay summoned a Synod of Churches to find the problem. This document portrays a long list of sins that the synod discovered and thereby throws some light on the sexuality of Massachusetts Bay colony.

Rush, Benjamin. THOUGHTS ON FEMALE EDUCATION. Boston: Samuel Hall, 1787. 32 p.

> Rush argues that since the United States had declared its political independence from England, so also should it declare its independence in social matters. He argues against finishing school education and proposed practical education in arithmetic, bookkeeping, government, and the principles of liberty.

Sewall, Samuel. THE DIARY OF SAMUEL SEWALL, 1674-1729. Edited by M. Halsey Thomas. 2 vols. New York: Farrar Straus and Giroux, 1973.

> Judge Samuel Sewall describes his life in minute detail. Although it is the life of a member of the upper class, it throws light on lesser people, including slaves and Indians. Originally published by the Massachusetts Historical Society in 3 volumes in the nineteenth century, this is the most complete edition. There are several abridgements available. Sewall describes courtship, marriage, and women in his circle.

Shippen, Nancy. NANCY SHIPPEN: HER JOURNAL. Edited by Ethel Armes. Philadelphia: J.B. Lippincott, 1935. Reprint. New York: Arno Press, 1968. 343 p.

> This is a diary of a fashionable Philadelphia woman from 1777 to 1800. There is a lengthy introduction about her life and times.

Spruill, Julia Cherry. WOMAN'S LIFE AND WORK IN THE SOUTHERN COLONIES. Chapel Hill: University of North Carolina Press, 1938. Reprint. New York: W.W. Norton, 1972. viii, 426 p.

> The author describes the need for women in the colonies, the pleasures, wardrobe, and education of women as well as courtship, marriage, and their participation in public affairs, the professions, and business. She describes the legal position of women in the courts.

Stanford, Ann. ANNE BRADSTREET: THE WORLDLY PURITAN: AN INTRODUCTION TO HER POETRY. New York: Burt Franklin and Co., 1974. 170 p.

> The author analyzes and describes the poems. There is a short biographical sketch of the first woman poet in America.

Starkey, Marion. THE DEVIL IN MASSACHUSETTS: A MODERN INQUIRY INTO THE SALEM WITCH TRIALS. New York: Knopf, 1949. Reprint. New York: Time Books, 1977. xvii, 310 p.

> Starkey uses the principles of psychology to seek understanding of the hysteria that sent several alleged witches to their deaths.

Wharton, Anne Hollingsworth. COLONIAL DAYS AND DAMES. 1895. Reprint. New York: Arno Press, 1977. xiii, 248 p.

> The author, writing in 1895, describes social life of the upper classes, basing her account on diaries and letters.

_____. SALONS: COLONIAL AND REPUBLICAN. 1900. Reprint. New York: . Arno Press, 1977. 220 p.

> The author describes the ladies who presided over society, thus shaping the art and literary people of the time.

Whitney, Janet Payne. ABIGAIL ADAMS. Boston: Little, Brown, and Co., 1947. Reprint. Westport, Conn.: Greenwood Press, 1978. xii, 357 p.

> This is the only full-length biography of a sturdy woman who advised her political husband, John Adams, on the rights of women.

Wright, Louis B. EVERYDAY LIFE IN COLONIAL AMERICA. New York: G.P. Putnam's, 1965. 255 p.

> Wright describes the "American Dream" of the colonists. He looks at the process of picking a homesite, the earliest housing, and life. He notes the progress of colonial life, their recreation, education, and life-style. He includes the lower classes as well as the rich.

# Chapter 7

# STRONG-MINDED WOMEN:

# THE ROMANTIC AGE, 1800-1860

Alcott, William A. THE YOUNG HUSBAND: OR, DUTIES OF MAN IN MAR-
RIAGE. 1841. Reprint. New York: Arno Press, 1972. 388 p.

   Alcott outlines the duties of a husband and illustrates the concept
   of domesticity in the Jacksonian era.

_____. THE YOUNG WIFE: OR, DUTIES OF WOMAN IN MARRIAGE RE-
LATION. 1837. Reprint. New York: Arno Press, 1972. 376 p.

   Alcott defines the male view of a woman's place in Jacksonian
   America. It is essentially the view that feminists argued against.
   The book sets forth the norms that many women had to accept with-
   in their limited choices.

Anthony, Kathryn Susan. MARGARET FULLER: A PSYCHOLOGICAL BIOG-
RAPHY. New York: Harcourt, Brace and Co., 1921. v, 213 p.

   Anthony tells the life story of Margaret Fuller, who dared to be
   an individual in a society which expected women to be in the
   background.

Barker-Benfield, G.J. THE HORRORS OF THE HALF-KNOWN LIFE: MALE
ATTITUDES TOWARD WOMEN AND SEXUALITY IN NINETEENTH-CENTURY
AMERICA. New York: Harper and Row, 1976. xiv, 352 p.

   The author ranges widely from the male-dominated society of the
   early nineteenth century to early gynecology and discrimination
   against women. The author suggests that males have achieved freedom by subordination of females.

Birney, Catherine H. THE GRIMKE SISTERS: SARAH AND ANGELINA GRIM-
KE, THE FIRST AMERICAN WOMEN ADVOCATES OF ABOLITION AND
WOMENS RIGHTS. 1885. Reprint. Westport, Conn.: Greenwood Press, 1969.
319 p.

   The Grimke sisters, both reared in the South, were in the vanguard
   of the antislavery and feminist movements.

Blackwell, Alice Stone. LUCY STONE: PIONEER OF WOMEN'S RIGHTS. Boston: Little, Brown and Co., 1930. Reprint. Detroit: Gale Research Co., 1971. viii, 313 p.

> This is the life of a feminist reformer. When Lucy Stone married, she kept her maiden name. She was instrumental in the early movement, including the Seneca Falls Convention.

Bloomer, D.C. THE LIFE AND WRITINGS OF AMELIA BLOOMER. Boston: Arena Publishing Co., 1895. 387 p.

> This volume is a biography of Amelia Bloomer (1818-1894), pioneer feminist. Known primarily for a revolt against Victorian dress, she designed a garb consisting of a short skirt and full ankle-length "Turkish trousers." She was active in other reform items including women's suffrage, temperance, and equality of women in employment. She promoted female identity of married women in having the right to use their own name.

Booth, Sally Smith. THE WOMEN OF '76. New York: Hastings House, 1973. 329 p.

> Booth includes familiar as well as obscure women in this popular account.

Brooks, Gladys. THREE WISE VIRGINS. New York: E.P. Dutton, 1957. 244 p.

> This is an account of Dorothea Lynde Dix, Elizabeth Palmer Peabody, and Catherine Maria Sedgwick, all women of note in the early nineteenth century. The author attaches importance to the fact that these women, all spinsters, escaped neuroses while sublimating their sexuality.

Child, Lydia. THE MOTHER'S BOOK. 1831. Reprint. New York: Arno Press, 1972. 168 p.

> This is a manual on child-rearing in the Jacksonian era.

Clarke, Adam. THE HOLY BIBLE, CONTAINING THE OLD AND NEW TESTAMENT, WITH A COMMENTARY AND CRITICAL NOTES. 8 vols. New York: Abingdon-Cokesbury Press, 1830.

> Clarke insisted in arguments based on Biblical texts that God had created man as preeminent. Because Adam was lonely, God created woman of his flesh as a gift to man. Thus, woman had no meaning apart from man.

Clement, Jesse, ed. NOBLE DEEDS OF AMERICAN WOMEN: WITH BIOGRAPHICAL SKETCHES OF SOME OF THE MORE PROMINENT. 1851. Reprint. New York: Arno Press, 1974. 480 p.

Clement provides 150 sketches of unsung heroines of America. Representing courage of the pioneer type, most are relatively unknown.

Clifford, Deborah Pickman. MINE EYES HAVE SEEN THE GLORY: A BIOGRAPHY OF JULIA WARD HOWE. Boston: Little, Brown and Co., 1978. 312 p.

Mrs. Howe is best known for having written the "Battle Hymn of the Republic." She was also active as an abolitionist and feminist. A friend of Emerson and other intellectuals of the time, she was the first woman elected to the American Academy of Arts and Sciences.

Conrad, Earl. HARRIET TUBMAN. Washington: Associated Press, 1943. 248 p.

Harriet Tubman (1820-1913) was born into slavery. She escaped and subsequently became famous for her exploits in helping other slaves to freedom. She later founded a home for indigent blacks.

Conrad, Susan Phinney. PERISH THE THOUGHT: INTELLECTUAL WOMEN IN ROMANTIC AMERICA, 1830-1860. New York: Oxford University Press, 1976. vi, 292 p.

Conrad believes that women of the generation of Margaret Fuller, Lydia Maria Child, and Elizabeth Cady Stanton represent the first generation of female intellectuals in the United States. She asserts that these intellectuals appeared because of the stimulus of the romantic revolution.

Cott, Nancy F. THE BONDS OF WOMANHOOD: "WOMAN'S SPHERE" IN NEW ENGLAND 1780-1835. New Haven, Conn.: Yale University Press, 1977. xii, 225 p.

Cott provides an account of middle-class women, dividing the book into five chapters that focus on work, domesticity, education, religion, and sisterhood. This is a scholarly work based on diaries, documents, and manuscripts as well as sermons of ministers to illustrate the male attitude toward women.

Crocker, Hannah Mather. OBSERVATIONS ON THE RIGHTS OF WOMEN. Boston: Printed for the author, 1818. 92 p.

The granddaughter of Cotton Mather, Crocker rejected the idea that women must be subordinate because of inherent shortcomings. Still she had doubts about women in public affairs and believed some subjects of study were beyond them.

Deiss, Joseph Jay. THE ROMAN YEARS OF MARGARET FULLER. New York: Crowell, 1969. 338 p.

Margaret Fuller (1810-50) went to Europe in 1846 and to Rome in 1847. There she met the Marchese d'Ossoli whom she eventually married and bore his son. She died in a marine accident in 1850 as she was coming to the United States. This is the story of the last four years of her life.

Dexter, Elisabeth Anthony. CAREER WOMEN OF AMERICA 1776-1840. Francestown, N.H.: Marshall Jones Co., 1950. xiii, 262 p.

Dexter describes the opportunities available to women particularly in teaching, health-related jobs, religion, entertainment, writing, business, and sewing as well as those engaged in "ornamental idleness." She describes the loss of status that some of these occupations brought to women.

Drury, Clifford Merrill, ed. FIRST WHITE WOMEN OVER THE ROCKIES: DIARIES, LETTERS, AND BIOGRAPHICAL SKETCHES OF THE SIX WOMEN OF THE OREGON MISSION WHO MADE THE OVERLAND JOURNEY IN 1836 AND 1838. 3 vols. Glendale, Calif.: Arthur H. Clarke, 1966.

These are the diaries and letters of Narcissa Prentiss Whitman, Mary Augusta Dix Gray, Sarah White Smith, Eliza Hart Spalding, Mary Richardson Walker, and Myra Fairbanks Eells. The editor provides biographical sketches.

DuBois, Ellen Carol. FEMINISM AND SUFFRAGE: THE EMERGENCE OF AN INDEPENDENT WOMEN'S MOVEMENT IN AMERICA, 1848-1869. Ithaca, N.Y.: Cornell University Press, 1978. 220 p.

DuBois, unlike other scholars, sees nineteenth-century feminism as a major factor in making the United States more democratic. She views the movement for suffrage as a social, rather than merely a political, reform.

Emerson, R.W., et al. MEMOIRS OF MARGARET FULLER OSSOLI. 2 vols. New York: Tribune Association, 1869.

This work is an assessment of the life of Margaret Fuller by her friends and associates in the New England transcendentalist group.

Farnham, Eliza Woodson. LIFE IN PRAIRIE LAND. 1846. Reprint. New York: Arno Press, 1972. 408 p.

The author describes a woman's life on the frontier in Illinois in the 1830s and 1840s. Farnham was active in a variety of reforms as well as the women's rights movement.

Fauset, Arthur. SOJOURNER TRUTH: GOD'S FAITHFUL PILGRIM. Chapel Hill: University of North Carolina Press, 1938. Reprint. Tampa, Fla.: Russell Publications, 1971. 187 p.

Sojourner Truth (1797-1883), abolitionist and reformer, was born a slave. She joined the women's rights movement, to which she added much because of her experience as a slave and her personality.

Finley, Ruth E. THE LADY OF GODEY'S: SARAH JOSEPHA HALE. Philadelphia: J.B. Lippincott, 1931. Reprint. New York: Arno Press, 1974. 318 p.

Among the few women of the nineteenth century to earn her living from writing, Sarah Hale (1788-1879) brought GODEY'S LADY'S BOOK, a periodical for women, to a high circulation rate. She gave the readers much of feminine style and traditional values as a means of cloaking campaigns for education for women, property rights for married women, and day care centers for working women.

Fischer, Christiane, ed. LET THEM SPEAK FOR THEMSELVES: WOMEN IN THE AMERICAN WEST, 1849-1900. Hamden, Conn.: Shoe String Press, 1977. 346 p.

This is an anthology of diaries, letters, and reminiscences of twenty-five female pioneer figures. It is the story of loneliness, hard work, and sometimes, despair. Yet on the frontier women achieved a measure of freedom.

Fuller, Edmund. PRUDENCE CRANDALL: AN INCIDENT OF RACISM IN NINETEENTH-CENTURY CONNECTICUT. Middletown, Conn.: Wesleyan University Press, 1971. 113 p.

In 1833 Prudence Crandall, a Quaker teacher, was arrested for accepting black females as students. Pressed by bigots, she was forced to close her school.

Fuller, Margaret. MARGARET FULLER: AMERICAN ROMANTIC. A SELECTION FROM HER WRITING AND CORRESPONDENCE. New York: Doubleday, 1963. Reprint. New York: W.W. Norton, 1971. 319 p.

Included in this volume are selections of Fuller's writings from her youth in Cambridge, Massachusetts, to her final years in Europe.

_____. THE WOMAN AND THE MYTH: MARGARET FULLER'S LIFE AND WRITINGS. Edited by Bell Gale Chavigny. Old Westbury, N.Y.: Feminist Press, 1976. 501 p.

This is a collection of Fuller's writings arranged by theme. Each section includes comments on Fuller and her work by her contemporaries, such as Emerson, William Henry Chavigny, and James Russell Lowell.

_____. WOMEN OF THE NINETEENTH CENTURY, WITH KINDRED PAPERS RELATING TO THE SPHERE, CONDITION AND DUTIES OF WOMEN. New York: Tribune Press, 1845. ix, 212 p.

Fuller urged the intellectual equality of women. She believed that

women were, in part, responsible for their own degradation, which
she saw as coming from love of fashion, flattery, and excitement.
On the other hand, she saw that men insisted on their patriarchal
role, educating daughters as servants. She urged women to be
independent of men.

Gattey, Charles Neilson. THE BLOOMER GIRLS. New York: Coward Mc-
Cann, 1968. 192 p.

Gattey provides a popular account of the feminist movement, particularly of Mrs. Bloomer. In the process, the author describes
much of the social history of women's dress.

Gilchrist, Beth. THE LIFE OF MARY LYON. Boston: Houghton Mifflin,
1910. 462 p.

Mary Lyon (1797-1849) founded Mount Holyoke Female Seminary
after long periods of study alternated with periods of teaching.
For many years she was both principal and teacher in the seminary,
which evolved into Mount Holyoke College.

Grimke, Sarah M. LETTERS ON THE EQUALITY OF THE SEXES, AND THE
CONDITION OF WOMEN. 1838. Reprint. New York: Source Book Press,
1970. 128 p.

Born into the patriarchal society of South Carolina, Sarah Grimke
observed the oppression of blacks and women. She became a
Quaker and an abolitionist. She also espoused the women's rights
crusade. In this book she uses many of the antislavery arguments
in connection with the oppression of women. She believed that
intellectual equality of the sexes enhanced feminism. She decried
the early training of girls for motherhood and marriage only. She
attacked the English common law view of the inferiority of women,
and believed these influences gave women a poor self-image.

Gurko, Miriam. THE LADIES OF SENECA FALLS: THE BIRTH OF THE
WOMEN'S RIGHTS MOVEMENT. New York: Macmillan, 1974. 328 p.

This is a popular account of the Seneca Falls Convention and its
participants.

Hare, Lloyd Custer Mayhew. THE GREATEST AMERICAN WOMAN, LUCRETIA
MOTT. New York: American Historical Society, 1937. Reprint. Westport,
Conn.: Greenwood Press, 1978. 307 p.

Hare describes Mott as the founder and soul of the women's rights
movement.

Hersey, Thomas. THE MIDWIFE'S PRACTICAL DIRECTORY: OR, WOMAN'S
CONFIDENTIAL FRIEND. COMPRISING EXTENSIVE REMARKS ON THE VARI-
OUS CASUALTIES AND FORMS OF DISEASE, PRECEDING, ATTENDING, AND

FOLLOWING THE PERIOD OF GESTATION. 1836. Reprint. New York: Arno Press, 1974. 336 p.

Hersey provides information about midwifery and nineteenth-century attitudes about conception, birth, and marriage.

Hersh, Blanche Glassman. THE SLAVERY OF SEX: FEMINIST ABOLITIONISTS IN AMERICA. Urbana: University of Illinois Press, 1978. 250 p.

Hersh, using the methods of intellectual history, studies the shared characteristics of fifty-one women who were leaders in the struggle for abolition and women's rights. She discusses equalitarian marriage, role models, and the reconciliation of these commitments to domesticity and activism.

Hollick, Frederick. THE MARRIAGE GUIDE, OR NATURAL HISTORY OF GEN-ERATION: A PRIVATE INSTRUCTOR FOR MARRIED PERSONS AND THOSE ABOUT TO MARRY, BOTH MALE AND FEMALE, IN EVERY THING CON-CERNING THE PHYSIOLOGY AND RELATIONS OF THE SEXUAL SYSTEM AND THE PRODUCTION OR PREVENTION OF OFF-SPRING--INCLUDING ALL THE NEW DISCOVERIES, NEVER BEFORE GIVEN IN THE ENGLISH LAN-GUAGE. 1850. Reprint. New York: Arno Press, 1974. 428 p.

Hollick was a widely read authority on sexual matters in the nine-teenth century. He imparts the traditional wisdom of his period.

Kemble, Frances A. JOURNAL OF A RESIDENCE ON A GEORGIAN PLANTA-TION IN 1838-1839. Edited by John A. Scott. 1864. Reprint. New York: Alfred A. Knopf, 1961. Reprint. New York: New American Library, 1975. lxi, 415 p.

Miss Kemble, a highly educated English woman, visited a Georgia plantation for a few months in 1838-1839. The volume was first published in 1863. She provides a careful description of life in the Deep South.

Jennings, Samuel K. THE MARRIED LADY'S COMPANION, OR POOR MAN'S FRIEND. 1808. Reprint. New York: Arno Press, 1972. 304 p.

Jennings illustrates the turn-of-the-century attitudes toward women and child rearing.

King, C. Richard. VICTORIAN LADY ON THE TEXAS FRONTIER: THE JOUR-NAL OF ANN RANEY COLEMAN. Norman: University of Oklahoma Press, 1971. xxi, 206 p.

This is the journal of a woman who came to Texas from England in 1832. She lived to be eighty-seven years old, witnessing the Civil War and going from prosperity to poverty.

Lerner, Gerda. THE GRIMKE SISTERS FROM SOUTH CAROLINA: PIONEERS FOR WOMEN'S RIGHTS AND ABOLITION. Boston: Houghton Mifflin, 1967. 479 p.

> Sarah (1792-1873) and Angelina (1805-1879) Grimke were well-educated women from a prosperous slave-owning family of South Carolina. They rebelled against their family background to become advocates of women's rights and abolitionism.

Loewenberg, Bert James, and Bogin, Ruth. BLACK WOMEN IN NINETEENTH CENTURY AMERICAN LIFE. University Park: Pennsylvania State University Press, 1976. 355 p.

> The authors present the lives of twenty-four black women born in pre-Civil War times. They include well known figures such as Charlotte Forten Grimke, Sojourner Truth, and Harriet Tubman, as well as black women whose lives have been hidden in history to a greater degree, like Ellen Craft, and Jarena Lee. Loewenberg and Bogin introduce the biographies with an analysis of the role of black women in America.

Lumpkin, Katharine DuPre. THE EMANCIPATION OF ANGELINA GRIMKE. Chapel Hill: University of North Carolina Press, 1974. 265 p.

> Lumpkin describes Grimke's work as an abolitionist and her rivalries with her sister Sarah.

Lutz, Alma. CRUSADE FOR FREEDOM: WOMEN OF THE ANTISLAVERY MOVEMENT. Boston: Beacon Press, 1968. 338 p.

> Lutz describes the participation of women in the abolitionist crusade, one of the few issues on which women were allowed to speak. The movement provided a springboard for other issues, particularly women's rights.

Marshall, Helen E. DOROTHEA L. DIX: FORGOTTEN SAMARITAN. Chapel Hill: University of North Carolina Press, 1937. x, 298 p.

> Marshall provides a biography of a major reformer, especially in the field of care of the mentally ill. She also provides insight into her life and times and the social attitudes toward defectives.

Martineau, Harriet. SOCIETY IN AMERICA. 3 vols. London: Saunders and Atby, 1837.

> Martineau travelled in the United States in the years 1834 to 1836. A keen observer, she visited most of the eastern states. She comments on the position of women, life-style of the people, children, religion, slavery, and the working classes.

Maverick, Mary A. MEMOIRS OF MARY A. MAVERICK. Edited by Rena Maverick Green. San Antonio, Tex.: Alamo Printing Co., 1921. 136 p.

This is the memoir of a woman in Texas during the period from 1836 to 1865. She describes the life of the people in various parts of Texas.

Melder, Keith E. BEGINNINGS OF SISTERHOOD: THE AMERICAN WOMAN'S RIGHTS MOVEMENT, 1800-1850. New York: Schocken Books, 1977. 199 p.

Melder portrays the feminist demand for suffrage and legal rights in the mid-nineteenth century as an outgrowth of other reforms in which women had participated.

More, Hannah. STRICTURES ON THE MODERN SYSTEM OF FEMALE EDUCATION. 2 vols. New York: E. Duyckinck, 1813.

Rejecting the feminist call for coeducation, More believed that innate differences in women called for distinct education. This education would deal with social and domestic skills and would also teach women how to think without violating the delicate physique and less-refined mind of women.

Perkins, A.J.G., and Wolfson, Theresa. FRANCES WRIGHT: FREE ENQUIRER. THE STUDY OF A TEMPERAMENT. New York: Harper and Brothers, 1939. Reprint. Philadelphia: Porcupine Press, 1972. 393 p.

This is a biography of Frances (Fanny) Wright (1795-1852) rebel against convention, friend of Robert Dale Owen, William McClure, and Lafayette. She was an antislavery activist and founder of the communitarian colony at Nashoba, Tennessee, which was integrated and widely believed to practice free love.

Ryan, Michael. THE PHILOSOPHY OF MARRIAGE IN ITS SOCIAL, MORAL AND PHYSICAL RELATIONS; WITH AN ACCOUNT OF THE GENITO-URINARY ORGANS, WITH THE PHYSIOLOGY OF GENERATION IN THE VEGETABLE AND ANIMAL KINGDOMS. 1839. Reprint. New York: Arno Press, 1974. 388 p.

Ryan summarizes the existing knowledge of 1839 on marriage, sexuality, and reproduction.

Shew, Joel. CONSUMPTION: ITS PREVENTION AND CURE BY WATER TREATMENT. New York: Fowler and Wells, 1851. xviii, 288 p.

Shew believed that neither sex had any predisposition to tuberculosis. He believed the higher incidence of the disease in women was due to faulty education, wrong clothing, bad living habits, and physical abuse by men, all of which lowered female resistence to disease.

Sklar, Kathryn Kish. CATHERINE BEECHER: A STUDY IN AMERICAN DO-
MESTICITY. New Haven, Conn.: Yale University Press, 1973. xv, 356 p.

> This is a biography of Catherine Beecher (1800-1878), a socially
> prominent woman, sister to Henry Ward Beecher and Harriet Beecher
> Stowe, who refused the stereotype which nineteenth-century
> America would have fastened on her. Active in education for
> women, she wrote "A lady should study, not to shine, but to act."

Stern, Madeleine B. THE LIFE OF MARGARET FULLER. New York: E.P.
Dutton and Co., 1942. Reprint. Brooklyn: Haskell House, 1969. xvi,
549 p.

> This is the biography of a feminist of the reform movement of the
> antebellum period. Miss Fuller was the author of WOMEN OF
> THE NINETEENTH CENTURY (1845), and embodied the principles
> of feminism in her own life.

Thorpe, Margaret Farrand. FEMALE PERSUASION: SIX STRONG MINDED
WOMEN. New Haven, Conn.: Yale University Press, 1949. x, 253 p.

> Thorpe provides sketches of Catherine Beecher, Jane Swisshelm,
> Amelia Bloomer, Grace Greenwood, Louisa McCord, and Lydia
> Marie Child.

Tillson, Christiana Holmes. A WOMAN'S STORY OF PIONEER ILLINOIS.
Edited by Milo Milton Quaife. Chicago: Lakeside Press, 1919. xxi, 169 p.

> This volume is the memoir of Mrs. Tillson, an educated and percep-
> tive woman, of her migration to Illinois and her life there in the
> 1820s. She describes the life-style on the frontier and the social
> disparity between the New Englanders, as represented by the Till-
> sons, and the southerners they found in Illinois.

Trollope, Frances M. DOMESTIC MANNERS OF THE AMERICANS. Edited by
Donald Smalley. New York: Knopf, 1949. Reprint. Gloucester, Mass.:
Peter Smith, 1979. lxxxiii, 454 p.

> Trollope, mother of novelist Anthony Trollope, came to America on
> a business venture which failed, which accounts in part for her
> choleric view of American manners and society. Bitterly resented
> when first published in 1832, the account is worth reading.

Truth, Sojourner. NARRATIVE OF SOJOURNER TRUTH, A BONDSWOMAN OF
OLDEN TIME, EMANCIPATED BY THE NEW YORK LEGISLATURE IN THE
EARLY PART OF THE PRESENT CENTURY: WITH A HISTORY OF HER LABORS
AND CORRESPONDENCE DRAWN FROM HER "BOOK OF LIFE." 1878. Re-
print. New York: Arno Press, 1968. 320 p.

> Sojourner Truth was one of the most remarkable women of the nine-
> teenth century. A former slave, she became a powerful spokes-
> woman for both abolition and women's rights.

Wade, Mason. MARGARET FULLER: WHETSTONE OF GENIUS. New York: Viking, 1940. Reprint. Clifton, N.J.: A.M. Kelley, 1973. xvi, 304 p.

>This is the standard biography of Fuller.

Wharton, Anne Hollingsworth. SOCIAL LIFE IN THE EARLY REPUBLIC. Philadelphia: J.B. Lippincott, 1902. Reprint. New York: Arno Press, 1976. 346 p.

>Wharton describes the social life in Boston, New York, Philadelphia, and other cities after the Revolution.

Wilson, Dorothy Clarke. STRANGER AND TRAVELER: THE STORY OF DOROTHEA DIX. Boston: Little, Brown and Co., 1975. 360 p.

>Involved in prison reform and care of mentally ill, Dix (1802-1887) was a notable woman in an era of reform. This is a popular account.

THE YOUNG LADY'S OWN BOOK: A MANUAL OF INTELLECTUAL IMPROVEMENT AND MORAL DEVELOPMENT. Philadelphia: Key, Meilke and Biddle, 1832. xi, 323 p.

>This is an extreme example of the concept that women are weak and capable only of domesticity. Advice is given on deportment, dress, education and reading, all of which must bring filial piety as well as the ability to please her husband by being attractive in dress and manner while also a "bustling person, who always has a good dinner and a clean house."

# Chapter 8

# THE WOMAN QUESTION:

# WOMEN IN THE VICTORIAN ERA

Alderson, Nannie T., and Smith, Helena H. A BRIDE GOES WEST. New York: Farrar and Rinehart, 1942. vii, 273 p.

> This is a description of pioneer life and the position of a woman on the Montana frontier in the 1880s.

Ames, Mary. FROM A NEW ENGLAND WOMAN'S DIARY IN DIXIE IN 1865. Norwood, Mass.: Plimpton Press, 1906. Reprint. Westport, Conn.: Greenwood Press, 1969. vi, 125 p.

> This is the diary of a teacher who served with the Freedman's Bureau on Edisto Island off South Carolina.

Anthony, Katharine Susan. SUSAN B. ANTHONY: HER PERSONAL HISTORY AND HER ERA. Garden City, N.Y.: Doubleday, 1954. 521 p.

> This volume describes the life and times of the suffragist.

Anthony, Susan B. AN ACCOUNT OF THE PROCEEDINGS ON THE TRIAL OF SUSAN B. ANTHONY, ON THE CHARGE OF ILLEGAL VOTING AT THE PRESIDENTIAL ELECTION IN NOVEMBER, 1872, AND ON THE TRIAL OF BEVERLY W. JONES, EDWIN T. MARSH AND WILLIAM B. HALL, THE IN-SPECTORS OF ELECTION BY WHOM HER VOTE WAS RECEIVED. 1874. Reprint. New York: Arno Press, 1974. 212 p.

> This is the record of Anthony's trial.

Arling, Emanie Sachs. THE TERRIBLE SIREN: VICTORIA WOODHULL (1838-1927). New York: Harper and Bros., 1928. Reprint. New York: Arno Press, 1972. 423 p.

> Marxist, suffragette, vegetarian, and candidate for president of the United States, Woodhull was regarded as outrageous by the staid of her time.

Baer, Helene G. THE HEART IS LIKE HEAVEN: THE LIFE OF LYDIA MARIA CHILD. Philadelphia: University of Pennsylvania Press, 1964. 339 p.

This is a sentimental biography of Lydia Maria Child (1802-1880), author and reformer.

Beecher, Catherine, and Stowe, Harriet Beecher. THE AMERICAN WOMAN'S HOME: OR, PRINCIPLES OF DOMESTIC SCIENCE. 1869. Reprint. New York: Arno Press, 1971. 500 p.

This was the standard how-to-do-it book for women in the mid-nineteenth century.

Blackford, L. Minor. MINE EYES HAVE SEEN THE GLORY: THE STORY OF A VIRGINIA LADY, MARY BERKELEY MINOR BLACKFORD, 1802-1896, WHO TAUGHT HER SONS TO HATE SLAVERY AND LOVE THE UNION. Cambridge, Mass.: Harvard University Press, 1954. xix, 293 p.

Blackford, matriarch of her family, hated slavery and supported the movement to colonize blacks in Africa. It is the story of an untypical southern woman.

Blackwell, Antoinette Louisa Brown. THE SEXES THROUGHOUT NATURE. 1875. Reprint. Westport, Conn.: Hyperion Press, 1976. 240 p.

Feminist and abolitionist, Antoinette Brown (1825-1921) became the first woman ordained as a minister in the United States. In this collection of essays she rejects the theories of Darwin and Spencer, who held women inferior because of their reproductive function and because of evolutionary factors. She denied any lack of reasoning capacity of women.

Blackwell, Elizabeth. ESSAYS IN MEDICAL SOCIOLOGY. London: E. Bell, 1902. Reprint. New York: Arno Press, 1972. 166 p.

This volume gives an understanding of the life of the first female physician in the United States.

Brothers, Mary Hudson. A PECOS PIONEER. Albuquerque: University of New Mexico Press, 1943. vii, 169 p.

This is a description of the life of a pioneer woman in Texas on a sheep ranch.

Brown, Dee. THE GENTLE TAMERS: WOMEN OF THE OLD WILD WEST. Lincoln: University of Nebraska Press, 1958. 317 p.

Brown provides a wide-ranging discussion of types of women on the frontier, including army dependents, entertainers, prostitutes, teachers, and the hard-working, long-suffering wives of the pioneers.

Burstall, Sara A. THE EDUCATION OF GIRLS IN THE UNITED STATES. 1894. Reprint. New York: Arno Press, 1971. 204 p.

An Englishwoman, Burstall studied the secondary and higher education available to young women in the United States at the end of the nineteenth century.

Call, Hughie. GOLDEN FLEECE. Boston: Houghton Mifflin, 1942. 250 p.

This is a description of the life of a Montana sheepherder at the end of the nineteenth century.

Campbell, Helen. PRISONERS OF POVERTY: WOMEN WAGE-WORKERS, THEIR TRADES AND THEIR LIVES. 1887. Reprint. Westport, Conn.: Greenwood Press, 1972. v, 257 p.

This book describes the social and working conditions of women in the nineteenth century. It is said to have been instrumental in bringing reforms in the Progressive era.

_____. WOMEN WAGE EARNERS: THEIR PAST, THEIR PRESENT, AND THEIR FUTURE. 1893. Reprint. New York: Arno Press, 1972. 257 p.

A home economist, Campbell studied the obstacles to the entry of women into industry late in the nineteenth century.

Chase, Richard. EMILY DICKINSON. New York: William Sloane Associates, 1951. 328 p.

This is a biography of one of the great poets of the United States.

Chestnut, Mary Boykin. A DIARY FROM DIXIE. Edited by Ben Ames Williams. Boston: Houghton Mifflin, 1949. xii, 572 p.

Chestnut, southern belle and wife of a senator, kept a diary with an account of society and life in Confederate Richmond.

Child, Lydia Maria. LETTERS OF LYDIA MARIA CHILD. 1883. Reprint. New York: Arno Press, 1969. 280 p.

Child (1802-1880), leading children's writer, gave up her career to promote the cause of abolition.

Clarke, Edward H. SEX IN EDUCATION: OR, A FAIR CHANCE FOR THE GIRLS. 1873. Reprint. New York: Arno Press, 1972. 181 p.

Clarke argued that education for women was harmful in that study and competition caused women to become unfit for motherhood.

Cleaveland, Agnes Morley. NO LIFE FOR A LADY. Boston: Houghton Mifflin, 1941. Reprint. Lincoln: University of Nebraska Press, 1977. ix, 356 p.

This is an account of frontier life in New Mexico at the end of the nineteenth century from a woman's point of view.

Cook, Tennessee Claflin. CONSTITUTIONAL EQUALITY: A RIGHT OF WOMEN. 1871. Reprint. Westport, Conn.: Hyperion Press, 1976. 148 p.

With her sister, Victoria Woodhull, Tennessee Claflin Cook published WOODHULL AND CLAFLIN'S WEEKLY, established in 1870, in which they advocated equal rights for women, a single standard of morality, legalized abortion, and prostitution. Cook insists that the Constitution guarantees women's suffrage. She also denounces unequal educational opportunities and restrictions visited on women by society.

Cooke, Nicholas Francis. SATAN IN SOCIETY: BY A PHYSICIAN. 1876. Reprint. New York: Arno Press, 1972. 412 p.

The author provides a catalog of nineteenth-century American sexual practices ranging through prostitution, masturbation, birth control, abortion, and sexual exploitation of wives.

Dall, Caroline H. THE COLLEGE, THE MARKET, AND THE COURT: OR, WOMAN'S RELATION TO EDUCATION, LABOR, AND LAW. 1867. Reprint. New York: Arno Press, 1972. 498 p.

The author describes the Anglo-Saxon traditions, cultural influences, and religious beliefs that impeded women's entry into the professions in the nineteenth century.

Dannett, Sylvia G.L., ed. NOBLE WOMEN OF THE NORTH. New York: Thomas Yoseloff, 1954. 419 p.

This is a collection of letters and narrative accounts of northern women during the Civil War, illustrating their hopes, services, and hardships.

Deshon, George. GUIDE FOR CATHOLIC YOUNG WOMEN: ESPECIALLY FOR THOSE WHO EARN THEIR OWN LIVING. 1897. Reprint. New York: Arno Press, 1972. 308 p.

Written by a Catholic Paulist priest, this is a manual instructing young girls on how to maintain their piety and purity.

Dillon, Mary. FRANCES WILLARD: FROM PRAYERS TO POLITICS. Chicago: University of Chicago Press, 1944. Reprint. Washington, D.C.: Zenger Publishing Co., 1975. 417 p.

Usually noted only as the temperance leader and founder of the Women's Christian Temperance Union, Willard (1839-1898) was also notable in the women's suffrage movement. Dillon believes Willard was the primary force in creating a national women's movement.

Douglas, Ann. THE FEMINIZATION OF AMERICAN CULTURE. New York: Alfred A. Knopf, 1977. x, 403 p.

The author sees a competition between liberal clergymen and sentimental female writers for the attention of Americans in the nineteenth century. She portrays this as corrupting American culture by flooding it with sentimentality. She analyzes in detail thirty women writers and thirty clergymen.

Duffey, Eliza B. THE RELATIONS OF THE SEXES. 1876. Reprint. New York: Arno Press, 1974. 320 p.

This is a nineteenth-century study of the relationship of sexuality, child-bearing, and the autonomy of women in such matters.

_____. WHAT WOMEN SHOULD KNOW: A WOMAN'S BOOK ABOUT WOMEN; CONTAINING PRACTICAL INFORMATION FOR WIVES AND MOTHERS. 1873. Reprint. New York: Arno Press, 1974. 320 p.

The author looks at the biological problems of women, making her views acceptable by cloaking them in nineteenth-century religious jargon.

Eastman, Elaine Goodale. SISTER TO THE SIOUX. Edited by Kay Grober. Lincoln: University of Nebraska Press, 1978. xiii, 175 p.

This is the memoir of Elaine Goodale Eastman (1863-1953), a New England woman who started a day school for Sioux children. The memoir covers the period 1885-1891.

Ellet, Elizabeth F. THE EMINENT AND HEROIC WOMEN OF AMERICA. 1873. Reprint. New York: Arno Press, 1974. 763 p.

This is a popular account of the activities of women in America.

Ellington, George. THE WOMEN OF NEW YORK: OR THE UNDER-WORLD OF THE GREAT CITY, ILLUSTRATING THE LIFE OF WOMEN OF FASHION, WOMEN OF PLEASURE, ACTRESSES AND BALLET GIRLS, SALOON GIRLS, PICKPOCKETS AND SHOPLIFTERS, ARTISTS' FEMALE MODELS, WOMEN-OF-THE-TOWN, ETC. 1869. Reprint. New York: Arno Press, 1972. 650 p.

This book purports to be an expose of the evil effects of New York on women.

Evans, Elizabeth Edson. THE ABUSE OF MATERNITY. 1875. Reprint. New York: Arno Press, 1975. 129 p.

Evans, a physician, urged that sexual abuses often marred marriages.

Frost, John. PIONEER MOTHERS OF THE WEST: OR, DARING AND HEROIC DEEDS OF AMERICAN WOMEN, COMPRISING THRILLING EXAMPLES OF

COURAGE, FORTITUDE, DEVOTEDNESS, AND SELF-SACRIFICE. 1869. Reprint. New York: Arno Press, 1974. 348 p.

> This volume consists of short biographical sketches of women who came from civilized backgrounds to the frontier with little or no preparation for the privation.

Gardner, Augustus K. CONJUGAL SINS AGAINST THE LAWS OF LIFE AND HEALTH AND THE EFFECTS UPON THE FATHER, MOTHER, AND CHILD. 1870. Reprint. New York: Arno Press, 1974. 240 p.

> Written by a physician, this is an antifeminist blast at birth control and abortion.

Graham, Abbie. GRACE H. DODGE: MERCHANT OF DREAMS. New York: Womans Press, 1926. 329 p.

> Grace Dodge (1856-1914) came from a wealthy copper mining family but chose to form in 1885 the Association of Working Girls Societies as a device to promote education and as an opportunity for self-expression for factory girls. She had a major part in founding the Teachers College of Columbia University. She also served as national president of YWCA.

Gray, Dorothy. WOMEN OF THE WEST. Milbrae, Calif.: Les Femmes Press, 1976. 180 p.

> This is a series of short biographies of American women in the West during the nineteenth and early twentieth centuries. It includes figures under such topics as minority women, women on the farm, woman ranchers, women in the professions, and women suffragettes of the West. Some well-known women portrayed are Sacajawea, Carrie Chapman Catt, and Willa Cather.

Hale, Sarah Josepha. MANNERS: OR, HAPPY HOMES AND GOOD SOCIETY ALL THE YEAR ROUND. 1868. Reprint. New York: Arno Press, 1972. 377 p.

> Hale provides a how-to book on manners, correct conversation, social duties, and obligations. She says that women can improve the world through moral strength. Although Hale aided in many campaigns for women's rights, she made a lot of money from promoting the traditional values.

Haller, John S., and Haller, Robin M. THE PHYSICIAN AND SEXUALITY IN VICTORIAN AMERICA. New York: W.W. Norton, 1977. 352 p. Paper.

> The authors find that Victorian physicians, all moralists, used their exalted status to add to the sexual fears of the time, helping to create the sexual stereotypes to which women were subjected. These fears and stereotypes were used as weapons against the feminist movement. The physicians generally preached restraint

even in marriage. They theorized that a man who used strength
in sexual activity would be less successful in other areas of life.
This limited the husband but diminished the wife's obligation to
submit.

Harper, Ida Husted. THE LIFE AND WORK OF SUSAN B. ANTHONY. 2
vols. Indianapolis: Bowen-Merrill Co., 1899.

This is a biography of the feminist leader by one of her coworkers
in the movement.

Haviland, Laura S. A WOMAN'S LIFE WORK: LABORS AND EXPERIENCES
OF LAURA S. HAVILAND. 1889. Reprint. New York: Arno Press, 1969.
559 p.

Haviland, a Civil War nurse, became an abolitionist and promoter
of black rights and equality.

Hays, Elinor Rice. THOSE EXTRAORDINARY BLACKWELLS: THE STORY OF
A JOURNEY TO A BETTER WORLD. New York: Harcourt, Brace and World,
1967. 349 p.

The Blackwell family of nine children produced some interesting
women including Elizabeth, the first woman physician in America.
Two of her brothers married Antoinette Brown and Lucy Stone.

Holmes, Emma. THE DIARY OF MISS EMMA HOLMES, 1861-1865. Baton
Rouge: Louisiana State University Press, 1979. 528 p.

Emma Holmes was the daughter of an aristocratic family of Charleston, South Carolina. She witnessed the bombardment of Ft. Sumter
and the destruction of her family home. She became a refugee and
records the role of southern women during the war.

Howe, Julia Ward. JULIA WARD HOWE AND THE WOMAN SUFFRAGE
MOVEMENT. Edited by Florence Howe Hall. Boston: D. Estes and Co.,
1913. Reprint. New York: Arno Press, 1969. 241 p.

This is a selection from speeches and writings of Julia Ward Howe
(1819-1910), edited by her daughter.

_____, ed. SEX AND EDUCATION: A REPLY TO DR. E.H. CLARKE'S "SEX
IN EDUCATION." THESE ARE THE DETERMINED RESPONSES TO ARGUMENTS
THAT INTELLECTUAL PURSUITS COULD WRECK WOMEN, TOGETHER WITH A
PLEA FOR MORE EDUCATIONAL POSSIBILITIES FOR WOMEN. THEY WERE
WRITTEN BY MEMBERS OF THE NEW ENGLAND WOMAN SUFFRAGE ASSO-
CIATION RALLIED BY JULIA WARD HOWE. 1874. Reprint. New York:
Arno Press, 1972. 203 p.

Clarke had written that education was detrimental to women (SEX
IN EDUCATION; OR, A FAIR CHANCE FOR GIRLS, 1873), par-

ticularly that it would render them unfit for child bearing and
rearing. This is a feminist response to him.

Jackson, James C. THE SEXUAL ORGANISM AND ITS HEALTHFUL MANAGE-
MENT. 1861. Reprint. New York: Arno Press, 1974. 279 p.

Jackson was a health reformer and advocate of women's rights.
He hoped to rationalize the sexual life of Americans.

Jeffrey, Julie Roy. FRONTIER WOMEN: THE TRANS-MISSISSIPPI WEST,
1840-1880. New York: Hill and Wang, 1979. xvi, 240 p.

Jeffrey provides an interpretive, historical study of women on the
frontier, their position, function, as well as attitudes toward women.

Jones, Katharine M., ed. HEROINES OF DIXIE: CONFEDERATE WOMEN
TELL THEIR STORY OF THE WAR. Indianapolis: Bobbs-Merrill, 1955. Reprint.
Westport, Conn.: Greenwood Press, 1973. xiv, 430 p.

The editor has woven together accounts of southern women during
the Civil War to form a picture of the life of women during the
war.

_____. WHEN SHERMAN CAME: SOUTHERN WOMEN AND THE "GREAT
MARCH." Indianapolis, Ind.: Bobbs-Merrill, 1964. 353 p.

Jones provides a selection of accounts of women about their experiences during Sherman's march to the sea.

Katzman, David M. SEVEN DAYS A WEEK: WOMEN AND DOMESTIC SER-
VICE IN INDUSTRIALIZING AMERICA. New York: Oxford University Press,
1978. xviii, 374 p.

Katzman writes about the experience of being a servant between
the Civil War and World War I. He also describes servants' collective efforts, strikes, boycotts, and organizations.

Kearney, Belle. A SLAVEHOLDERS DAUGHTER. 1900. Reprint. Westport,
Conn.: Greenwood Press, 1973. 269 p.

The autobiography of the daughter of a prominent Mississippi family,
Kearney traces her life through Reconstruction and as a speaker for
the Women's Christian Temperance Union.

Leslie, Eliza. MISS LESLIE'S BEHAVIOR BOOK: A GUIDE AND MANUAL
FOR LADIES. 1859. Reprint. New York: Arno Press, 1972. 336 p.

This volume provides an insight into what was expected of young
women by the traditionalists of the mid-nineteenth century.

Livermore, Mary A. THE STORY OF MY LIFE: OR, THE SUNSHINE AND SHADOW OF SEVENTY YEARS. 1899. Reprint. New York: Arno Press, 1974. 730 p.

> This is the autobiography of Mary Rich Livermore (1820–1905), a worker for suffrage, peace, temperance. The book includes some of her lectures.

Long, Mary Alves. HIGH TIME TO TELL IT: "AH, DISTINCTLY I REMEMBER." Durham, N.C.: Duke University Press, 1950. xi, 319 p.

> This memoir recounts life in the South just after the Civil War. It is household history, thus covering the role of women.

Lutz, Alma. EMMA WILLARD. Boston: Houghton Mifflin, 1929. Reprint. Washington, D.C.: Zenger Publishing Co., 1976. 291 p.

> Emma Hart Willard (1787–1870), born on a farm, grew up with inadequate educational opportunities. She taught herself and became a teacher and a major proponent of educational opportunity. She founded Troy Female Seminary, a model of the ideas she promoted.

_____. SUSAN B. ANTHONY: REBEL CRUSADER, HUMANITARIAN. Boston: Beacon Press, 1959. 340 p.

> The story of the participation of a great reformer in the feminist as well as other movements of the time.

McCracken, Elizabeth. THE WOMEN OF AMERICA. New York: Macmillan, 1903. xi, 397 p.

> The author provides a series of essays and accounts of women in the West, in the small town, and of the women's suffrage movement in Colorado. She describes club women, college women, women in the theatre, and women writers, as well as their work in education and philanthropy. She also deals with women in tenements, on the farm, and in the professions.

Massey, Mary Elizabeth. BONNET BRIGADES. New York: Knopf, 1966. xxi, 371 p.

> This is a description of the role of women in the Civil War--both in the North and South, Negro and white. Generally women, as always in war, were in demand to perform all kinds of tasks that had formerly been done by men, including teaching. Many women, especially in the south, suffered great hardships because of the war.

Mauriceau, A.M. THE MARRIED WOMAN'S PRIVATE MEDICAL COMPANION: EMBRACING THE TREATMENT OF MENSTRUATION, OR MONTHLY TURNS, DURING THEIR STOPPAGE, IRREGULARITY, OR ENTIRE SUPPRESSION; PREGNANCY, AND HOW IT MAY BE DETERMINED; WITH THE TREATMENT OF

VARIOUS DISEASES; DISCOVERY TO PREVENT PREGNANCY; THE GREAT
AND IMPORTANT NECESSITY WHERE MALFORMATION OR INABILITY EXISTS
TO GIVE BIRTH. 1847. Reprint. New York: Arno Press, 1974. 238 p.

> Mauriceau was a promoter of birth control. This marriage manual
> was popular in the mid-nineteenth century.

Mayo, Amory D. SOUTHERN WOMEN IN THE RECENT EDUCATIONAL MOVE-
MENT IN THE SOUTH. 1892. Reprint. Baton Rouge: Louisiana State University Press, 1978. 305 p.

> Mayo, a clergyman, promoted the idea that southern white women
> were the ideal vehicle to transmit education, American culture,
> and values to black children.

Meltzer, Milton. TONGUE OF FLAME: THE LIFE OF LYDIA MARIA CHILD.
New York: Thomas Y. Crowell Co., 1965. 210 p.

> This is a biography of Child who was an author, abolitionist,
> feminist.

Meyer, Annie Nathan, ed. WOMAN'S WORK IN AMERICA. 1891. Reprint.
New York: Arno Press, 1972. 457 p.

> This book contains eighteen articles by women such as Julia Ward
> Howe, Mary Livermore, Clara Barton, and Frances Willard. They
> describe the modest start in opening up professions to women.

Muncy, Raymond Lee. SEX AND MARRIAGE IN UTOPIAN COMMUNITIES:
19TH CENTURY AMERICA. Bloomington: Indiana University Press, 1973.
275 p.

> Muncy describes a variety of practices varying from the abstinence
> of the Rappites to the polygamy of the Mormons, the complex mar-
> riage of Oneida, and the free and easy scene of Fanny Wright's
> Nashoba. He places all of this against the standards of outside
> society.

Oakley, Mary Ann. ELIZABETH CADY STANTON. Old Westbury, N.Y.:
Feminist Press, 1972. 148 p.

> Stanton (1815-1902) inspired many of the nineteenth-century direc-
> tions of the suffragist movement. She worked for property rights
> for women, lenient divorce laws, and tried to correct sexist bias.

Peel, Robert. MARY BAKER EDDY: THE YEARS OF DISCOVERY. New York:
Holt, Rinehart and Winston, 1966. 372 p.

> This describes the life of Eddy (1821-1910) up to the point of
> founding the Christian Science Church.

_____. MARY BAKER EDDY: THE YEARS OF TRIAL. New York: Holt, Rinehart and Winston, 1971. 391 p.

> This book covers the years from 1876 to 1891, the period following publication of Eddy's first book. She emerges as the leader of the Christian Science movement.

Penny, Virginia. HOW WOMEN CAN MAKE MONEY, MARRIED OR SINGLE IN ALL BRANCHES OF THE ARTS AND SCIENCES, PROFESSIONS, TRADES, AGRICULTURAL PURSUITS. 1870. Reprint. New York: Arno Press, 1971. 500 p.

> The author sought to prove that there are at least five hundred jobs which women can do as well as men. She provides an inventory of such trades, jobs, and skills. She also compares the United States with other countries.

_____. THINK AND ACT: A SERIES OF ARTICLES PERTAINING TO MEN AND WOMEN, WORK AND WAGES. 1869. Reprint. New York: Arno Press, 1971. 372 p.

> The author argues that woman's work role must be more than domestic servant or school teacher.

Pivar, David. PURITY CRUSADE: SEXUAL MORALITY AND SOCIAL CONTROL, 1868-1900. Westport, Conn.: Greenwood Press, 1973. x, 308 p.

> Pivar relates the purity crusade to the woman's movement.

Radin, Edward D. LIZZIE BORDEN: THE UNTOLD STORY. New York: Simon and Schuster, 1961. 271 p.

> Lizzie Borden, in 1892, was accused of brutally murdering her mother and stepfather with an axe. The author raises doubts as to her guilt.

Rayne, Martha Louise. WHAT CAN A WOMAN DO; OR, HER POSITION IN THE BUSINESS AND LITERARY WORLD. 1893. Reprint. New York: Arno Press, 1974. 528 p.

> The author lists genteel jobs open to women, particularly in the office or governmental agency.

Richards, Clarice E. A TENDERFOOT BRIDE. 1920. Garden City, N.Y.: Doubleday, Page and Co., 1927. 189 p.

> This is an account of the experiences of a rancher's wife on the frontier.

Royce, Sarah. A FRONTIER LADY: RECOLLECTIONS OF THE GOLD RUSH AND EARLY CALIFORNIA. Edited by Ralph Henry Gabriel. New Haven,

Conn.: Yale University Press, 1932. Reprint. Lincoln: University of Nebraska Press, 1977. xiv, 217 p.

> Sarah Royce was the mother of Josiah Royce, American philosopher. She comments on the trip West, the gold rush, and manners, morals, and life-style of women on the frontier.

Ross, Nancy. WESTWARD THE WOMEN. New York: Knopf, 1945. 199 p.

> This is an account of pioneer women of the Pacific Northwest. The author adds a bibliography of published journals and diaries.

Salmon, Lucy Maynard. DOMESTIC SERVICE. 1897. Reprint. New York: Arno Press, 1972. 307 p.

> The author analyzes the life of domestic servants in the late nineteenth century.

Sanford, Mollie Dorsey. MOLLIE: THE JOURNAL OF MOLLIE DORSEY SANFORD IN NEBRASKA AND COLORADO TERRITORIES, 1857-1866. Lincoln: University of Nebraska Press, 1958. ix, 199 p.

> This little volume is the diary of Mollie Dorsey Sanford, 1838-1915.

Saxton, Martha. LOUISA MAY: A MODERN BIOGRAPHY OF LOUISA MAY ALCOTT. Boston: Houghton Mifflin, 1977. viii, 428 p.

> Louisa May Alcott became a popular writer, often supporting her destitute family. She was also a feminist of consequence, taking an interest in suffrage and other women's causes.

Sears, Hal D. THE SEX RADICALS: FREE LOVE IN HIGH VICTORIAN AMERICA. Lawrence: Regents Press of Kansas, 1977. xi, 342 p.

> Sears describes the concept in the late nineteenth century that there should be no coercion in relationships between men and women. There are brief sketches of sex radicals of the period.

Shaw, Anna Howard. THE STORY OF A PIONEER. New York: Harper and Brothers, 1915. 337 p.

> Anna Howard Shaw (1847-1919), a minister, was ordained by the Methodist Protestant Church in 1880. She graduated from medical school, and she was equally interested in the suffrage movement.

Stanton, Theodore, and Blatch, Harriott Stanton, eds. ELIZABETH CADY STANTON AS REVEALED IN HER LETTERS, DIARY AND REMINISCENCES. 2 vols. New York: Harper and Brothers, 1922.

> This is the life and times of one of the feminist leaders. The book contains much material on other feminist leaders, as well as the problems of women of the times.

Stern, Madeline B. LOUISA MAY ALCOTT. 1950. Norman: University of Oklahoma Press, 1971. xiii, 424 p.

This biography traces Alcott from childhood and includes the influence of her father, Bronson Alcott. There is an excellent bibliography of Louisa May Alcott's writings.

_____. WE THE WOMEN: CAREER FIRSTS OF NINETEENTH CENTURY AMERICA. New York: Schulte Publishing Co., 1963. xi, 402 p.

The author describes women pioneers in various fields: ballet, literature, architecture, telegraphy, dentistry, chemistry, academe, stenography, law, business, and industry.

Stewart, Elinore Pruitt. LETTERS OF A WOMAN HOMESTEADER. Boston: Houghton Mifflin, 1914. Reprint. Lincoln: University of Nebraska Press, 1961. vii, 282 p.

Elinore Pruitt Stewart lost her husband in a railway accident in 1909 and became the sole support of an infant daughter. She later became housekeeper and wife of a rancher.

Storer, Horatio Robinson. THE CAUSATION, COURSE, AND TREATMENT OF REFLEX INSANITY IN WOMEN. 1871. Reprint. New York: Arno Press, 1974. 154 p.

This volume is less useful in psychiatry than it is in the history of attitudes toward women. Storer believed mental illness in women was due to their reproductive systems.

Storer, Horatio Robinson, and Heard, Franklin Fiske. CRIMINAL ABORTION: ITS NATURE, ITS EVIDENCE, AND ITS LAW. 1868. Reprint. New York: Arno Press, 1974. 215 p.

This volume reveals the basic assumptions of the mid-nineteenth century toward abortion and women.

Sumner, William Graham. FOLKWAYS. Boston: Ginn, 1940. xiv, 642 p.

Using Darwinian arguments, Sumner maintained there were contrasts between men and women which were immutable. They had complementary but different abilities from birth. Thus feminists were making irresponsible demands, violating social arrangements based on sexual differences. He emphasized the process of sexual selection whereby the fittest males developed stronger bodies to attract the healthiest and most beautiful females.

Wallace, Irving. THE TWENTY SEVENTH WIFE. New York: Simon and Schuster, 1961. 400 p.

This is a biography of Ann Eliza Webb Young (b. 1844), the twenty-seventh wife of Brigham Young, Mormon leader. Married to Young

in 1869, she caused a sensation by suing for divorce in 1873.
She went on a lecture tour denouncing polygamy.

Walters, Ronald, ed. PRIMERS FOR PRUDERY: SEXUAL ADVICE TO VICTO-
RIAN AMERICA. Englewood Cliffs, N.J.: Prentice-Hall, 1974. 175 p.

Walters provides selections from sex manuals, medical journals,
and homemaking guides that reflect Victorian attitudes toward sex.

Ward, Lester Frank. THE PSYCHIC FACTORS OF CIVILIZATION. Boston:
Ginn, 1897. xxiii, 369 p.

Ward argued that women are intuitive while men reason. Because
of this, men have the characteristics of action, progress, positive-
ness, shrewdness, and diplomacy. A woman, on the other hand,
is cautious, negative, emotional, timid, conservative, and fearful
of innovation. Women desire to please while men are original.

Wiley, Bell Irwin. CONFEDERATE WOMEN. Westport, Conn.: Greenwood
Press, 1975. xiv, 204 p.

Wiley deals specifically with Mary Boykin Chestnut (1822-1886),
a South Carolina intellectual; Virginia Turnstall Clay (1825-1915),
an Alabama socialite; and Varina Howell Davis (1826-1913), the
wife of Jefferson Davis. One chapter gives a general account of
women in the South and the privation of the Civil War.

Woodhull, Victoria, and Claflin, Tennessee. WOODHULL AND CLAFLIN'S
WEEKLY. THE LIVES AND WRITINGS OF NOTORIOUS VICTORIA WOOD-
HULL AND TENNESSEE CLAFLIN. Edited by Arlene Kisner. Washington,
N.J.: Times Change Press, 1972. 63 p.

Kisner selects passages which place the notorious sisters in the
stream of feminism.

Worthington, Marjorie. MISS ALCOTT OF CONCORD. Garden City, N.Y.:
Doubleday, 1958. 330 p.

This biography of Louisa May Alcott emphasizes her connection with
Emerson, Thoreau, and Hawthorne. It deals with the privation of
the Alcott family and Alcott's service as a nurse during the Civil
War.

Wright, Carrol D. THE WORKING GIRLS OF BOSTON. 1889. Reprint.
New York: Arno Press, 1969. 133 p.

This study presents in detail the working conditions, income, and
financial difficulties of women who worked in business and industry.

Young, Agatha. THE WOMEN AND THE CRISIS: WOMEN OF THE NORTH
IN THE CIVIL WAR. New York: McDowell, Abolensky, 1959. 389 p.

Young concludes that the women of the Civil War period did not fit the Victorian stereotype of the frail, consumptive, and incompetent. The women met the demands of war in ways which dispell this view. These demands came from the battlefield as well as the home front.

Young, Kimball. ISN'T ONE WIFE ENOUGH? New York: Henry Holt, 1954. Reprint. Westport, Conn.: Greenwood Press, 1972. xiv, 476 p.

Young provides a detailed and sensitive study of Mormon polygamy.

# Chapter 9

# WOMEN ACHIEVE THE RIGHT TO VOTE:

# THE PROGRESSIVE ERA

Abbott, Lyman. THE RIGHTS OF MAN: A STUDY IN TWENTIETH CENTURY PROBLEMS. New York: Houghton Mifflin, 1901. xi, 375 p.

> Among the problems that Abbott describes are those of Indians, Negroes, and women. The volume is useful to achieve a view of problems at the beginning of the twentieth century. Equating democracy and "political Christianity," Abbott believes the problems can be solved.

Addams, Jane. THE SECOND TWENTY YEARS AT HULL HOUSE. New York: Macmillan, 1930. xiii, 413 p.

> Miss Addams deals with the Hull House settlement in Chicago during the years 1909 to 1929. She supported many of the current reform movements.

_____. THE SOCIAL THOUGHT OF JANE ADDAMS. Edited by Christopher Lasch. Indianapolis: Bobbs-Merrill, 1965. 266 p.

> Lasch brings together items of Addams's writing that illustrate her social thought in relation to reforms of the Progressive era.

_____. TWENTY YEARS AT HULL HOUSE WITH AUTOBIOGRAPHICAL NOTES. New York: Macmillan, 1912. xvii, 462 p.

> This is the story of Miss Addams, her establishment of Hull House, and her struggle to bring social reform to Chicago through the neighborhood concept.

Anderson, Mary. WOMAN AT WORK: THE AUTOBIOGRAPHY OF MARY ANDERSON AS TOLD TO MARY N. WINSLOW. Minneapolis: University of Minnesota Press, 1951. 266 p.

> This is the biography of a Swedish immigrant girl who got to Chicago at the time of the 1893 World's Fair. She worked in a factory, entered into the Hull House scene, became a part of the trade union movement, particularly the Chicago Women's Trade

Union League, and later, through the New Deal era, was head of the Women's Bureau in Washington.

Anthony, Katharine. MOTHERS WHO MUST EARN. New York: Survey Associates, 1914. 223 p.

Anthony describes the condition of women on New York's west side in the years after 1900. She describes the work women did, their home life, the physical and human cost of low wages, long hours, in addition to maintaining a home.

Beard, Mary Ritter. WOMAN'S WORK IN MUNICIPALITIES. New York: D. Appleton and Co., 1915. Reprint. New York: Arno Press, 1972. 344 p.

Beard recounts the work of women in social movements in her time.

Blatch, Harriot Eaton Stanton. CHALLENGING YEARS: THE MEMOIRS OF HARRIOT STANTON BLATCH. New York: G.P. Putnam's Sons. 1940. Reprint. Westport, Conn.: Hyperion Press, 1976. xvi, 347 p.

The daughter of Elizabeth Cady Stanton, Harriot Blatch (1856-1920) was a feminist and suffragist in her own right. After living in England for two decades, Blatch returned to the United States in 1902 where she continued feminist activities, including founding the Equality League of Self-Supporting Women, a militant group.

Blumberg, Rose. FLORENCE KELLEY: THE MAKING OF A SOCIAL PIONEER. New York: Kelley, 1966. 194 p.

Kelley (1859-1932) lived at Hull House, became a socialist and a leader in reform of working conditions in factories and abolition of child labor.

Bosworth, Louise Marion. THE LIVING WAGE OF WOMEN WORKERS: A STUDY OF INCOMES AND EXPENDITURES OF 450 WOMEN IN THE CITY OF BOSTON. New York: Longmans, Green and Co., 1911. Reprint. New York: Arno Press, 1976. 90 p.

This study offers insights into living patterns and problems faced by urban women workers.

Brandeis, Louis D., and Goldmark, Josephine. WOMEN IN INDUSTRY. New York: National Consumer's League. 1908. Reprint. New York: Arno Press, 1969. 118 p.

This is Brandeis's historic defense of the Oregon law that limited the female work day to ten hours.

Busbey, Katherine. HOME LIFE IN AMERICA. London: Methuen and Co., 1911. x, 410 p.

This volume gives a stereotyped view of girls and women of the upper middle class about 1910. It describes also, in an idealized way, household expenditures, recreation, resorts, housing, and colleges of the same class.

Campbell, Barbara K. THE "LIBERATED" WOMAN OF 1914: PROMINENT WOMEN OF THE PROGRESSIVE ERA. Ann Arbor, Mich.: UMI Research Press, 1979. 202 p.

Campbell studied nine thousand active women, relating their education and families to their careers to ascertain their reason for achievement.

Coolidge, Mary Roberts. WHY WOMEN ARE SO. New York: Henry Holt and Co., 1912. viii, 371 p.

Dr. Coolidge examined the conventions of her day, the role of stereotyping of the sexes, and the position to which these relegated women. She urges every man to "ask himself whether he is really a god, that he should presume to set for women the limits of capacity and duty."

Crow, Martha Foote. THE AMERICAN COUNTRY GIRL. New York: Frederick A. Stokes Co., 1915. Reprint. New York: Arno Press, 1974. viii, 367 p.

The story of women on the farms and in the small towns in the era before World War I, this book shows both the cultural disadvantages and the advantages.

Davis, Allen F. AMERICAN HEROINE: THE LIFE AND LEGEND OF JANE ADDAMS. New York: Oxford University Press, 1973. 339 p.

Davis sets out to write a realistic biography which lays to rest the myths about Addams.

_____. SPEARHEADS FOR REFORM: THE SOCIAL SETTLEMENTS AND THE PROGRESSIVE MOVEMENT, 1890-1914. New York: Oxford University Press, 1967. xviii, 322 p.

Davis tells the story of a group of idealists who sought to solve problems of lower-class neighborhoods by establishing residences there and teaching the workers and their families how to cope with society. Many of these settlement house people were women and many contributed to broader reform movements.

Dell, Floyd. WOMEN AS WORLD BUILDERS: STUDIES IN MODERN FEMINISM. Chicago: Forbes and Co., 1913. Reprint. Westport, Conn.: Hyperion Press, 1976. 104 p.

Dell, novelist, playwright, and critic, pays tribute to feminists of his time. He deals with some non-Americans but includes Jane Addams, Charlotte Perkins Gilman, Emma Goldman, Isadora Duncan, and Margaret Dreier Robins, founder of the National Woman's Trade Union League. Dell denounced the ideology by which women were idealized and at the same time dehumanized. Later Dell recanted this position.

Drake, Emma. WHAT A YOUNG WIFE OUGHT TO KNOW. Philadelphia: Vir Publishing, 1908. 288 p.

Drake believed that women were innately more moral than men, thus giving her the capacity to teach man right from wrong, show him cleanliness and order, and help him to peace.

Dreier, Mary E. MARGARET DREIER ROBINS: HER LIFE, LETTERS AND WORK. New York: Island Press Cooperative, 1950. xviii, 278 p.

This is a biography of Mrs. Raymond Robins who was active in settlement house work at Hull House, associate of many in the movement, organizer of the National Women's Trade Union, and in many crusades for women and labor. The book is indispensible for study of reform movements of early twentieth century.

Drinnon, Richard. REBEL IN PARADISE: A BIOGRAPHY OF EMMA GOLD-MAN. Chicago: University of Chicago Press, 1961. 349 p.

Emma Goldman (1869-1940) was one of the best known anarchists of her day. She also promoted feminist causes, birth control, and the arts.

DuBois, W.E. Burghardt, ed. THE NEGRO AMERICAN FAMILY. Atlanta: Atlanta University Press, 1908. Reprint. New York: Negro Universities Press, 1969. 156 p.

DuBois brings together a group of articles written by his students in 1909 and 1910 at the Atlanta University. They studied the condition of the family, the size of the family, sexual mores, the home, and family economics.

Eastman, Crystal. CRYSTAL EASTMAN ON WOMEN AND REVOLUTION. Edited by Blanche Wiesen Cook. New York: Oxford, 1978. xxii, 468 p.

Crystal Eastman (1881-1928) was a feminist, social worker, attorney, peace advocate, and promoter of industrial reform. She supported most progressive and radical causes. For a time, she was managing editor of the LIBERATOR, a radical journal published by her brother, Max Eastman. This is a collection of her feminist writings.

Farrell, John C. BELOVED LADY: A HISTORY OF JANE ADDAMS' IDEAS ON REFORM AND PEACE. Baltimore: Johns Hopkins Press, 1967. 272 p.

Jane Addams was active in many reforms of the Progressive era in-cluding the settlement house movement, feminism, and international peace. This book is a study of her ideas on these and other ideas.

Fetherling, Dale. MOTHER JONES, THE MINER'S ANGEL: A PORTRAIT. Carbondale: Southern Illinois University Press, 1974. viii, 263 p.

> Born in Ireland, Mary Jones (1830-1930) was well-educated for her time despite the somewhat coarse reputation that was put on her. She could speak the workingman's language and showed up at nearly every strike and labor disturbance to cheer on the workers and sometimes to organize their wives. Despite the hatred of the operators of mines and mills, she was much loved by the workers.

Finch, Edith. CAREY THOMAS OF BRYN MAWR. New York: Harper, 1947. 342 p.

> Martha Carey Thomas (1857-1935) was an educator and feminist. She became dean of Bryn Mawr in 1885 and president in 1894. She was determined that the college maintain standards equivalent to or better than the best men's colleges. She was active for women's suffrage.

Frankfort, Roberta. COLLEGIATE WOMEN: DOMESTICITY AND CAREER IN TURN-OF-THE-CENTURY AMERICA. New York: New York University Press, 1977. xix, 121 p.

> The author describes Elizabeth Palmer Peabody as "a precollegiate woman" and Alice Freeman Palmer and Martha Carey Thomas as examples of college-educated women. Further she describes education at Bryn Mawr and Wellesley in the years 1885 to 1908.

Friedman, Bernard H. GERTRUDE VANDERBILT WHITNEY: A BIOGRAPHY. Garden City, N.Y.: Doubleday, 1978. xi, 684 p.

> The daughter of one of the richest families in America and the wife of another of the richest families, Gertrude Vanderbilt Whitney (1875-1942) became a well-known sculptress. The book is encyclopedic and gives much of the life of a rich woman.

Fuller, Paul. LAURA CLAY AND THE WOMEN'S RIGHTS MOVEMENT. Lexington: University of Kentucky Press, 1975. xi, 217 p.

> Laura Clay (1849-1941), daughter of Cassius M. Clay, worked for woman's suffrage and other feminist causes, primarily in Kentucky. The book also contains much on Laura Clay's sisters Annie Clay, Sally Clay Bennett, and Mary B. Clay.

Gelb, Barbara. SO SHORT A TIME: A BIOGRAPHY OF JOHN REED AND LOUISE BRYANT. New York: W.W. Norton, 1973. 304 p.

> Bryant (1890-1936), well-educated daughter of an upper middle-class family, rebelled against the established way to follow the radical path. She became a Marxist and lived with John Reed, perhaps the only American buried in the Kremlin.

Gilman, Charlotte Perkins. HIS RELIGION AND HERS: A STUDY OF THE FAITH OF OUR FATHERS AND THE WORK OF OUR MOTHERS. New York: Century Co., 1923. Reprint. Westport, Conn.: Hyperion Press, 1976. xi, 300 p.

> Often described as the leading feminist intellectual, Gilman discusses religion in a sociological context. She argues that religion has been perverted by men by overemphasis on death and fate, which she believes are predominantly masculine concepts.

_____. IN THIS OUR WORLD. 1899. Reprint. New York: Arno Press, 1974. 120 p.

> Gilman had to support her family by lecturing, writing, and keeping boarders. Because of the prejudice at the turn of the century, she was socially and economically ostracized. Her autobiography reveals the difficulties of the self-supporting woman in San Francisco in that era.

_____. THE LIVING OF CHARLOTTE PERKINS GILMAN: AN AUTOBIOGRAPHY. New York: D. Appleton-Century Co., 1935. Reprint. New York: Arno Press, 1972. 341 p.

> This is the autobiography of the leading feminist intellectual. She believed that man could control the evolutionary process. She speaks of the female's cooperative nature and berates woman's economic independence on men.

_____. THE MAN-MADE WORLD OR, OUR ANDROCENTRIC CULTURE. New York: Charlton Co., 1911. 260 p.

> Gilman writes of the stereotype of women and of the fears of men that liberated women would bring him to a position of subservience. Gilman refutes this fear. She believed free women will bring a better life for all without sacrificing the family.

Gluck, Sherna, ed. FROM PARLOR TO PRISON: FIVE AMERICAN SUFFRAGISTS TALK ABOUT THEIR LIVES. New York: Vintage Books, 1976. x, 285 p.

> Using the technique of oral history, the editor provides reminisences of five women who were active in the suffrage movement: Sylvie Thygeson (Minnesota), Jessie Haver Butler (Colorado), Miriam Allen deFord (Pennsylvania), Laura Ellsworth Senter (New York), and Ernestine Hara Kettler (New York). From these accounts comes good information about the varied backgrounds of the feminists of the early twentieth century.

Goldman, Emma. LIVING MY LIFE. New York: A.A. Knopf, 1951. Reprint. New York: New American Library, 1977. 754 p.

> This is the autobiography of Emma Goldman (1869-1940), anarchist,

feminist, birth control advocate, and popularizer of the arts. Born in Russia of Jewish parents, she knew virtually every person of note in radical circles and the arts. This book is a mine of information not only about Goldman but also about many other women of the times.

Grimes, Alan P. THE PURITAN ETHIC AND WOMAN SUFFRAGE. New York: Oxford University Press, 1967. xiii, 159 p.

Grimes argues that woman suffrage was achieved for the same reason that black suffrage was denied--the desire of the establishment to maintain their position. He argues that the addition of women to the voter lists, particularly in the West, added to the numbers who would support the status quo.

Hale, Beatrice Forbes-Robertson. WHAT WOMEN WANT: AN INTERPRETATION OF THE FEMINIST MOVEMENT. New York: Frederick A. Stokes Co., 1914. ix, 307 p.

Hale viewed feminism in terms of freedom of choice, as a part of the progress of democratic freedom. She advocates the achievement of this through love rather than hate.

Hill, Joseph Adna. WOMEN IN GAINFUL OCCUPATIONS 1870 TO 1920. Washington, D.C.: Government Printing Office, 1929. Reprint. Westport, Conn.: Greenwood Press, 1976. xii, 416 p.

This is a study of the trends in numbers, occupational distribution, and family relationship of women reported in the census as following a gainful occupation.

Illinois. General Assembly. Senate. Vice Committee. REPORT OF THE SENATE VICE COMMITTEE. CREATED UNDER AUTHORITY OF THE SENATE OF THE FORTY-NINTH GENERAL ASSEMBLY AS A CONTINUATION OF THE COMMITTEE CREATED UNDER THE AUTHORITY OF THE SENATE OF THE FORTY-EIGHTH GENERAL ASSEMBLY, STATE OF ILLINOIS. Chicago: 1916. 979 p.

In the Progressive era, it was commonly believed that women went into prostitution because of the low pay in jobs available to them. This committee was established to study prostitution in Illinois and took their approach from that theory. The committee learned little about prostitution, but they turned up an immense amount of information about working women, their jobs, wages, working conditions, and life-style. They studied conditions in Washington, D.C., New York, and Illinois.

Irwin, Inez Haynes. THE STORY OF THE WOMAN'S PARTY. New York: Harcourt, Brace, 1921. 486 p.

In 1913 Alice Paul and Lucy Burns founded a new organization called the Congressional Union for the purpose of promoting the federal suffrage amendment. This group evolved into the Woman's party, which generally compaigned against Democratic congressional condidates and against President Wilson in 1916.

Jastrow, Joseph. THE PSYCHOLOGY OF CONVICTION. Boston: Houghton Mifflin, 1918. xix, 387 p.

A University of Wisconsin psychologist, Jastrow said that women have twin instincts of maternity and the desire to please. Thus childbearing is her greatest fulfillment which leads to problems through the divided loyalty to children and husband.

Jones, Mary Harris. THE AUTOBIOGRAPHY OF MOTHER JONES. 1926. Chicago: Charles H. Kerr, 1972. 242 p.

Mary "Mother" Jones (1830-1930) was a labor organizer, primarily known for her work with miners. She was better educated than most women of her time, although she could speak the profane language of the miners and other workers.

Keller, Helen [Adams]. HELEN KELLER, HER SOCIALIST YEARS: WRITINGS AND SPEECHES. Edited by Philip S. Foner. New York: International Publishers, 1967. 128 p.

Foner has collected Keller's writings from 1911 to 1929 that reflect her Socialist ideas.

_____. MIDSTREAM: MY LATER LIFE. Garden City, N.Y.: Doubleday, Doran and Co., 1929. Reprint. Westport, Conn.: Greenwood Press, 1968. xxiii, 362 p.

This book is the autobiographical account of Helen Keller in the twenty-five years after she left Radcliffe College.

Kelley, Florence. SOME ETHICAL GAINS THROUGH LEGISLATION. New York: Macmillan Co., 1905. Reprint. New York: Arno Press, 1969. 341 p.

Kelley was the first factory inspector in Illinois. She provided a first hand account of the exploitation of women and children and how the use of the information brought labor legislation.

Kraditor, Aileen S. THE IDEAS OF THE WOMAN SUFFRAGE MOVEMENT, 1890-1920. New York: Columbia University Press, 1965. xii, 313 p.

Kraditor describes the movement, its leaders, and the ideas used by the movement to advance the cause as well as the arguments used against equality.

Lane, Ann J. MARY RITTER BEARD: A SOURCE BOOK. New York: Schocken Books, 1977. 252 p.

Lane gives a brief biography of Beard, the early twentieth-century feminist, and provides a large selection of her writings and speeches.

Laughlin, Clara E. WORK-A-DAY GIRL: A STUDY OF SOME PRESENT DAY CONDITIONS. New York: Fleming H. Ravell Co., 1913. Reprint. New York: Arno Press, 1974. 320 p.

This is an account of the exploitation of young women who came to the big city seeking employment. Many turned to prostitution for survival.

Levine, David. JANE ADDAMS AND THE LIBERAL TRADITION. Madison: State Historical Society of Wisconsin, 1971. 277 p.

Levine details the thought of Jane Addams as she participated in the settlement house movement, housing reform, child labor legislation, progressive education, feminism, and pacifism. He poses Addams as a radical who operated within the liberal framework.

MacLean, Annie Marion. WAGE-EARNING WOMEN. New York: Macmillan Co., 1910. Reprint. New York: Arno Press, 1974. 202 p.

This survey by the Young Women's Christian Association considered four hundred establishments employing 135,000 women. The industries considered were paper, shoe, textile, agriculture, and mining. The survey deals with wages, social life, and problems of sexual discrimination suffered by the workers.

Marat, Helen. AMERICAN LABOR UNIONS, BY A MEMBER. New York: Henry Holt and Co., 1914. 275 p.

This is a general survey of labor unions in the early twentieth century, but told from the viewpoint of a woman worker and union member.

Martin, John, and Martin, Prestonia. FEMINISM: ITS FALLACIES AND FOLLIES. New York: Dodd, Mead, 1916. 359 p.

The authors argue that women who wanted college degrees and self-fulfillment outside the home forfeited maternity. Thus feminism was a threat to society. They argued that nature had ordained that men have a stronger sex urge than women so that race extinction could be avoided. Equal employment would bring the death of the human race.

Morgan, David. SUFFRAGISTS AND DEMOCRATS. East Lansing: Michigan State University Press, 1972. 225 p.

Morgan deals with the period between 1916 and 1920, the critical period preceding ratification of the nineteenth Amendment. He describes the political battle and the broadening of the base of the movement.

Noun, Louise R. STRONG MINDED WOMEN: THE EMERGENCE OF THE WOMAN SUFFRAGE MOVEMENT IN IOWA. Ames: Iowa State University Press, 1969. 322 p.

Noun relates the suffrage movement in Iowa to the national scene.

Ovington, Mary White. THE WALLS CAME TUMBLING DOWN. New York: Harcourt, Brace, 1947. Reprint. New York: Arno Press, 1969. 307 p.

Debutante turned reformer, Ovington worked in settlement houses and was one of the founders of the NAACP. This is her auto-biography.

Paulson, Ross Evans. WOMEN'S SUFFRAGE AND PROHIBITION: A COM-PARATIVE STUDY OF EQUALITY AND SOCIAL CONTROL. Glenview, Ill.: Scott, Foresman, 1973. 212 p.

Paulson describes his subjects in terms of social control of the com-munity. He also analyzes social reform and includes a discussion of feminism.

Peck, Mary Gray. CARRIE CHAPMAN CATT: A BIOGRAPHY. New York: H.W. Wilson Co., 1944. 495 p.

This is a biography of Carrie Chapman Catt (1859-1947), the feminist leader who succeeded Susan B. Anthony as president of the National American Woman's Suffrage Association in 1900. She provided much of the leadership in the final years of the struggle for the right to vote for women. She was also active in the move-ment for peace and disarmament after that time. With the suffrage struggle over, Catt founded the League of Women Voters.

Pennington, Patience. A WOMAN RICE PLANTER. Cambridge, Mass.: Har-vard University Press, 1961. xxxii, 446 p.

This is the account of Elizabeth Allston Pringle of South Carolina, who tried desperately but unsuccessfully from 1903 to 1907 to make a rice plantation profitable. She worked in the muddy fields with her laborers.

Rappaport, Philip. LOOKING FORWARD, A TREATISE ON THE STATUS OF WOMAN AND THE ORIGIN AND GROWTH OF THE FAMILY AND THE STATE. Chicago: C.H. Kerr and Co., 1913. 234 p.

This is an attempt to examine the status of women and the family as social institution in relation to the state using the theory of eco-nomic determinism. Rappaport believes that men presumptuously limit the sphere of women out of fear of competition and for economic motives. He examines the status of women, prostitution, the family, and divorce as they existed in 1913.

Riegel, Robert E. AMERICAN FEMINISTS. Lawrence: University of Kansas Press, 1963. 233 p.

Riegel describes the beginnings of the feminist reform movement, devoting a chapter each to three of the early feminists, Elizabeth Cady Stanton, Susan B. Anthony, and Lucy Stone. He takes note of the professional and literary women in the post-Civil War era and concludes with a chapter on why only a small minority of women became feminists and the nature of their movement.

Rogers, Anna B. WHY AMERICAN MARRIAGES FAIL. Boston: Houghton Mifflin, 1909. 213 p.

Rogers believed marriages fail because women had become devoted to the "cult of individualism" and thus their selfishness caused marriage to break down.

Sewell, May Wright. WOMEN, WORLD WAR AND PERMANENT PEACE. San Francisco: J.J. Newbegin, 1915. Reprint. Westport, Conn.: Hyperion Press, 1976. xxx, 206 p.

Sewell, feminist and pacifist, established a girls school in Indianapolis to better prepare girls for college on the same basis as boys. President of the International Woman's Congress in 1900, she also participated in the peace movement prior to 1900. This book is an account of the International Conference of Women Workers to Promote Permanent Peace held in San Francisco in 1915.

Sochen, June. THE NEW WOMAN: FEMINISM IN GREENWICH VILLAGE, 1910-1920. New York: Quadrangle, 1972. xi, 175 p.

Sochen describes the life and activities of Crystal Eastman, Henrietta Rodman, Ida Rank, Neith Boyce, and Susan Glaspell as well as their associates Max Eastman and Floyd Dell. These feminists espoused the causes of child care facilities, equal professional opportunities for women, and women's equality in sexual matters.

Stanton, Elizabeth Cady, et al. HISTORY OF WOMAN SUFFRAGE. 6 vols. New York: Fowler and Wells, National Womans Suffrage Association, 1881-1922.

The authors provide an amazingly detailed history of the feminist movement from the London Anti-Slavery Convention in 1840 and the Seneca Falls convention of 1848 to the eve of the achievement of women's suffrage. The successes and failures of the movement are portrayted as seen by its leaders.

Taft, Jessie. THE WOMAN MOVEMENT FROM THE POINT OF VIEW OF SOCIAL CONSCIOUSNESS. Chicago: University of Chicago Press, 1916. 62 p.

Taft notes the stereotype that women must be selfless and suffer. She writes that in the nineteenth-century feminine ideal, the element of sacrifice is treated as a virtue and glory of the perfect woman, whose function was only as wife and mother.

Tarbell, Ida. THE BUSINESS OF BEING A WOMAN. New York: Macmillan, 1912. 242 p.

Ida Tarbell was a journalist and historian of the muckraker school. Her life and career was the epitome of the feminist goal, but in this book she rejected feminism on the grounds that nature and society had assigned to women the role of marriage and motherhood.

Wald, Lillian D. WINDOWS ON HENRY STREET. Boston: Little, Brown and Co., 1934. xi, 348 p.

Lillian Wald was the force behind the Henry Street settlement house in New York City. It became a model and training ground of personnel for other settlements. Miss Wald was active in nearly every movement for social reform in New York. This book is the story of her activity.

Walsh, Correa Moylan. FEMINISM. New York: Sturgis and Walton, 1917. 396 p.

Walsh argues that feminists came from asexual women who would have fewer children than women who did not deny their femininity. Thus, the feminists were, in her view, not a threat to be concerned with because the problem they caused would be cured by nature. However, if this movement spread to the upper classes, said Walsh, this would limit progress, so feminism should be fought vigorously.

Wilson, Margaret Gibbons. THE AMERICAN WOMAN IN TRANSITION: THE URBAN INFLUENCE, 1870-1920. Westport, Conn.: Greenwood Press, 1979. 280 p.

Wilson studies the change in the social and economic roles of women and the resulting change in self-image as the United States emerged from a primarily agricultural society into an industrialized, urban society.

# Chapter 10

# FROM THE 19TH AMENDMENT TO 1963

Abbott, Edith. THE TENEMENTS OF CHICAGO, 1908-1935. Chicago: University of Chicago Press, 1936. Reprint. New York: Arno Press, 1970. xx, 503 p.

> Abbott describes the population changes of Chicago, the arrival and change of various waves of ethnic groups, both European and American blacks. Abbott studied a crescent-shaped area from the near north side, west past Hull House and the stockyards, and south to the steel mills on the South Side. She describes the congestion, the unsanitary conditions, and high rents. She notes some improvements made with modern technology, the automobile, electricity, gas, and plumbing.

Allen, Ruth Alice. THE LABOR OF WOMEN IN THE PRODUCTION OF COTTON. Austin: University of Texas Press, 1933. Reprint. New York: Arno Press, 1976. 285 p.

> Allen describes women farm workers in Texas.

Barnett, Avrom. FOUNDATIONS OF FEMINISM. New York: Robert M. McBride and Co., 1921. 245 p.

> Barnett looks at the biological, psychological, and sociological foundations of feminism. He ends with a plea for feminism and freedom from the "tyranny of sex customs, caste customs, of the customs the elders created for their own protection."

Beard, Mary Ritter. AMERICA THROUGH WOMEN'S EYES. New York: Macmillan Co., 1933. 558 p.

> Beard puts forth feminism and the history of women as a part of the growing emphasis on social history and the growing demand for the integration of knowledge by combining forces of history with the social sciences. She proposes to remedy earlier omissions by illustrating the role of women in the development of American society.

Beebe, Gilbert Wheeler. CONTRACEPTION AND FERTILITY IN THE SOUTH-ERN APPALACHIANS. Baltimore, Md.: Williams and Wilkins, 1942. Reprint. New York: Arno Press, 1972. 274 p.

> This is a sociological survey of birth control methods in low-income families during the era of the Great Depression.

Breckinridge, Sophonisba P. WOMEN IN THE TWENTIETH CENTURY: A STUDY OF THEIR POLITICAL, SOCIAL, AND ECONOMIC ACTIVITIES. New York: McGraw-Hill, 1933. Reprint. New York: Arno Press, 1977. xi, 364 p.

> This monograph surveys the changing roles of women's clubs and professional organizations.

Chafe, William Henry. THE AMERICAN WOMAN: HER CHANGING SOCIAL, ECONOMIC, AND POLITICAL ROLES, 1920-1970. New York: Oxford University Press, 1972. xiii, 351 p.

> The author notes that despite the passage of the 19th Amendment, the conditions of women did not improve drastically, especially as the Depression reinforced prejudice against employment of women. Despite the fact that the numbers of employed women increased, working conditions and role stereotypes of women did not change much. He notes the revival of feminism after World War II.

_____. WOMEN AND EQUALITY: CHANGING PATTERNS IN AMERICAN CULTURE. New York: Oxford University Press, 1977. xiii, 207 p.

> In several essays, the author explores the development of sex roles in America. He examines the manner in which political movements intervene and assesses the potential for sex equality in America. He sees World War II as a watershed in the women's movement. He believes that, at that point, women refused to be content with an attack on legal and political problems, rather confronting sex stereotyping at all levels. Chafe is hopeful that equality may be achieved.

Day, Dorothy. THE LONG LONELINESS. New York: Harper, 1952. 288 p.

> This is the autobiography of Dorothy Day, founder of the Catholic Worker's Movement in 1933 and editor of the CATHOLIC WORKER. Day describes the loneliness of the radical life and the connection of the religious, political, and social impulses of her life.

Dix, Dorothy. HOW TO WIN AND HOLD A HUSBAND. New York: Double-day, Doran and Co., 1939. Reprint. New York: Arno Press, 1979. 268 p.

> Dix wrote an advice-to-the-lovelorn column in newspapers during the 1920s and 1930s. This is her solution to what she regarded as the goal of every woman.

Donovan, Frances R. THE SALESLADY. Chicago: University of Chicago Press, 1929. Reprint. New York: Arno Press, 1974. 267 p.

> This is a sociological study of the problems of the female sales-person in the retail stores. This was one of the positions readily available to women in the 1920s.

_____. THE SCHOOLMA'AM. New York: Frederick A. Stokes Co., 1938. Reprint. New York: Arno Press, 1974. 355 p.

> Teaching on the elementary level was one of the professions open to women. This book is a study of that profession.

_____. THE WOMAN WHO WAITS. Boston: R.G. Badger, 1920. Reprint. New York: Arno Press, 1974. 228 p.

> The job of waitress is always available to women. This book looks at the long hours, fatigue, low pay, and humiliation at the hands of customers.

Elliott, Maud Howe. THIS WAS MY NEWPORT. Cambridge, Mass.: Mythology Co., 1944. xxiv, 279 p.

> Elliott describes the "social capital" of the United States. Newport became the resort of the rich Bostonians and New York social-ites. She describes the life and sports of the rich.

Filene, Catherine, ed. CAREERS FOR WOMEN. New York: Houghton Mifflin Co., 1920. Reprint. New York: Arno Press, 1974. 576 p.

> This is the report of a series of Intercollegiate Conferences on Vocations for Women held just before 1920. It lists 174 career descriptions under thirty-two general headings. The very fact that such conferences were held is indicative of the increasing interest of women in careers outside the home in the post-World War I era.

Glick, Paul. AMERICAN FAMILIES. New York: John Wiley, 1957. xiv, 240 p.

> This volume is based on statistical studies derived from census records. Some of it is historical but most deals with the post-World War II period.

Gregory, Chester W. WOMEN IN DEFENSE WORK DURING WORLD WAR II: AN ANALYSIS OF THE LABOR PROBLEMS AND WOMEN'S RIGHTS. New York: Exposition Press, 1974. xxii, 243 p.

> This looks at the kinds of jobs women had in the defense industry, how they were trained and worked, the problems and benefits of this employment, and government policy in relation to women workers.

Hagood, Margaret Jarman. MOTHERS OF THE SOUTH: PORTRAITURE OF THE WHITE TENANT FARM WOMAN. Chapel Hill: University of North Carolina Press, 1939. 252 p.

> Hagood places the woman within the context of southern share-cropping in the Depression era. Beyond their work in the fields, she describes them as mothers and wives. She cites the problems of childbearing and child rearing and the worries of these women. The book is based on interviews done in the South in the 1930s.

Hairwich, Andrea Taylor, and Palmer, Gladys L., eds. I AM A WOMAN WORKER: A SCRAPBOOK OF AUTOBIOGRAPHIES. New York: Affiliated School for Workers, 1936. 152 p.

> This volume is a collection of women's experiences as workers which grew out of the summer schools for workers run by a coalition of labor movement groups. The women speak out about life in the factory, losing their jobs, organizing unions, and strikes they have been involved in.

Hamilton, Mary E. THE POLICEWOMAN: HER SERVICE AND IDEALS. New York: Frederick A. Stokes Co., 1924. Reprint. New York: Arno Press, 1971. 200 p.

> Hamilton, a New York policewoman, explains why she entered a profession previously reserved to men. She describes her work, especially with juveniles.

Hareven, Tamara. ELEANOR ROOSEVELT: AN AMERICAN CONSCIENCE. Chicago: Quadrangle, 1968. 326 p.

> Hareven makes the point that without special training or brilliance Eleanor Roosevelt became a world leader, partly because of her personality.

Henry, Alice. THE TRADE UNION WOMAN. New York: D. Appleton and Co., 1915. xxiv, 314 p.

> Henry describes the trade union movement for women, the woman organizer, immigrant women, vocational training for women, and the working woman and marriage.

_____. WOMEN AND THE LABOR MOVEMENT. New York: George H. Doran Co., 1923. xix, 241 p.

> This is a survey of women's participation in the labor movement throughout American history up to 1923.

Kirchwey, Freda, ed. OUR CHANGING MORALITY: A SYMPOSIUM. 1930. Reprint. New York: Arno Press, 1972. 249 p.

> Reflecting the conservative concern with the alleged sexual freedom

of the 1920s, this symposium of leading social thinkers explored the links between sexual behavior and the increased freedom of women.

LaFollette, Suzanne. CONCERNING WOMEN. New York: Albert and Charles Boni, 1926. 306 p.

> Demanding full and equal freedom for every individual, LaFollette called for a new feminism which went beyond the suffragist mentality. She believed the new woman of the twenties who enjoyed new freedom in clothing, pleasures, and employment could not relate well to the old ideas now that suffrage had been achieved. La-Follette has been called the most original feminist of the 1920s.

Lash, Joseph P. ELEANOR AND FRANKLIN. New York: W.W. Norton and Co., 1971. xvii, 765 p.

> This is a biography of Eleanor Roosevelt from her childhood through the death of Franklin Roosevelt.

Lemons, J. Stanley. THE WOMAN CITIZEN: SOCIAL FEMINISM IN THE 1920S. Urbana: University of Illinois Press, 1973. xiii, 266 p.

> Beginning his description of feminism at the time of the ratification of the 19th Amendment, Lemons deals with social welfare activities of the feminists to increase education, health, and work opportunities. He describes the activities of the League of Women Voters, National Consumers League, Women's Trade Union League, and Women's Joint Congressional Committee. He contrasts the social feminists who fought these battles with the hard core feminists who concentrated on the Equal Rights Amendment.

Levine, Louis. THE WOMEN'S GARMENT WORKERS: A HISTORY OF THE INTERNATIONAL LADIES' GARMENT WORKERS' UNION. New York: B.W. Huebach, 1924. Reprint. New York: Arno Press, 1969. 608 p.

> The author provides, based on union records and interviews, a history of an industry and union comprised of women and immigrants. He emphasizes the strike of 1910 which still provides precedents in industrial relations.

Lindbergh, Anne Morrow. BRING ME A UNICORN: DIARIES AND LETTERS OF ANNE MORROW LINDBERGH, 1922-1928. New York: Harcourt Brace Jovanovich, 1971. xxv, 259 p.

> This is the study of Lindbergh's college years at Smith and meeting her husband.

_____. THE FLOWER AND THE NETTLE. DIARIES OF ANNE MORROW LINDBERGH, 1936-1939. New York: Harcourt Brace Jovanovich, 1976. xxix, 605 p.

After the kidnapping of their son, the Lindberghs' lived abroad for many years. This is the record of part of that life.

_____. HOUR OF GOLD, HOUR OF LEAD: DIARIES AND LETTERS 1929-1932. New York: Harcourt Brace Jovanovich, 1973. xi, 340 p.

These diaries and letters describe the exhilaration of life with Lindbergh and the despair from her son being kidnapped and killed in 1932.

Lobsenz, Johanna. THE OLDER WOMAN IN INDUSTRY. New York: Charles Scribner's Sons, 1929. Reprint. New York: Arno Press, 1974. 281 p.

Lobsenz describes the double discrimination that women over thirty-five suffered--age and sex.

McCurry, Dan C. CANNERY CAPTIVES: WOMEN WORKERS IN THE PRO-DUCE PROCESSING INDUSTRY. Washington, D.C.: U.S. Women's Bureau, 1926, 1927, 1930, 1940. Reprint. New York: Arno Press, 1974. 396 p.

This examines women in the fruit industries of Washington and Hawaii, women in the vegetable industry of Delaware, and relevant labor legislation.

Manning, Caroline. THE IMMIGRANT WOMAN AND HER JOB. Washington, D.C.: Government Printing Office, 1920. Reprint. New York: Arno Press, 1970. ix, 179 p.

Manning interviewed two thousand immigrant women, chiefly in Philadelphia and eastern Pennsylvania, in 1925, in an attempt to find their role in and contribution to the industrial system. She analyzes the shift from housewife to industrial workers.

Miller, William D. A HARSH AND DREADFUL LOVE: DOROTHY DAY AND THE CATHOLIC WORKER MOVEMENT. New York: Liveright, 1973. xvi, 370 p.

This is the standard history of the radical Catholic Worker movement and the part of Dorothy Day in its founding.

Mowry, George E., ed. THE TWENTIES: FORDS, FLAPPERS & FANATICS. Englewood Cliffs, N.J.: Prentice-Hall, 1963. v, 186 p.

Mowry pulls together articles from contemporary magazines which illustrate much of the social history of the twenties. He includes fads, recreation, the sexual revolution, religion, prohibition, and the heroes of the era.

Myerson, Abraham. THE NERVOUS HOUSEWIFE. Boston: Little, Brown and Co., 1927. Reprint. New York: Arno Press, 1972. 273 p.

Myerson, a psychiatrist, found that women in the 1920s were becoming neurotic as they were stirred by feminism and individualism but found only frustration with housework or discrimination in the business world.

Pruette, Lorine. WOMEN AND LEISURE: A STUDY OF SOCIAL WASTE. New York: E.P. Dutton and Co., 1924. Reprint. New York: Arno Press, 1972. 225 p.

This author is concerned that at a time when mechanical devices promised to free women from household work, sex discrimination would turn the free time into useless leisure.

Reed, Ruth. THE ILLEGITIMATE FAMILY IN NEW YORK CITY: ITS TREATMENT BY SOCIAL AND HEALTH AGENCIES. New York: Columbia University Press, 1934. Reprint. New York: Arno Press, 1971. 385 p.

This volume provides some of the scarce historical information on illegitimacy.

Rogers, Agnes. WOMEN ARE HERE TO STAY. New York: Harper, 1949. 220 p.

This is a largely pictorial account of the changing role of women in America. It doesn't do much for women's liberation, but serves to illustrate attitudes and standards of the period immediately after World War II.

Roosevelt, Eleanor. THE YEARS ALONE. New York: Norton, 1972. 368 p.

This autobiography deals with Eleanor Roosevelt's years after the death of her husband. She served as representative to the United Nations, supported Adlai Stevenson, worked as a journalist and college lecturer.

Strong, Anna Louise. I CHANGE WORLDS: THE REMAKING OF AN AMERICAN. New York: Henry Holt and Co., 1935. 422 p.

Coming from an upper middle class but liberal activist family, Strong graduated from Oberlin at nineteen and at twenty-three was the youngest student to receive a Ph.D. degree from the University of Chicago. She became a labor reporter and after firsthand contact with the Everett, Washington, massacre, became radicalized and opposed World War I. By 1921 she was in Russia and spent much of her life in China. She died in Peking in 1970.

Weber, Gustavus A. THE WOMEN'S BUREAU: ITS HISTORY, ACTIVITIES AND ORGANIZATION. Baltimore: Johns Hopkins Press, 1923. 31 p.

This is a short description of the early history of the Women's Bureau of the Department of Labor in the years 1919 to 1923. It includes a list of the bureau's publications of the period.

Weisbord, Vera Buch. A RADICAL LIFE. Bloomington: Indiana University Press, 1977. xviii, 330 p.

> This is the autobiography of Weisbord--writer, teacher, artist, factory worker, and sometime Socialist and Communist.

Westin, Jeanne. MAKING DO: HOW WOMEN SURVIVED IN THE '30S. Chicago: Follett Publishing Co., 1976. xi, 331 p.

> This book describes the position of women in the Depression of the 1930s. Women often had to feed the family with little resources. Westin describes the problems, the ways of making food and money stretch, and the search for a better life.

Yellis, Kenneth A. "Prosperity's Child: Some Thoughts On The Flapper." AMERICAN QUARTERLY 21 (Spring 1969): 49-64.

> This is a description of the revolt of the flapper of the 1920s against the Gibson girl image of the 1890s. The revolt in costume symbolized the revolt against the sexual role of the woman of the late Victorian period. The Gibson girl image was one of chastity and femininity while the flapper portrayed a boyish and free image that was "at least capable of sin if not actually guilty of it."

# Chapter 11

# 1963 TO PRESENT

Arofat, Ibtihay, and Yorburg, Betty. THE NEW WOMEN: ATTITUDES, BE-HAVIOR AND SELF-IMAGE. Columbus: Charles E. Merrill, 1976. vii, 149 p.

> This book explores the life-styles of women in the 1970s and how women have changed, in part because of the influence of feminist values.

Bardwick, Judith. IN TRANSITION: HOW FEMINISM, SEXUAL LIBERATION, AND THE SEARCH FOR SELF-FULFILLMENT HAVE ALTERED OUR LIVES. New York: Holt, Rinehart and Winston, 1976. 203 p.

> Bardwick, a psychologist, examines how women's lives have changed through the women's movement.

Carden, Maren Lockwood. THE NEW FEMINIST MOVEMENT. New York: Russell Sage Foundation, 1974. xviii, 234 p.

> Carden discusses the ideas, issues, and trends of the current women's movement. She focuses especially on the history of the National Organization of Women.

Chafe, William H. WOMEN AND EQUALITY: CHANGING PATTERNS IN AMERICAN CULTURE. New York: Oxford University Press, 1972. xiii, 207 p.

> Chafe describes the manner in which women have been denied equality and the challenge they have made against their traditional role. Chafe compares sex and race as means of understanding the oppression of women. He examines the obstacles in the way of equality.

Deckard, Barbara Sinclair. THE WOMEN'S MOVEMENT: POLITICAL, SOCIO-ECONOMIC AND PSYCHOLOGICAL ISSUES. New York: Harper and Row, 1979. 484 p.

> Deckard devotes one lengthy section to the status of women in America in the 1970s. This work also describes the women's movement throughout history. Her aim, however, is to place the con-

temporary women's movement in context. The last three chapters of the book are on the movement since 1960 and the issues with which it is concerned.

Denmark, Florence, ed. WHO DISCRIMINATES AGAINST WOMEN? Beverly Hills, Calif.: Sage Publications, 1974. 143 p.

This book grew out of the meeting of the American Psychological Association in 1972. The papers deal with some sources of discrimination against women, for example, parents, men, institutions, and other women.

Evans, Sara. PERSONAL POLITICS: THE ROOTS OF WOMEN'S LIBERATION IN THE CIVIL RIGHTS MOVEMENT AND THE NEW LEFT. New York: Alfred A. Knopf, 1979. xii, 274 p.

Evans examines the origins of contemporary feminism in the other left movements of the 1960s. She finds a significant connection between the two social forces, although some of the women's struggle was a reaction to the oppressive attitudes of the men on the left.

Freeman, Jo. THE POLITICS OF WOMEN'S LIBERATION. New York: Longram, 1975. xvi, 268 p.

Freeman explores the beginnings of the contemporary feminism, its goals, organizations, and impact on public policy.

Frieden, Betty. IT CHANGED MY LIFE: WRITINGS ON THE WOMEN'S MOVEMENT. New York: Random House, 1976. xix, 388 p.

Frieden brings together her articles on the women's movement, mostly published after FEMININE MYSTIQUE (1963). She concludes with a chapter, "An Open Letter to the Women's Movement --1976." She warns of the dangers of dissent, too much emphasis on lesbianism, and the fear engendered in women in general by too radical an approach. She also discusses the impact of the movement in her life.

Goodman, Ellen. TURNING POINTS: HOW PEOPLE CHANGE THROUGH CRISIS AND COMMITMENT. New York: Doubleday, 1979. 290 p.

Goodman interviewed nearly a hundred women to determine the impact of recent feminism upon them both personally and in their relationships with others. She found most were exhilarated by the freedoms offered but were afraid to take advantage of these because it might jeopardize their marriages. These felt duty bound to adhere to traditional sex roles upon which these relationships were based. In many instances, husbands and wives have reached a compromise solution whereby some growth is tolerated. Other women in this group still feel rage as their desire for independence and

respect are thwarted. Others, for instance, Marabel Morgan, re-
sist change. Many women in this group have so little self-esteem
that they believe they deserve only a subservient position. On
the other extreme are those who are willing to risk their secure
lives for new challenges. Goodman believes still further redefini-
tion of roles is necessary so that men and women can have a true
partnership in life.

Hole, Judith, and Levine, Ellen. REBIRTH OF FEMINISM. New York:
Quadrangle Books, 1971. xiii, 488 p.

This is an analysis of the roots of the contemporary women's movement and its growth during the 1960s. It also examines some issues facing contemporary feminists, such as the image of women,
abortion, child care, education, and entry into professions.

Mead, Margaret, and Kaplan, Frances Bagley, eds. AMERICAN WOMEN:
REPORT OF THE PRESIDENT'S COMMISSION ON THE STATUS OF WOMEN
AND OTHER PUBLICATIONS OF THE COMMISSION. New York: Scribner's,
1965. xi, 274 p.

In 1960 President John F. Kennedy established the Commission on
the Status of Women chaired by Eleanor Roosevelt. This volume
is the report of that commission. Heavily statistical, it deals with
economic, social, and political issues, and recommends the right
of women to choose in all areas. It deals with education, the
home, child care centers, employment and wages, health, and
legal status.

Morgan, Robin. GOING TOO FAR. THE PERSONAL CHRONICLE OF A
FEMINIST. New York: Vintage Books, 1978. xiii, 333 p.

Morgan writes a series of essays, both personal and political, that
describe what it means to be a feminist and the implications of
having a feminist world view. She analyzes numerous social issues through a radical feminist ideology. This book was written
after Morgan's immersion in feminism and it reflects the changes
wrought on her personally and in her thought.

National Commission on the Observance of International Women's Year. THE
SPIRIT OF HOUSTON: THE FIRST NATIONAL WOMEN'S CONFERENCE.
Washington, D.C.: 1978. 308 p.

This is the report from the Houston conference held in November
1977. It includes final proposals and excerpts from speeches given.

Snyder, Eloise, ed. THE STUDY OF WOMEN: ENLARGING PERSPECTIVES
OF SOCIAL REALITY. New York: Harper and Row, 1979. xx, 379 p.

Several authors deal with minority women, sexism and racism,
women in history and religion, unfulfilled women, physical sex differ-

ences, constitutional rights, federal laws, women in the work force, and the anatomy of the women's movement.

West, Uta, ed. WOMEN IN A CHANGING WORLD. New York: McGraw-Hill, 1975. 170 p.

This is a collection of writings which examine the impact of the shifting sex roles on women's experience. It looks at how women have changed and how they feel about themselves and the new definition of their roles. It is primarily intended to speak to those who embrace some degree of feminism in order to reassure and share means of coping.

Wortin, Helen, and Rabinowitz, Clara, eds. THE WOMAN MOVEMENT: SOCIAL AND PSYCHOLOGICAL PERSPECTIVES. New York: Halsted, 1972. 151 p.

This is a collection of essays from the AMERICAN JOURNAL OF ORTHOPSYCHIATRY which explores the changing definition of women's role in society.

# Chapter 12

# CONTEMPORARY FEMINIST THOUGHT
# AND ANALYSIS

Atkinson, Ti-Grace. AMAZON ODYSSEY. New York: Links, 1974. 226 p.

This is a collection of writings which document Atkinson's increas-
ingly radical position in the feminist community.

Billings, Victoria. THE WOMANSBOOK. Greenwich, Conn.: Fawcett-Crest
Books, 1974. 266 p.

This is a very practical book oriented towards the specifics of liberation. It asks its readers to look at their lives to determine the
degree of independence.

Brogger, Suzanne. DELIVER US FROM LOVE. New York: Dell Publishing
Co., 1976. x, 298 p.

Brogger, a radical Danish feminist, discusses the impossibility of a
free and equalitarian personal life in the oppressive, sexist society.

Burton, Gabrielle. I'M RUNNING AWAY FROM HOME, BUT I'M NOT AL-
LOWED TO CROSS THE STREET. Pittsburgh: KNOW, 1972. 206 p.

Burton wrote an informal story of her growing-feminist beliefs and
how she made changes in her life.

Carroll, Berenice A., ed. LIBERATING WOMEN'S HISTORY: THEORETICAL
AND CRITICAL ESSAYS. Urbana: University of Illinois Press, 1976. xiv,
434 p.

This volume is a collection of wide-ranging essays mostly written
since the beginning of the new feminism of the 1960s. Many of
them deal with the need for the study of women's history and some
aim at a methodology.

Cassell, Joan. A GROUP CALLED WOMEN: SISTERHOOD AND SYMBOLISM
IN THE FEMINIST MOVEMENT. New York: David McKay Co., 1977. xiv,
240 p.

Cassell uses an anthropological approach to describe what it is like to become a feminist and the new systems of meaning that occur in women once radicalized.

Daly, Mary. BEYOND GOD THE FATHER: TOWARD A PHILOSOPHY OF WOMEN'S LIBERATION. Boston: Beacon Press, 1973. xii, 225 p.

Daly describes the condition of women and the uses of a theological or religious perspective in defining a new, feminist world view.

_____. GYN/ECOLOGY: THE METAETHICS OF RADICAL FEMINISM. Boston: Beacon Press, 1978. 185 p.

Daly analyzes patriarchy as the predominant religion throughout history. She believes patriarchy has led women and society to fragmentation and proposes a new cultural mythology of connection which will alter the state of consciousness in society.

DeBeauvoir, Simone. THE SECOND SEX. New York: Vintage Books, 1974. xxxiv, 814 p., xii.

DeBeauvoir's classic book analyzes women in history and mythology and the state of women's life in the mid-twentieth century.

Dreifus, Claudia. WOMEN'S FATE: RAPS FROM A FEMINIST CONSCIOUS-NESS-RAISING GROUP. New York: Bonfern, 1973. 277 p.

Dreifus describes the theory of a consciousness-raising group and the experience of one actual C-R group.

Dworkin, Andrea. OUR BLOOD: PROPHECIES AND DISCOURSES ON SEXUAL POLITICS. New York: Harper and Row, 1976. 118 p.

Dworkin writes a series of essays on issues facing women today utilizing a radical-feminist perspective. She addresses such topics as rape, nonviolence, lesbianism, and the causes of oppression.

_____. WOMAN HATING. New York: G.P. Dutton, 1974. 217 p.

Dworkin delineates the history of misogyny.

Freeman, Jo, ed. WOMEN: A FEMINIST PERSPECTIVE. Palo Alto, Calif.: Mayfield Publishing, 1975.

This series of essays presents a feminist analysis of many aspects of women's lives--their bodies, marriage, growing up female, work, the double standards, and others.

Friedan, Betty. THE FEMININE MYSTIQUE. New York: W.W. Norton and Co., 1963. 410 p.

Often credited with starting the new militant feminism of the 1960s,

Friedan argued that women were discontented because housework was boring. Rejecting Freudianism, she denied that women had any special ability in raising children. She blamed advertisers, women's magazines, and the media for the mystique that marriage and the good life would bring fulfillment.

Fritz, Leah. DREAMERS AND DEALERS. Boston: Beacon Press, 1979. xvii, 293 p.

Fritz looks at the whole of the women's movement from the inside and criticizes some of its elitism and middle-class assumptions. She proposes the movement struggle towards the most utopian goals, and links the oppression of women to patriarchy.

_____. THINKING LIKE A WOMAN. New York: WIN Books, 1975. 160 p.

This is a group of essays which express Fritz's growth as a feminist.

Gornick, Vivian. ESSAYS IN FEMINISM. New York: Harper and Row, 1978. 234 p.

This is a collection of essays written from 1969 to 1977 on a variety of topics of concern to the emerging new feminist movement. These essays originally appeared in MS. MAGAZINE, THE VILLAGE VOICE, and THE NEW YORK TIMES MAGAZINE. Gornick's perspective is basically liberal.

Gornick, Vivian, and Moran, Barbara K., eds. WOMEN IN SEXIST SOCIETY: STUDIES IN POWER AND POWERLESSNESS. New York: Basic Books, 1971. xxv, 515 p.

The editors have brought together articles by thirty-three authors, all female. Most are scholars in one discipline or another. Their topics range from prostitution to depression of middle-aged mothers, the image of women in various media to creativity of women and the feminist movement.

Gould, Carol C., and Wartofsky, Marx W., eds. WOMEN AND PHILOSOPHY: TOWARD A THEORY OF LIBERATION. New York: G.P. Putnam and Sons, 1976. 364 p.

This collection of essays attempts to outline the fundamental philosophic assumptions of the women's liberation movement and how they apply to specific issues.

Greer, Germaine. THE FEMALE EUNUCH. New York: McGraw-Hill, 1971. x, 349 p.

Greer devotes most of the book to dispelling male stereotypes of female sexuality, illustrating her points with quotations from various novels, both good and bad.

Griffin, Susan. WOMAN AND NATURE: THE LION ROARING INSIDE HER. New York: Harper and Row, 1978. 263 p.

Griffin analyzes the connection of feminism and ecology, and makes parallels with the disturbing of the environment and the oppression of women throughout history. She sees patriarchy as the cause of both.

Heilbrun, Carolyn G. RE-INVENTING WOMANHOOD. New York: W.W. Norton and Co., 1979. 244 p.

Heilbrun writes a book-essay on how women's identity has been lost in history. She suggests some possible ways to understand womanhood independently of the pervasive male definition.

_____. TOWARD A RECOGNITION OF ANDROGYNY. New York: Harper and Row, 1973. 189, v p.

Heilbrun has written an essay challenging traditional sex roles on philosophic grounds.

Herschberger, Ruth. ADAM'S RIB. New York: Harper and Row, 1970. 238 p.

The author challenges many of the assumptions about women, particularly their sexuality.

Janeway, Elizabeth. BETWEEN MYTH AND MORNING: WOMEN AWAKENING. New York: William Morrow and Co., 1975. 279 p.

Janeway describes some changes brought about by the women's movement and what new issues arise from the changes.

_____. MAN'S WORLD. WOMAN'S PLACE: A STUDY IN SOCIAL MYTHOLOGY. New York: Delta, 1971. 319 p.

Janeway writes about the contemporary situation of women and the way in which the whole social network depends upon the myth of inequality.

Koldt, Anne, et al., eds. RADICAL FEMINISM. New York: Quadrangle Books, 1973. viii, 424 p.

The editors provide nearly fifty selections written by a variety of women on questions affecting women and the radical response to these problems. The issues range from the problems of black women to women in the arts, from sexuality to feminist graffiti.

Lakoff, Robin. LANGUAGE AND WOMAN'S PLACE. New York: Colaphon Books, 1975. 83 p.

Lakoff examines language, consciousness, sexism, and the mechanisms of oppression.

Meade, Marion. BITCHING. Frogmore, St. Albans, Engl.: Panther Books, 1976. 222 p.

> Meade describes in graphic language the games between men and women. Space is also devoted to allowing women to comment on what they think about male-female interaction.

Miller, Casey, and Swift, Kate. WORDS AND WOMEN. Garden City, N.Y.: Anchor Books, 1976. xiii, 197 p.

> This book examines the sexism inherent in the English language. It takes the position that language, reflecting consciousness, is a serious issue.

Millett, Kate. SEXUAL POLITICS. Garden City, N.Y.: Doubleday, 1970. xii, 393 p.

> Millett believes that the problems of women go much deeper than the economic issue. She calls for a revolution in attitudes to rid the nation of sexism. She believes that legislation could not solve the problem. She proposes a revolution in family structure, the economy, and social institutions to accomplish the goal.

Morgan, Robin, ed. SISTERHOOD IS POWERFUL: AN ANTHOLOGY OF WRITINGS FROM THE WOMEN'S LIBERATION MOVEMENT. New York: Random House, 1970. xii, 602 p.

> Morgan brings together a variety of writings by members of the movement. They deal with psychology, law, education, and birth control.

Negrin, Su. BEGIN AT START: SOME THOUGHTS ON PERSONAL LIBERA-TION AND WORLD CHANGE. New York: Times Change Press, 1972.

> Negrin articulates the idea that the personal is political and that the political is personal, a key idea in the contemporary women's movement.

Newland, Kathleen. THE SISTERHOOD OF MAN. New York: W.W. Norton and Co., 1979. 242 p.

> Newland analyzes women's role in several spheres--law, education, politics, work, and others--and the way economic issues are inter-twined.

Rich, Adrienne. ON LIES, SECRETS AND SILENCE: SELECTED PROSE 1966-1978. New York: W.W. Norton and Co., 1979. 310 p.

> This is a collection of Rich's essays which aim at a definition of a new women's culture. Rich has a radical, lesbian-feminist ideology which binds the essays together. She comments on work, educa-tion, literature, power, motherhood, and woman's culture.

Sabrosky, Judith A. FROM RATIONALITY TO LIBERATION: THE EVOLU-
TION OF FEMINIST IDEOLOGY. Westport, Conn.: Greenwood Press, 1979.
viii, 175 p.

> Sabrosky looks at the origins of feminist thought in the Enlighten-
> ment philosophy of the eighteenth century. She goes on to analyze
> contemporary feminist ideology as a coherent set of beliefs and
> proposes some guidelines for strengthening the new feminism as an
> ideology.

Safilios-Rothschild, Constantina. LOVE, SEX AND SEX ROLES. Englewood
Cliffs, N.J.: Prentice-Hall, 1977. x, 150 p.

> The author examines issues of sexuality and love and the way in
> which the social conventions of both have served to oppress women.

Solanas, Valerie. S.C.U.M. MANIFESTO. New York: Olympia Press, 1970.
xxxvi, 52 p.

> Solanas, who was once charged with the attempted murder of pop
> artist Andy Warhol, articulates the idea that women can be free
> only by destroying men and the all-male culture. This is the view
> of the Society for Cutting Up Men.

Stanbler, Sookie, ed. WOMEN'S LIBERATION: BLUEPRINT FOR THE FUTURE.
New York: Ace, 1970. 283 p.

> This is a group of writings done by many contemporary feminists,
> such as Susan Brownmiller and Kate Millett.

Thompson, Mary Lou, ed. VOICES OF THE NEW FEMINISM. Boston: Beacon Press, 1970. 216 p.

> This is an anthology of works by feminists who touch on a wide
> range of issues.

Ware, Cellestine. WOMAN POWER: THE MOVEMENT FOR WOMEN'S LIB-
ERATION. New York: Tower Publications, 1970. 176 p.

> Ware portrays in general terms the state of the women's movement
> in 1970.

Yates, Gayle Graham. WHAT WOMEN WANT: THE IDEAS OF THE MOVE-
MENT. Cambridge, Mass.: Harvard University Press, 1975. xi, 230 p.

> This work briefly discusses the women's movement, past and present,
> and finds three main perspectives in the movement: the feminist
> perspective, the women's liberationist perspective, and the androgy-
> nous perspective.

# Chapter 13

# CONTEMPORARY SOCIALIST FEMINISM

Andreas, Carol. SEX AND CASTE IN AMERICA. Englewood Cliffs, N.J.: Prentice-Hall, 1971. xiv, 146 p.

Andreas analyzes sexism and its roots in the economic system.

Ballan, Dorothy. FEMINISM AND MARXISM. New York: World View Publishers, 1971. 72 p.

This is a publication of the Youth Against War and Facism. It supplies a feminist-materialist analysis of current world conditions. It also traces the development of oppression of women in the tradition of Marxist history. It postulates the existence of a matriarchal society in early history.

Benston, Margaret. THE POLITICAL ECONOMY OF WOMEN'S LIBERATION. Somerville, Mass.: New England Free Press, 1970. 15 p.

This pamphlet is a reprint from the September 1969 issue of MONTHLY REVIEW. It discusses the role of housewives and housework in the capitalist system. Using a Marxist perspective, the author advocates socialism as at least a partial answer to the solution of women's oppression.

Bernard, Jessie. WOMEN AND THE PUBLIC INTEREST: AN ESSAY ON POLICY AND PROTEST. New York: Atherton, 1971. viii, 293 p.

Bernard looks at the sexual division of labor and the functions of women. She also examines the necessary adaptations women must make for the social system and the possibilities of protest and change.

Bunch, Charlotte, and Myron, Nancy, eds. CLASS AND FEMINISM. Baltimore: Diana Press, 1974. 90 p.

This book is a group of articles written by the Furies, a lesbian-feminist collective, on the efforts to deal with issues of class in their collective. The articles are a combination of theoretical analysis of class and women's oppression and a reporting of the personal experiences of the writers.

Cook, Blanche Wiesen. WOMEN AND SUPPORT NETWORKS. Brooklyn, N.Y.: Out and Out Books, 1979. 41 p.

This small book consists of two essays, "Women Against Economic and Social Repression: The Two Front Challenge" and "Female Support Networks and Political Activism: Lillian Wald, Crystal Eastman, Emma Goldman, Jane Addams." The main thesis of both is the importance of woman to woman relationships for support in the feminist struggle.

Dixon, Marlene. WOMEN IN CLASS STRUGGLE. San Francisco: Synthesis Publications, 1978. 47 p.

This is a collection of essays originally printed in the journal, SYNTHESIS. It discusses the role women have played in socialist movements and criticizes the women's movement as revisionist.

Eisenstein, Zillah R., ed. CAPITALIST PATRIARCHY AND THE CASE FOR SOCIALIST FEMINISM. New York: Monthly Review Press, 1979. 394 p.

This book is a collection of essays on feminist-socialist theory and its applications to specific historical contexts, like antebellum America, the nineteenth-century women's suffrage movement and others. It includes statements of principles by several contemporary feminist-socialist collectives.

Figes, Eva. PATRIARCHIAL ATTITUDES. London: Virago, 1978. 191 p.

Figes analyzes the situation of women historically and finds the defining factor to be the patriarchial society.

Firestone, Shulamith. THE DIALETIC OF SEX: THE CASE FOR FEMINIST REVOLUTION. New York: Morrow, 1970. 274 p.

Firestone analyzes, historically, culturally, and politically, the persecution of women.

Foreman, Ann. FEMININITY AS ALIENATION: WOMEN AND THE FAMILY VS. MARXISM AND PSYCHOANALYSIS. London: Plato Press, 1977. 168 p.

This book examines the current status of the women's movement and its relation to the whole radical tradition. It argues that the women's struggle must move to the forefront of the movement for change. It is also a critique of Marx and Freud in relation to women's issues.

Guettel, Charnie. MARXISM AND FEMINISM. Toronto: Canadian Women's Educational Press, 1974. 62 p.

This book examines the state of the women's movement in Canada and the United States in theoretical terms and suggests the women's movement must unite with other radical movements.

Jenness, Linda. SOCIALISM AND THE FIGHT FOR WOMEN'S RIGHTS. New York: Pathfinder Press, 1976. 15 p.

This pamphlet is written by the 1972 presidential candidate of the Socialist Workers party. It explores the source of the oppression of women and concludes that an autonomous mass movement of women is necessary to fight sexism, but that this movement must coordinate itself in some fashion with the overall socialist struggle.

_____, ed. FEMINISM AND SOCIALISM. New York: Pathfinder Press, 1972. 160 p.

This is a collection of essays on many issues from a socialist-feminist viewpoint.

Kuhn, Annette, and Wolpe, Ann Marie, eds. FEMINISM AND MATERIALISM: WOMEN AND MODES OF PRODUCTION. Boston: Routledge and Kegan Paul, 1978. 328 p.

This book is a series of essays which all have a feminist-socialist perspective. The essays cover a variety of topics, especially patriarchy, paid and unpaid labor, the family, and the state.

Mandle, Joan D. WOMEN AND SOCIAL CHANGE IN AMERICA. Princeton, N.J.: Princeton Book Co., 1979. 228 p.

This book examines women in various aspects of American society using a theoretical framework drawn from Marx, Freud, and the women's movement. It proposes a new ideology for social change.

Red Collective. THE POLITICS OF SEXUALITY IN CAPITALISM. London: Red Collective and Publications Distribution Cooperative, 1978. 146 p.

This volume is a republication of two pamphlets which examine the impact of capitalism on personal relationships. It is a socialist-feminist analysis of the family and other interpersonal units. It includes both analytic discussions and personal life stories.

Reed, Evelyn. PROBLEMS OF WOMEN'S LIBERATION: A MARXIST APPROACH. New York: Pathfinder Press, 1970. 96 p.

Reed writes of the economic and social origin of the oppression of women from a socialist viewpoint.

REVOLUTIONARY FEMINISM: WOMEN AS REASON. New York: Women's Liberation News and Letters, 1970. 21 p.

This group of short essays on a wide variety of topics includes one on the origins of International Women's Day. The essays are introduced as having the aim of presenting a total picture of women's revolutionary activity and potential.

Rowbotham, Sheila. WOMAN'S CONSCIOUSNESS, MAN'S WORLD. Baltimore: Penguin Books, 1973. xvi, 136 p.

Rowbotham is a British feminist-socialist; however, her analysis is relevant to the United States and an important element of the contemporary women's movement.

Stone, Betsey. SISTERHOOD IS POWERFUL. New York: Pathfinder Press, 1970. 15 p.

This short essay is part of an address given to the Social Activists and Educational Conference held at Oberlin College in the summer of 1970. Its main thesis is that the whole radical socialist movement needs to recognize and encourage the growing women's movement.

"Third Special Issue on the Political Economy of Women." THE RADICAL REVIEW OF POLITICAL ECONOMICS 9 (Fall 1977): entire issue.

This is a collection of articles on feminist-materialist economics; it includes material on Britain and the United States.

Weinbaum, Batya. THE CURIOUS COURTSHIP OF WOMEN'S LIBERATION AND SOCIALISM. Boston: South End Press, 1978. ix, 168 p.

Weinbaum has written a theoretical work on the relationship between the women's movement and the traditional Marxist struggle. She proposes a strategy which encompasses Marx, Freud, and radical feminism.

Weisstein, Naomi, et al. THE GODFATHERS: FREUDIANS, MARXISTS AND THE SCIENTIFIC AND POLITICAL PROTECTION SOCIETIES. New Haven, Conn.: Belladonna Publishing, 1975. 94 p.

The authors critique Marx and Freud as inadequate in understanding the situation of women.

WOMEN'S LIBERATION AND THE SOCIALIST REVOLUTION. New York: Pathfinder Press, 1979. 93 p.

This book is a series of proposals by the Socialist Workers party prepared for its world conference in the summer of 1979. It analyzes the current conditions of women from a Marxist-feminist perspective.

# Chapter 14

# WOMEN, LAW, AND POLITICS

Abzug, Bella S. BELLA! MS. ABZUG GOES TO WASHINGTON. New York: Saturday Review Press, 1972. 314 p.

> Abzug discusses the issues she faced as a congresswoman. The book is organized as a diary for the year 1971.

Babcock, Barbara Allen, et al., eds. SEX DISCRIMINATION AND THE LAW: CAUSES AND REMEDIES. Boston: Little, Brown and Co., 1975. ix, 1,092 p.

> This is a law casebook which reports on wide-ranging aspects of the law and sex discrimination. It is organized to some degree like a law school text; its inclusion of popular press resources differs, however.

Boles, Janet K. THE POLITICS OF THE EQUAL RIGHTS AMENDMENT: CONFLICTS AND THE DECISION PROCESS. New York: Longmans, 1979. x, 214 p.

> Boles examines the factions involved in the ERA controversy.

California. Commission on the Status of Women. IMPACT ERA: LIMITATIONS AND POSSIBILITIES. Millbrae, Calif.: Les Femmes Publishing, 1976. 287 p.

> The commission presents arguments on the political, economic, social, and psychological impact of the equal rights amendment.

Cary, Eve, and Peratis, Kathleen Willert. WOMAN AND THE LAW. Skokie, Ill.: National Textbook Co., 1977. xii, 202 p.

> This volume was done in conjunction with the American Civil Liberties Union. It looks at the history of women and law, constitution issues, and law pertaining to women and employment, education, commerce, families, and reproductive freedom.

Chamberlin, Hope. A MINORITY OF MEMBERS: WOMEN IN THE U.S.

CONGRESS. New York: Praeger Publishers, 1973. 374 p.

> The author studies the eighty-five women who have served in Congress up to 1973.

Chisholm, Shirley. THE GOOD FIGHT. New York: Harper and Row, 1973. 206 p.

> Chisholm tells the story of her campaign to be the first black woman president.

_____. UNBOUGHT AND UNBOSSED. Boston: Houghton Mifflin, 1970. 177 p.

> This is the political autobiography of the black congresswoman from New York.

DeCrow, Karen. SEXIST JUSTICE. New York: Random House, 1974. xii, 329 p.

> DeCrow, feminist activist and lawyer, has written a description of the injustices of the American legal system.

Dennis, Peggy. THE AUTOBIOGRAPHY OF AN AMERICAN COMMUNIST: A PERSONAL VIEW OF A POLITICAL LIFE, 1925-1975. Westport, Conn.: Lawrence Hill and Co., 1977. 302 p.

> This is one woman's story of her life in the Communist party and her involvement in many radical causes of half a century. It concludes with her resignation from the party in 1976.

Diamond, Irene. SEX ROLES IN THE STATE HOUSE. New Haven, Conn.: Yale University Press, 1977. xii, 214 p.

> Diamond analyzes the role of the woman state legislator as a reflection of social reality and catalyst for change in sex role stereotypes.

Edmundson, Madeleine, and Cohen, Alden Duer. THE WOMEN OF WATERGATE. New York: Stein and Day, 1975. 228 p.

> This book is a series of brief chapters on the women involved directly and indirectly in Watergate. It describes the nature of their involvement and their beliefs and feelings about the scandals of the Nixon era. The figures portrayed include among others such women as Martha Mitchell, Deborah Sloane, Julie Nixon Eisenhower, Katharine Graham, Barbara Jordan, and Elizabeth Holtzman.

Eisler, Riane Tennenhaus. THE EQUAL RIGHTS HANDBOOK. New York: Avon Books, 1978. xii, 257 p.

This is a guide to the equal rights amendment controversy. The first half deals with concerns and questions about ERA; the second is a strategy and organizing reference.

Flynn, Elizabeth Gurley. MY LIFE AS A POLITICAL PRISONER: THE ALDERSON STORY. New York: International Publishers, 1976. 223 p.

This is the story of Flynn's life in prison following her conviction under the Smith Act for her Communist beliefs.

Githeas, Marianne, and Prestage, Jewel L., eds. A PORTRAIT OF MARGINALITY: THE POLITICAL BEHAVIOR OF THE AMERICAN WOMAN. New York: David McKay, 1977. xvii, 427 p.

The editors have assembled a collection of articles on many facets of contemporary women in politics, including socialization, recruitment, participation, and black women in politics.

Goldstein, Leslie Freedman. THE CONSTITUTIONAL RIGHTS OF WOMEN: CASES IN LAW AND SOCIAL CHANGES. New York: Longmans, 1979. xii, 414 p.

This book, organized as a casebook, looks at the U.S. Constitution and its use in the struggle for women's rights.

Gruberg, Martin. WOMEN IN AMERICAN POLITICS: AN ASSESSMENT AND SOURCEBOOK. Oshkosh, Wis.: Academia Press, 1968. 336 p.

This examines women's role in politics since 1920. It covers achievements by women in politics, women as party members, women's political organizations, and women in government.

Jaquette, Jane, ed. WOMEN IN POLITICS. New York: John Wiley and Sons, 1974. vii, 367 p.

This is a collection of articles surveying many aspects of women and politics. Some topics covered include women in the Daley organization, contemporary feminism, and women as voters. One section of the book is devoted to comparative politics--international issues.

Johnson, Marilyn, and Stanwick, Kathy. PROFILE OF WOMEN HOLDING OFFICE. 2d ed. Metuchen, N.J.: Scarecrow Press, 1978. xix, 510 p.

This is a description of women who held public office in the United States during 1974 and 1975.

Josephson, Hannah. JEANNETTE RANKIN: FIRST LADY IN CONGRESS: A BIOGRAPHY. Indianapolis: Bobbs-Merrill, 1974. 227 p.

This book describes the life and career of Rankin, a crusader for women's rights and other causes and the first woman in Congress.

Kanowitz, Leo. SEX ROLES IN LAW AND SOCIETY: CASES AND MATERIALS. Albuquerque: University of New Mexico Press, 1973. 706 p.

This is Kanowitz's test done privately for law students on the law, women, sex roles, and equality.

_____. WOMEN AND THE LAW: THE UNFINISHED REVOLUTION. Albuquerque: University of New Mexico Press, 1969. ix, 312 p.

Kanowitz deals with the legal aspects of employment of women, rape, abortion, prostitution, divorce, rights of single women. He treats the problem historically, beginning with William Blackstone, the great English writer, and traces precedents through various court cases. He believes the law mirrors and perpetuates the prevailing social idea of male dominance.

Kelly, Rita Mae, and Boutilier, Mary, eds. THE MAKING OF POLITICAL WOMEN: A STUDY OF SOCIALIZATION AND ROLE CONFLICT. Chicago: Nelson-Hall, 1978. x, 368 p.

This examines the forces which motivate women to political participation.

Kennedy, Rose Fitzgerald. TIMES TO REMEMBER. Garden City, N.Y.: Doubleday, 1974. 536 p.

This is the autobiography of Rose Kennedy. It is her personal reflection on her life and faith.

Kincaid, Diane D. SILENT HATTIE SPEAKS: THE PERSONAL JOURNAL OF SENATOR HATTIE CARAWAY. Westport, Conn.: Greenwood Press, 1979. 160 p.

Caraway seldom spoke in the Senate but her journal reveals political awareness and ambition. Her public reticence was a shield against ridicule.

Kirkpatrick, Jeane J. POLITICAL WOMEN. New York: Basic Books, 1974. xiii, 274 p.

Kirkpatrick describes what it is like for women participants in the political world of campaigns and legislative bodies.

Lamson, Peggy. FEW ARE CHOSEN: AMERICAN WOMEN IN POLITICAL LIFE TODAY. Boston: Houghton Mifflin, 1968. 240 p.

Lamson interviewed ten American women in politics and focused in on the stereotypes they have had to cope with.

Lash, Joseph P. ELEANOR: THE YEARS ALONE. New York: W.W. Norton and Co., 1972. 368 p.

Lash writes the story of Eleanor Roosevelt's life from the time of F.D.R.'s death until her own. It discusses her continuing public service, her private self, and many friendships.

Lester, David. THE LONELY LADY OF SAN CLEMENTE: THE STORY OF PAT NIXON. New York: Thomas Y. Crowell, 1978. 235 p.

This is the biography of Pat Nixon, from childhood to the post-Watergate era.

McCarthy, Abigail. PRIVATE FACES/PUBLIC PLACES. Garden City, N.Y.: Doubleday, 1972. 448 p.

McCarthy, the exwife of the unsuccessful presidential candidate Eugene McCarthy, wrote about her life as a political spouse.

McCourt, Kathleen. WORKING-CLASS WOMEN AND GRASS-ROOTS POLITICS. Bloomington: Indiana University Press, 1977. 256 p.

McCourt examines the attitudes and actions of working class women from Chicago's southwest side who are politically active.

McGovern, Eleanor. UPHILL: A PERSONAL STORY. Boston: Houghton Mifflin, 1974. 234 p.

This is the autobiography of the wife of George McGovern, the 1972 Democratic presidential nominee.

Reston, James Jr. THE INNOCENCE OF JOAN LITTLE: A SOUTHERN MYSTERY. New York: New York Times Books, 1977.

Reston presents evidence on all sides of the issue in the Joan Little case--the black woman accused of murdering her white prison guard who she claimed attempted to rape her.

Rhoades, Kathy, and Beardry, Ann, eds. LEGISLATIVE HANDBOOK ON WOMEN'S ISSUES. Washington, D.C.: Institute for Policy Studies, 1976. 159 p.

This looks at legislation affecting women, most specifically on economic issues--work, education, family law, child care, and equal rights.

Roosevelt, Eleanor. ON MY OWN: THE YEARS SINCE THE WHITE HOUSE. Vol. 3. New York: Dell Publishing, 1958. 288 p.

In the final volume of her autobiography, Roosevelt describes her work for the United Nations, in the Stevenson campaigns, and her other interests.

_____. THIS I REMEMBER. Vol. 2. New York: Harper and Brothers, 1949. x, 387 p.

This volume of Roosevelt's life details her years as first lady.

_____. THIS IS MY STORY. Vol. 1. New York: Harper and Brothers, 1937. x, 365.

This volume covers the first forty years of Eleanor Roosevelt's life.

Ross, Susan Deller. THE RIGHTS OF WOMEN: AN AMERICAN CIVIL LIBER-TIES UNION HANDBOOK. New York: Avon Books, 1973. 263 p.

This ACLU-authorized volume delineates women's rights under contemporary law. It focuses on such issues as discrimination, the criminal justice system, marriage, divorce, and control of women's own bodies.

Sanders, Marion K. THE LADY AND THE VOTE. Boston: Houghton Mifflin, 1956. 172 p.

The author argues that women who seek political success should work through party organization.

Schwartz, Helene E. LAWYERING. New York: Farrar, Straus and Giroux, 1975. x, 308 p.

This is a woman lawyer's account of her career.

Stimpson, Catharine, ed. WOMEN AND THE "EQUAL RIGHTS AMENDMENT." New York: R.R. Bowker, 1972. xvi, 538 p.

Stimpson has edited for publication the Senate hearings of the 91st Congress on the equal rights amendment. It includes statements by many noted feminists in support and by organizations such as the National Council of Catholic Women in opposition.

Switzer, Ellen. THE LAW FOR A WOMAN. New York: Charles Scribner's Sons, 1976. 246 p.

Written in cooperation with a lawyer, this book describes the law as it applies to women on the contemporary scene.

Thomas, Dorothy, ed. WOMEN LAWYERS IN THE UNITED STATES. New York: Scarecrow Press, 1957. 747 p.

This somewhat outdated volume is an alphabetical listing of women lawyers. It includes their degrees, practice, and address.

Timothy, Mary. JURY WOMAN: THE STORY OF THE TRIAL OF ANGELA Y. DAVIS. San Francisco: Glide, 1975. 276 p.

Timothy was a member of the jury at Angela Davis's trial. The book not only provides commentary on the issues presented in the Davis case, but describes the experience of serving on a jury.

Tolchin, Susan, and Tolchin, Martin. CLOUT: WOMAN POWER AND POLI-TICS. New York: Coward, McCann and Geoghegan, 1974. 320 p.

> This book, written soon after the 1972 presidential election, ex-amines the role of women in the party connections of that year, the ongoing exclusion of women from party politics, the equal rights amendment, and women's liberation.

WOMEN STATE LEGISLATORS. New Brunswick, N.J.: Center for American Woman and Politics, 1972. 31 p.

> This is a report from a Conference for Women in Public Life held in 1972 at Rutgers University. It discusses women legislators as candidates and officeholders.

# Chapter 15

# WOMEN IN SCIENCE AND MEDICINE

Alsop, Gulielma F. HISTORY OF THE WOMAN'S MEDICAL COLLEGE, PHILA-DELPHIA, PA., 1850-1950. Philadelphia: Lippincott, 1950. xi, 256 p.

> Founded in 1850, this pioneering medical college was responsible for the training of many early female physicians.

Baker, Nina Brown. CYCLONE IN CALICO: THE STORY OF MARY ANN BICKERDYKE. Boston: Little, Brown and Co., 1952. 278 p.

> This is the biography of Bickerdyke (1817-1901), a Civil War nurse.

Blackwell, Elizabeth. PIONEER WORK IN OPENING THE MEDICAL PROFES-SION TO WOMEN. London: J.M. Dent and Sons, 1895. Reprint. New York: Schocken Books, 1977. 236 p.

> This is the autobiography of the first female graduate in medicine in the United States. She details the struggle of female physicians to attract patients. In 1857 she founded the New York Infirmary for women and children.

Bolzan, Emma Lydia. ALMIRA HART LINCOLN PHELPS: HER LIFE AND WORK. Philadelphia: Science Press, 1936. xi, 534 p.

> Almira Phelps (1793-1884), sister of Emma Willard, American educator, was the author of textbooks and popular books in botany.

Clarke, Mary A. MEMORIES OF JANE A. DELANO. New York: Lakeside Publishing, 1934. 62 p.

> Jane Arminda Delano (1862-1919), a registered nurse who engaged in industrial nursing, was superintendent of the Army Nurse Corps, and after 1912 worked full time with the Red Cross, where she insisted on high standards for Red Cross nurses.

Clarke, Robert. ELLEN SWALLOW: THE WOMAN WHO FOUNDED ECOLOGY. Chicago: Follett Publishing Co., 1973. 362 p.

> Ellen Swallow Richards (1842-1911), a chemist, graduated from

Vassar in 1870 and did graduate work at the Massachusetts Institute of Technology. She is especially noted for the application
of chemistry to nutrition and environmental matters, including
sanitation.

Donegan, Jane B. WOMEN AND MEN MIDWIVES. MEDICINE, MORALITY
AND MISOGYNY IN EARLY AMERICA. Westport, Conn.: Greenwood Press,
1978. viii, 316 p.

Donegan writes of the takeover of the profession of midwifery by
men. She believes that the history of midwifery is closely related
to the history of feminism.

Grady, Roy I., and Chittun, John W., eds. THE CHEMIST AT WORK. Easton,
Pa.: Journal of Chemical Education, 1940. xv, 422 p.

Although somewhat outdated, this volume devotes eleven chapters
to women in chemistry.

Hume, Ruth Fox. GREAT WOMEN OF MEDICINE. New York: Random
House, 1964. 268 p.

Hume includes Americans Dr. Elizabeth Blackwell and Dr. Mary
Putnam Jacobi.

Hurd-Mead, Kate Campbell. MEDICAL WOMEN OF AMERICA. New York:
Froben Press, 1933. 95 p.

This is a survey of women midwives, physicians, and nurses from
the colonial period to the 1930s. It includes biographical information on individual women, their careers, and the status of the professions in the different periods.

Kendall, Phebe Mitchell. MARIA MITCHELL: LIFE, LETTERS AND JOURNALS.
Boston: Lee and Shepard, 1896.

Maria Mitchell (1818-1889), pioneer astronomer, discovered a
comet in 1847 which was named for her, leading to her election
to the American Academy of Arts and Sciences, the first woman
so honored.

Knapp, Sally. WOMEN DOCTORS TODAY. New York: Thomas Y. Crowell,
1947. 184 p.

Knapp describes the life and work of twelve women doctors who
were practicing in the 1940s. Not all were Americans, but over
half were.

Kreinberg, Nancy. I'M MADLY IN LOVE WITH ELECTRICITY AND OTHER
COMMENTS ABOUT THEIR WORK BY WOMEN IN SCIENCE AND ENGINEER-
ING. Berkeley and Los Angeles: University of California Press, 1977. vi, 37 p.

This volume contains women's thoughts on their jobs as scientists.
It also contains a resource guide for women in science–related
fields.

Lathan, Jean. RACHEL CARSON: WHO LOVED THE SEA. Champaign, Ill.:
Coward, 1973. 80 p.

This is a biography of the biologist, naturalist, and environmentalist.

Litoff, Judy Barrett. AMERICAN MIDWIVES: 1860 TO THE PRESENT. Westport, Conn.: Greenwood Press, 1978. xi, 197 p.

In 1900 midwives attended half the births in the United States.
In the ensuing years middle- and upper-class women abandoned the
use of midwives, accepting the argument of physicians that they
provided the only safe delivery.

Lopate, Carol. WOMEN IN MEDICINE. Baltimore: Johns Hopkins University
Press, 1968. 204 p.

Lopate looks at the status of women in the medical professions and
urges the admission of greater numbers.

Lovejoy, Esther Pohl. WOMEN DOCTORS OF THE WORLD. New York:
Macmillan, 1957. x, 413 p.

Lovejoy examines women doctors in history and in international
perspective. She devotes several chapters to the United States,
including one on the first American women doctors and one on
doctors by geographic region in the U.S.

Marks, Geoffrey, and Beatty, William K. WOMEN IN WHITE. New York:
Charles Scribner's Sons, 1972. 239 p.

The authors deal with female physicians, nurses, and medicine.
A section is devoted to women's rights in medicine.

Mattfield, Jacquelyn A., and Van Aben, Carol G., eds. WOMEN AND THE
SCIENTIFIC PROFESSIONS. Cambridge, Mass.: MIT Press, 1965. Reprint.
Westport, Conn.: Greenwood Press, 1976. xvii, 250 p.

This volume contains the proceedings of the MIT symposium on
American Women and Engineering held in the mid-sixties. Notable
participants included Jessie Bernard, Bruno Bettelheim, and Erik
Erikson. The discussions relate to both opportunities and difficulties
of women in the scientific and technical professions.

Osen, Lynn M. WOMEN IN MATHEMATICS. Cambridge, Mass.: MIT Press,
1974. 224 p.

Although Osen does not deal only with American mathematicians

some of the women included are Americans. Osen describes their
work, contributions and life-styles.

Reed, Evelyn. SEXISM AND SCIENCE. New York: Pathfinder Press, 1978.
190 p.

This collection of essays by a socialist anthropologist focuses on
the presence of sexist stereotypes in the supposedly objective
natural and social sciences.

Richards, Linda. REMINISCENCES OF LINDA RICHARDS. Boston: Whitcomb
and Barrows, 1911. xvi, 121 p.

Linda Richards (1841-1930), a pioneer in nursing education, served
as a medical missionary in Japan. She is regarded as the first
nurse in the United States to receive a diploma.

Roberts, Mary M. AMERICAN NURSING: HISTORY AND INTERPRETATION.
New York: Macmillan, 1954. 688 p.

Roberts traces the development of nursing from 1900-1952. She
notes the professionalization of nurses, the development of schools
of nursing, and the influence of religious and military groups, as
well as international groups such as the World Health Organization.
She dates the professionalization of nursing from the first journal
of nursing. She appends a lengthy bibliography at the end of each
chapter.

Robinson, Victor. WHITE CAPS: THE STORY OF NURSING. Philadelphia:
Lippincott, 1946. xvi, 425 p.

Robinson traces the history of nursing from antiquity. The last
half of the book applies to the United States. He carries the story
in encyclopedic fashion through World War II.

Ross, Ishbel. ANGEL OF THE BATTLEFIELD: CLARA BARTON. New York:
Harper, 1956. xi, 305 p.

Barton (1821-1912), a Civil War nurse, was founder and president
of the Red Cross for twenty-three years. She also promoted feminist
causes.

_____. CHILD OF DESTINY: THE LIFE OF ELIZABETH BLACKWELL. New
York: Harper, 1949. 309 p.

Elizabeth Blackwell, M.D., graduated from the medical school of
Geneva College in 1859, the first woman to graduate in medicine.
The biography also contains information about Emily Blackwell,
M.D., her sister.

Sayre, Anne. ROSALIND FRANKLIN AND DNA. New York: W.W. Norton and Co., 1975. 221 p.

> This is the story of Franklin (1920-1958) and her contribution to the DNA theory.

Stage, Sarah. FEMALE COMPLAINTS: LYDIA PINKHAM AND THE BUSINESS OF WOMEN'S MEDICINE. New York: W.W. Norton and Co., 1979. 304 p.

> Stage examines the life of Pinkham and her successful enterprise of selling the Pinkham vegetable compound as women's medicine. She analyzes Pinkham's story in terms of the changing attitudes towards women and health.

Walsh, Mary Ruth. "DOCTORS WANTED: NO WOMEN NEED APPLY": SEXUAL BARRIERS IN THE MEDICAL PROFESSION, 1835-1975. New Haven, Conn.: Yale University Press, 1977. xxiii, 303 p.

> Walsh describes the sexual stereotypes accepted and strengthened by male physicians. Despite hostility women made some inroads in the profession and made real gains after 1970. Much of the book deals with Boston and New England in the late nineteenth and early twentieth centuries.

Wilson, Dorothy Clarke. PALACE OF HEALING: THE STORY OF DR. CLARA SWAIN. New York: McGraw-Hill, 1968. x, 245 p.

> Clara Swain (1834-1910), who graduated from the medical department of Western Reserve College in 1855, became a medical missionary in India.

Wright, Helen. SWEEPER IN THE SKY. New York: Macmillan, 1949. 253 p.

> This is a biography of Maria Mitchell (1818-1889), astronomer and first woman elected to the American Academy of Arts and Sciences. She taught at Vassar, was a spokesman for women's rights, and became president and founder of the Association for the Advancement of Women in 1873.

Yost, Edna. AMERICAN WOMEN OF SCIENCE. New York: Frederick A. Stokes, 1943. xviii, 234 p.

> This volume contains brief biographies of Ellen H. Richards, Annie Jump Cannon, Alice Hamilton, Florence Reva Sabin, Mary Engle Pennington, Lillian Moller Gilbreth, Libbie Henrietta Hyman, Wanda K. Farr, Hazel K. Stiebling, Florence B. Seibert, Katharine Burr Blodgett, and Margaret Mead.

# Chapter 16

# WOMEN AND THE ARTS

Anderson, Margaret. MY THIRTY YEARS WAR. New York: Covici, Friede, 1930. 274 p.

This is the autobiography of Margaret Anderson, who rebelled against the restriction of small-town life and moved to Chicago where she edited THE LITTLE REVIEW, an important journal in the days before World War I. She later lived much of her life abroad.

Anthony, Katharine Susan. LOUISA MAY ALCOTT. New York: Alfred A. Knopf, 1938. Reprint. Westport, Conn.: Greenwood Press, 1977. xiii, 304 p.

This is a biography of a famous female writer of the nineteenth century.

Baym, Nina. WOMAN'S FICTION: A GUIDE TO NOVELS BY AND ABOUT WOMEN IN AMERICA, 1820-1870. Ithaca: Cornell University Press, 1978. 320 p.

This is a history of the role of women as authors and as subjects in the fiction of the period 1820-1870, a time when popular woman's fiction blossomed.

Bolton-Smith, Robin, and Truettner, William H. LILY MARTIN SPENCER, 1822-1902: THE JOYS OF SENTIMENT. Washington, D.C.: National Gallery of Fine Arts, 1973. 253 p.

Spencer was a popular and sentimental painter of dogs and children in the nineteenth century. For the most part, this is an exhibition catalog.

Botta, Vincenzo, ed. MEMOIRS OF ANNE C.L. BOTTA WRITTEN BY HER FRIENDS WITH SELECTIONS FROM HER CORRESPONDENCE AND FROM HER WRITINGS IN PROSE AND POETRY. New York: J.S. Tait and Sons, 1894. 99 p.

Anne Charlotte Lynch Botta, 1815 to 1891, was an author of poetry, travel pieces and literary criticism. She was an important figure in the literary world, acting as hostess for gatherings of such notables as Julia Ward Howe, Poe, Emerson, Margaret Fuller, and William Cullen Bryant.

Boyle, Regis Louise. MRS. E.D.E.N. SOUTHWORTH, NOVELIST. Washington, D.C.: Catholic University, 1939. vii, 171 p.

This is a study of Emma Dorothy Eliza Neiutte Southworth the nineteenth-century popular novelist. Her fiction was usually serialized in THE NEW YORK LEDGER; one of her most popular efforts was THE HIDDEN HAND, 1859.

Brown, Alice. LOUISE IMOGEN GUINEY. New York: Macmillan, 1921. 111 p.

This is a biography of Guiney, the poet and literary scholar, by her literary friend and colleague, Alice Brown.

Buck, Pearl S. A BRIDGE FOR PASSING. Vol. 2. New York: John Day Co., 1962. 256 p.

_____. MY SEVERAL WORLDS. Vol. 1. New York: Day, 1954. 407 p.

Buck was a novelist whose books were mainly set in Asia.

Bullard, E. John. MARY CASSATT: OILS AND PASTELS. New York: Wilson-Guptil Publications, 1972. 87 p.

This volume contains a substantial introduction to the life and work of Mary Cassatt, and includes thirty-two color reproductions of her work, each with a comment and description.

Brown, Edward K. WILLA CATHER: A CRITICAL BIOGRAPHY. New York: Alfred A. Knopf, 1953. xxiv, 351 p.

This is a literary biography of Cather, who wrote about life on the frontier.

Butscher, Edward. SYLVIA PLATH: METHOD AND MADNESS. New York: Seabury Press, 1976. xix, 388 p.

This biography of Plath looks at her psychological problems and the impact they had on her life and work.

_____, ed. SYLVIA PLATH: THE WOMAN AND THE WORK. New York: Dodd, Mead and Co., 1977. xiii, 242 p.

This book is divided into two parts, the first on Plath's life, the second on her art. There are several pieces by those who knew the poet.

Campbell, Helen. ANNE BRADSTREET AND HER TIME. Boston: D. Lathrop, 1841. 373 p.

> Anne Bradstreet, 1612–72, was one of the earliest women poets on the American colonial scene.

Carr, Virginia Spencer. THE LONELY HUNTER: A BIOGRAPHY OF CARSON McCULLERS. Garden City, N.Y.: Doubleday and Co., 1975. xix, 598 p.

> This is a substantial biography of the twentieth-century playwright, novelist, and literary figure.

Cheney, Anne. MILLAY IN GREENWICH VILLAGE. University: University of Alabama Press, 1975. xi, 160 p.

> Cheney describes Millay's seven years in Greenwich Village as a time of passage into maturity. In this period, Millay's views were radicalized and she began to live a very bohemian life-style.

Chicago, Judy. THROUGH THE FLOWER: MY STRUGGLE AS A WOMAN ARTIST. Garden City, N.Y.: Doubleday, 1975. 226 p.

> This volume is the autobiography of a contemporary, feminist artist and her efforts to create a new alternative art form that reflects the emerging woman's culture.

Damon, S. Foster. AMY LOWELL: A CHRONICLE. Boston: Houghton Mifflin, 1935. xxi, 773 p.

> This is the story of the poet's life. It includes selections of her letters.

Deland, Margaret. GOLDEN YESTERDAYS. New York: Harper and Brothers, 1941. 351 p.

> This is the autobiography of Margaret Deland, 1857–1945, who wrote poetry and fiction. Her work is considered to have greater literary merit than that of most of her popular contemporaries.

Ferber, Edna. A PECULIAR TREASURE. New York: Doubleday, Doran, 1939. 392 p.

> This is an autobiography of a writer who was popular in the first half of the twentieth century. Ferber also functioned as a journalist during the early years of the century.

Fitzgerald, Zelda. SAVE ME THE WALTZ. New York: Signet Books, 1967. 206 p.

> This is an autobiography written while Zelda Fitzgerald was in a mental hospital. She reconstructs her frenetic marriage to Scott Fitzgerald.

Forrest, Mary. WOMEN OF THE SOUTH: DISTINGUISHED IN LITERATURE. 1861. Reprint. New York: Garnett Press, 1969. xvi, 511 p.

> This volume includes selections from thirty-six southern women authors of the antebellum period and a biographical sketch of each.

Glasgow, Ellen. LETTERS OF ELLEN GLASGOW. Edited by Blair Rouse. New York: Harcourt, Brace and Co., 1958. 384 p.

> This is a selected collection of Glasgow's correspondence with family, friends, and literary figures.

Glimcher, Arnold B. LOUISE NEVELSON. New York: E.P. Dutton and Co., 1976. 105 p.

> This volume includes biography and aesthetic criticism as well as reproductions of Nevelson's work.

Godbold, E. Stanley, Jr. ELLEN GLASGOW AND THE WOMAN WITHIN. Baton Rouge: Louisiana State University Press, 1972. xii, 322 p.

> This is a biography of Glasgow, the southern novelist of the early twentieth century.

Goodrich, Lloyd, and Bry, Doris. GEORGIA O'KEEFE. New York: Praeger Publishers, 1970. 195 p.

> This is a catalog of O'Keefe's work which was exhibited in the Whitney Museum of American Art in 1970. It includes an introduction which discusses her life and work.

Gould, Jean. THE POET AND HER BOOK: A BIOGRAPHY OF EDNA ST. VINCENT MILLAY. New York: Dodd, Mead and Co., 1969. xii, 308 p.

> Millay was a poet who lived a free and bohemian life.

Greer, Germaine. THE OBSTACLE RACE: THE FORTUNES OF WOMEN PAINTERS AND THEIR WORK. New York: Farrar, Straus and Giroux, 1979. 373 p.

> Greer surveys the work of American and European artists and advances the thesis that their work has been overlooked because of sexism.

Guiney, Louise Imogen. LETTERS. 2 vols. New York: Harper and Brothers, 1926.

> This is a collection of Guiney's letters. Guiney (1861-1920) was a poet and literary critic.

Gurko, Miriam. RESTLESS SPIRIT: THE LIFE OF EDNA ST. VINCENT MILLAY. New York: Thomas Y. Crowell, 1962. 271 p.

> This is a biography of Millay's life as a poet.

Harris, Ann Sutherland, and Nochlin, Linda. WOMEN ARTISTS 1550-1950. New York: Alfred A. Knopf, 1978. 368 p.

> This volume catalogs an exhibition of women artists at the Los Angeles County Museum in 1976. It was an international show, but the book labels the nationality of the painters; some are American.

Hart, John S. FEMALE PROSE: WRITERS OF AMERICA! Philadelphia: E.H. Butler, 1870. Reprint. Detroit: Gale Research Co., 1976. 536 p.

> This is a collection of nineteenth century-women authors which includes portraits, biographical notices, and specimens of their writings. The women are authors of both fiction and nonfiction.

Hellman, Lillian. PENTIMENTO. Vol. 2. Boston: Little, Brown and Co., 1973. 297 p.

_____. AN UNFINISHED WOMAN: A MEMOIR. Boston: Little, Brown and Co., 1969. 280 p.

> Hellman brought together a group of writings on her own life as a playwright and literary figure and her friendships with Dashiell Hammett and Dorothy Parker.

Hess, Thomas B., and Baker, Elizabeth C., eds. ART AND SEXUAL POLITICS: WOMEN'S LIBERATION, WOMEN ARTISTS AND ART HISTORY. New York: Macmillan, 1973. ix, 150 p.

> This is a collection of essays on women as artists and the social forces they contend with and express in their work.

Hoyt, Nancy. ELINOR WYLIE: THE PORTRAIT OF AN UNKNOWN LADY. Indianapolis: Bobbs-Merrill, 1935. 363 p.

> This is a biography of the literary figure of the early twentieth century written by her sister. It is chatty and sentimental, yet factual.

Jewett, Sarah Orne. LETTERS OF SARAH ORNE JEWETT. Edited by Annie Fields. Boston: Houghton Mifflin, 1911. 259 p.

> This is a small incomplete collection of Jewett's letters. Jewett was an important literary figure by the last half of the nineteenth century.

Josephson, Matthew. RUTH GIBOW. New York: Random House, 1970. 32 p.

This book contains a biographical sketch and plates of paintings of Ruth Gibow.

Kallir, Otto, ed. ART AND LIFE OF GRANDMA MOSES. New York: A.S. Barnes, 1969. 168 p.

This is an anthology of the writings of and about Anna Mary Robertson Moses (1860-1961), primitive painter.

Keats, John. YOU MIGHT AS WELL LIVE: THE LIFE AND TIMES OF DOROTHY PARKER. New York: Simon and Schuster, 1970. 318 p.

Poet, critic, and humorist, Dorothy Parker was one of those who had lunch almost daily at the famed Round Table in the Algonquin Hotel. She was one of the few women who had the courage to match wits with such men as Heywood Broun, Alexander Woollcott, or James Thurber.

Lewis, Edith. WILLA CATHER: LIVING: A PERSONAL RECORD. New York: Alfred A. Knopf, 1953. xviii, 197 p.

This is the recollection of the author Willa Cather. It is more than a biography and contains information about others of the time, including Mabel Dodge Luhan.

Lewis, Robert W.B. EDITH WHARTON: A BIOGRAPHY. New York: Harper and Row, 1975. xiv, 592 p.

Edith Wharton was a novelist and literary figure of the 1920s and 1930s. This biography was done by a well-known literary scholar and critic.

Luhan, Mabel Dodge. INTIMATE MEMORIES. 4 vols. New York: Harcourt Brace, 1933-37.

Luhan befriended writers and artists and provided financial support for many of them during her unconventional life.

McCall, Muhal Moses. "The Sociology of Female Artists: A Study of Female Painters, Sculptors and Printmakers in St. Louis." Ph.D. dissertation, University of Illinois, 1975.

McCall conducted a sociological observation of contemporary women fine artists. He particularly examined the social role of these artists in one community, St. Louis.

McKenzie, Barbara. MARY McCARTHY. New York: Twayne Publishers, 1966. 191 p.

This is a biography of McCarthy, literary critic, author, and liberated woman.

McMichael, George L.  JOURNEY TO OBSCURITY:  THE LIFE OF OCTAVE
THANET.  Lincoln:  University of Nebraska, 1965.  v, 259 p.

> This is a biography of Alice French, 1850 to 1934, whose pen
> name was Octave Thanet.  She wrote novels which were thinly-
> veiled social criticisms.

Matthiessen, F.O.  SARAH ORNE JEWETT.  Boston:  Houghton Mifflin, 1929.
460 p.

> This is an informal biography of Jewett, the nineteenth-century
> novelist.

Mellow, James R.  CHARMED CIRCLE:  GERTRUDE STEIN AND COMPANY.
New York:  Praeger Publishers, 1974.  528 p.

> This is the story of Gertrude Stein and her entourage as they lived
> in Paris.

Millay, Edna St. Vincent.  LETTERS OF EDNA ST. VINCENT MILLAY.  Edited
by Allan Ross MacDougall.  New York:  Harper and Brothers, 1952.  xii, 384 p.

> This is a collection of Millay's correspondences from her childhood
> to her death.

Moise, Penina.  SECULAR AND RELIGIOUS WORK OF PENINA MOISE WITH
A BRIEF SKETCH OF HER LIFE.  Charleston, S.C.:  N.G. Duffy, 1911.  xi,
313 p.

> Moise, 1797-1880, was a Jewish poet and composer of hymns.
> This book was compiled by the Charleston, S.C., Council of
> Jewish Women.

Monroe, Harriet.  A POET'S LIFE:  SEVENTY YEARS IN A CHANGING WORLD.
New York:  Macmillan, 1938.  viii, 488 p.

> This is the autobiography of the founder of POETRY MAGAZINE.
> Monroe's life touched almost every aspect of the arts in the early
> decades of the twentieth century.  Not the least of her contributions
> was the financial support of many struggling poets.

Moses, Anna Mary Robertson.  GRANDMA MOSES:  MY LIFE HISTORY.  New
York:  Harper, 1948.  140 p.

> This is the autobiography of the primitive painter, including details
> of her country life and her late recognition as an artist.

Munsterberg, Hugo.  A HISTORY OF WOMEN ARTISTS.  New York:  Clarkson
N. Potter, 1975.  ix, 150 p.

> This is a general history of women, but does include references to
> Americans.

Nason, Elias. A MEMOIR OF MRS. SUSANNA ROWSON. Albany, N.Y.: J. Munsell, 1970. 212 p.

Rowson, 1762-1824, was an educator and novelist. Often her novels dealt with the status of women's lives.

Nevelson, Louise. DAWNS AND DUSKS: TAPED CONVERSATIONS. New York: Charles Scribner's Sons, 1976. 207 p.

Nevelson, the painter and sculptress, discusses her life, and her work with her collaborator, Diana MacKoun. Included in the book are photographs of Nevelson's art and pictures of the artist herself.

Olsen, Tillie. SILENCES. New York: Delta, 1979. 300 p.

Olsen, a poet, writes about creativity, aesthetics, and how being female affects art.

Overton, Grant. THE WOMEN WHO MAKE OUR NOVELS. New York: Dodd, Mead, 1938. viii, 352 p.

Overton describes the life and work of sixty-three American women writers of the early twentieth century, some literary, others popular.

Papashuily, Helen Waite. ALL THE HAPPY ENDINGS: A STUDY OF THE DOMESTIC NOVEL IN AMERICA, THE WOMEN WHO WROTE IT, THE WOMEN WHO READ IT, IN THE NINETEENTH CENTURY. New York: Harper and Brothers, 1956. xvii, 231 p.

This examines the popular novels of nineteenth-century America which were written primarily by and for women. Papashuily analyzes the novels as reflections of the beliefs of the period.

Pincus-Whitman, Robert. ALICE TRUMBULL MASON. New York: Whitney Museum of American Art, 1973. 8 p.

This pamphlet was issued for an exhibit of Mason's abstract paintings. Minimal biographical material is included. Mason's life spanned the years from 1904 to 1971.

Plath, Sylvia. LETTERS HOME: CORRESPONDENCE 1950-1963. Edited by Aurelia Siboken Plath. New York: Harper and Row, 1975. 500 p.

This is a collection of letters which Plath wrote to her mother.

Rogers, William G. LADIES BOUNTIFUL. New York: Harcourt, Brace and World, 1968. 236 p.

Rogers discusses the lives and interests of a variety of women who subsidized literary figures. Most lived unconventional lives. Included are women such as Mabel Dodge Luhan, Edith Rockefeller McCormick, Harriet Monroe, Natalie Barney, and Sylvia Beach.

Ross, Isabel. SILHOUETTE IN DIAMONDS: THE LIFE OF MRS. POTTER PALMER. New York: Harper, 1960. 276 p.

This is a biography of a social leader and art patron, Bertha Honore Palmer (1849-1918). She was the undisputed social leader of Chicago. More importantly, advised by Mary Cassatt, Palmer collected an array of French impressionist paintings, most of which became part of the collection of the Chicago Art Institute. The book portrays the life of a woman of unlimited wealth in the late nineteenth and early twentieth century.

Ruihley, Glenn Richard. THE THORN OF A ROSE: AMY LOWELL RECONSIDERED. Hamden, Conn.: Shoe String Press, 1975. 191 p.

Ruihley proposes to restore the artistic reputation of this flamboyant poet.

Secrest, Meryle. BETWEEN ME AND LIFE: A BIOGRAPHY OF ROMAINE BROOKS. Garden City, N.Y.: Doubleday, 1974. 432 p.

This is a study of the life of Brooks, the lesbian artist of the early twentieth century.

Sergeant, Elizabeth Shepley. WILLA CATHER: A MEMOIR. New York: J.B. Lippincott, 1953. 288 p.

This is the story of Cather's life and work as told by a friend from the literary world.

Sexton, Anne. ANNE SEXTON: A SELF-PORTRAIT IN LETTERS. Edited by Linda Gray Sexton and Lois Ames. Boston: Houghton Mifflin, 1977. 433 p.

This is a collection of the poet's letters from 1928 to 1974, done in part by her daughter.

Seyersted, Per. KATE CHOPIN: A CRITICAL BIOGRAPHY. Baton Rouge: Louisiana State University Press, 1969. 246 p.

This is a literary biography of Chopin's life and work as a novelist in the American realism tradition.

Spencer, Cornelia. THE EXILE'S DAUGHTER: A BIOGRAPHY OF PEARL S. BUCK. New York: Coward-McCann, 1944. 228 p.

This is a biography of the popular novelist done in narrative fashion by her sister.

Sweet, Frederick A. MISS MARY CASSATT: IMPRESSIONIST FROM PENN-SYLVANIA. Norman: University of Oklahoma Press, 1966. xix, 242 p.

>This is a biography of the impressionist painter. It includes some illustrations of her work.

Toklas, Alice B. STAYING ON ALONE: LETTERS OF ALICE B. TOKLAS. Edited by Edward Burns. New York: Liveright, 1973. xxii, 426 p.

>This is a collection of Toklas's letters from the time of Gertrude Stein's death in 1946 to 1966 when Toklas died.

_____. WHAT IS REMEMBERED. London: Michael Joseph, 1963. 192 p.

>Toklas tells the story of her life and her relationship with Gertrude Stein.

Tyler, Parker. FLORINE STETTHEIMER: A LIFE IN ART. New York: Farrar and Straus, 1963. 194 p.

>Stettheimer (1871-1944) was a whimsical decorative painter. This book is a study of her life and painting.

Van Alstyne, Frances June Crosby. MEMORIES OF EIGHTY YEARS. Boston: J.H. Earl, 1906. 253 p.

>This is the autobiography of Fanny Crosby, 1820-1915, who is best known as a hymn writer. She also wrote some poetry.

Vernon, Hope J., ed. THE POEMS OF MARIA LOWELL, WITH UNPUBLISHED LETTERS AND A BIOGRAPHY. Providence, R.I.: Brown University, 1936. 252 p.

>Maria White Lowell, wife of James Russell Lowell, was a poet in her own right.

Watts, Emily Stipes. THE POETRY OF AMERICAN WOMEN FROM 1632 TO 1945. Austin: University of Texas Press, 1977. xvi, 218 p.

>The selections of poetry are included in a text that connects the biography of each poet and the literary trends of poetry and women poets in America.

Webster, Jeannette L., and Grumman, Joan. WOMAN AS WRITER. Boston: Houghton Mifflin, 1978. xvi, 451 p.

>This book consists primarily of selections from the work of women authors of the twentieth century, both American and British. The first half of the volume consists of articles by women writing about writing. The main interest here is the biographical sketches of writers which precede each selection. Authors represented include Eudora Welty, Flannery O'Connor, Margaret Atwood, Mary McCarthy, Joan Didion, and many others.

Wheatley, Phillis. POEMS AND LETTERS. Edited by Charles F. Heartman. New York: C.F. Heartman, 1915. Reprint. New York: Arno Press, 1972. 44 p.

> This is a collection of Phillis Wheatley's poetry and correspondence. Wheatley was a black poet of the revolutionary period.

Williams, Ellen. HARRIET MONROE AND THE POETRY RENAISSANCE: THE FIRST TEN YEARS OF POETRY, 1912-1922. Urbana: University of Illinois Press, 1977. xiv, 312 p.

> Williams details the relationship of Harriet Monroe and POETRY MAGAZINE to the poets of the time. Monroe, a staid woman of upper middle-class background, helped many of the young poets after 1912.

Wilson, Robert Forrest. CRUSADER IN CRINOLINE: THE LIFE OF HARRIET BEECHER STOWE. Philadelphia: J.B. Lippincott Co., 1941. Reprint. Westport, Conn.: Greenwood Press, 1972. 706 p.

> Harriet Beecher Stowe, a member of the famous family, is noted as an author, particularly of UNCLE TOM'S CABIN. The author places Stowe in the context of her times and her family.

Wolff, Cynthia Griffin. A FEAST OF WORDS: THE TRIUMPH OF EDITH WHARTON. New York: Oxford University Press, 1977. 425 p.

> Wolff analyzes Edith Wharton and her problems, both as a woman and as a literary figure.

# Chapter 17

# WOMEN IN THE PERFORMING ARTS

Albertson, Chris. BESSIE. New York: Stein and Day, 1972. 253 p.

This is a biography of Bessie Smith, the black blues singer.

Anderson, Marian. MY LORD WHAT A MORNING: AN AUTOBIOGRAPHY.
New York: Viking, 1956. 312 p.

Anderson describes her life and career as she battled racial prejudice to become a world renowned singer.

Astor, Mary. MY STORY: AN AUTOBIOGRAPHY. Garden City, N.Y.:
Doubleday, 1959. 332 p.

This is the autobiography of a movie star from the 1920s and 1930s.

Bacall, Lauren. BY MYSELF. New York: Alfred A. Knopf, 1979. 377 p.

Bacall tells the story of her rise as an actress, starting as an usher,
then modelling and going to Hollywood when she was nineteen.
She writes about her marriage to Humphrey Bogart and the tragedy
of his death.

Barrymore, Ethel. MEMORIES: AN AUTOBIOGRAPHY. New York: Harper
and Row, 1955. 310 p.

Barrymore writes of her short childhood and the sudden decision to
lead a life in the theatre with her brother actors. She discusses
the many roles of her long career as leading lady on stage and
screen.

Binns, Archie. MRS. FISKE AND THE AMERICAN THEATRE. New York:
Crown Publishers, 1955. 436 p.

This is the story of Fiske as an actress and proponent of theatre in
the late nineteenth century. It portrays her struggle to create a
vital theatre in the United States and to educate the audiences to
the then avant-garde works of such playwrights as Ibsen.

Davenport, M. Marguerite. AZALIA: THE LIFE OF MADAME E. AZALIA HOCKLEY. Boston: Chapman and Grimes, 1947. 196 p.

> This is a biography of Emma Azalia Smith Hockley (1867-1922), black singer and choir director. Obtaining education with difficulty, she taught school for a time while studying music and, after her marriage, received the Bachelor of Music degree in 1900.

Davis, Bette. THE LONELY LIFE: AN AUTOBIOGRAPHY. New York: G.P. Putnam's Sons, 1962. 254 p.

> This is the autobiography of one of the great actresses of the twentieth century.

Dressler, Marie. MY OWN STORY. Introduction by Will Rogers. Edited by Mildred Harrington. Boston: Little, Brown and Co., 1934. 290 p.

> Dressler told this story to Harrington who wrote it for her. She described the intrigue and glamour of her stage and movie life and her acquaintances with other stars of the period.

Edwards, Anne. JUDY GARLAND. New York: Simon and Schuster, 1975. 349 p.

> This is a biography of Garland, the singer and movie actress.

_____. VIVIEN LEIGH: A BIOGRAPHY. New York: Simon and Schuster, 1977.

> Edwards writes of Leigh, the story of the movie GONE WITH THE WIND, her Hollywood life, and personal romances.

French, Brandon. ON THE VERGE OF REVOLT: WOMEN IN AMERICAN FILMS OF THE FIFTIES. New York: Ungar, 1978. xxv, 165 p.

> French hypothesizes that seeds of the women's movement were germinating in the 1950s, finding evidence in the popular images of film.

Friedman, Myra. BURIED ALIVE: THE BIOGRAPHY OF JANIS JOPLIN. New York: William Morrow and Co., 1973. 333 p.

> Friedman was Joplin's manager for the last two years of her life. The book describes Joplin's career as a rock singer in the sixties, her involvement with drugs, and her death in 1970 from an overdose of heroin.

Garden, Mary, and Biancolli, Louis. MARY GARDEN'S STORY. New York: Simon and Schuster, 1951. xiii, 302 p.

> This is the autobiography of Garden, a famous opera star who sang in France, New York and, for most of her career, at the Chicago Opera. For one year she was musical director there.

Gipson, Richard McCandless. THE LIFE OF EMMA THURSBY. New York: New York Historical Society, 1940. xxii, 470 p.

> Emma Thursby (1845-1931) was a concert singer and music teacher. Born in New York, she frequently toured the United States in concert.

Glackens, Ira. YANKEE DIVA: LILLIAN NORDICA AND THE GOLDEN DAYS OF OPERA. New York: Coleridge Press, 1936. xiv, 366 p.

> Nordica (1857-1914), born in Maine, sang opera in the United States and Europe. She was in the Metropolitan Company from 1893-1907 as a Wagnerian soprano.

Gordon, Ruth. MY SIDE: THE AUTOBIOGRAPHY OF RUTH GORDON. New York: Harper and Row, 1976. 502 p.

> This is the story of Gordon as an actress and figure in the theatre for most of the twentieth century.

Hauk, Minnie. MEMORIES OF A SINGER. London: A.M. Philpot, 1925. 295 p.

> Minnie Hauk, (1851-1924), operatic soprano, studied and performed in the United States and Europe.

Hayes, Helen. ON REFLECTION: AN AUTOBIOGRAPHY. New York: M. Evans and Co., 1968. 253 p.

> Hayes writes the story of her life, both personal and professional. She relates anecdotes about her family, her career on the stage and in the movies, and her friendships with other well-known people of the acting world.

Higham, Charles. KATE: THE LIFE OF KATHARINE HEPBURN. New York: W.W. Norton and Co., 1975. 244 p.

> Higham creates an authoritative portrait of the actress Hepburn, emphasizing her ability as an actress and her personal qualities. He downplays her relationship with Spencer Tracy. Hepburn authorized this biography.

Homer, Sidney. MY WIFE AND I. THE STORY OF LOUISE AND SIDNEY HOMER. New York: Macmillan, 1939. xii, 269 p.

> Louise Dilworth Beatty Homer (1871-1947), born in Pennsylvania, was a member of the Metropolitan Opera Company from 1900 to 1919.

Jones, Hettie. BIG STAR FALLIN' MAMA: FIVE WOMEN IN BLACK MUSIC. New York: Viking Press, 1974. 150 p.

Jones tells the story of Ma Rainey, Bessie Smith, Mahalia Jackson, Billie Holiday, and Aretha Franklin.

Kellogg, Clara Louise. MEMOIRS OF AN AMERICAN PRIMA DONNA. New York: Putnam's, 1913. xiii, 382 p.

Clara Louise Kellogg (1842-1916) writes of her life and career in anecdotal fashion, leaving out many essential biographical details. She had considerable critical acclaim in Europe.

Klein, Herman. GREAT WOMEN SINGERS OF MY TIME. New York: Dutton, 1931. vi, 244 p.

Klein's selection is international but he includes a number of singers associated with the United States, including Adelina Patti, Lillian Nordica, Ernestine Schumann-Heink.

_____. THE REIGN OF PATTI. New York: Century Co., 1920. ix, 470 p.

This is the biography of Adelina Patti (1843-1919), a great opera star of the turn of the century. Born in Spain, she made her debut in New York in 1859. She sang for several seasons in the United States.

Lawton, Mary. SCHUMANN-HEINK: THE LAST OF THE TITANS. New York: Macmillan, 1928. ix, 390 p.

Lawton writes in autobiographical form of one of the great opera singers. Born in Bohemia in 1861, Schumann-Heink launched her operatic career in the United States in 1898. She sang for five seasons for the Metropolitan. Later she performed, mostly in concert, in New York and Chicago. She was a star until 1932, when she gave her last operatic performance. Later, to revive her fortunes, she sang in vaudeville and made some motion pictures. She died in 1936.

McBride, Mary Margaret. OUT OF THE AIR. Garden City, N.Y.: Doubleday, 1960. 384 p.

This is the autobiography of McBride who conducted early day talk shows via radio.

Mailer, Norman. MARILYN: A BIOGRAPHY. New York: Grosset and Dunlop, 1973. 270 p.

Mailer, the novelist, writes commentary on the life of Marilyn Monroe. He matches his words to an extensive collection of photographs of the film actress.

Malvern, Gladys. CURTAIN GOING UP: THE STORY OF KATHARINE CORNELL. New York: Julius Messner, 1943. 244 p.

This is the biography of the actress from her childhood in upstate New York at the turn of the century through her early days on the stage to her success as an actress in the 1930s and 1940s.

Martin, Sadie E. THE LIFE AND PROFESSIONAL CAREER OF EMMA ABBOTT. Minneapolis: L. Kimball, 1891. 192 p.

Emma Abbott (1850-1891), an opera singer, born in New England, achieved greater success in England than in the United States, although she sang in New York, Baltimore, Washington, D.C., and Philadelphia. Beginning in 1878, she organized an opera company to give performances in smaller towns in the United States. Called the "peoples prima donna," she sang from Iowa to Utah with acclaim.

Maynard, Olga. AMERICAN MODERN DANCERS, THE PIONEERS. Boston: Little, Brown and Co., 1956. 218 p.

Maynard describes the antecedents of modern dance in America and its great figures, Ruth St. Denis, Ted Shawn, Martha Graham, and others.

Milinowski, Marta. TERESA CARRENO, "BY THE GRACE OF GOD." New Haven, Conn.: Yale University Press, 1940. xvi, 410 p.

Carreno (1853-1917), born in Venezuela and raised in New York, became a concert pianist. She performed in both the United States and Europe to great popular acclaim.

Moore, Grace. YOU'RE ONLY HUMAN ONCE. Garden City, N.Y.: Doubleday, 1944. 275 p.

Grace Moore (1898-1947), born in Tennessee, sang several seasons at the Metropolitan, performed in musical comedy, made some movies, and sang for radio.

Nash, Alanna. DOLLY. Los Angeles: Reed Books, 1978. 275 p.

This is the biography of Dolly Parton, the contemporary country singer. It details her childhood in rural Tennessee, entry into the singing world in Nashville, and rise to stardom as a pop singer. It also discusses her troubled personal life through marriages and divorces.

Paine, Albert Bigelow. LIFE AND LILLIAN GISH. New York: Macmillan, 1932. 303 p.

Paine describes the life of Gish on the stage and at home. He is eloquent about the beauty and art of this early twentieth-century actress.

Parish, James Robert. THE FOX GIRLS. New Rochelle, N.Y.: Arlington House, 1971. 722 p.

These biographical sketches of actresses who worked for Twentieth Century-Fox Studio range in time from Theda Bara to Raquel Welch. A list of feature films is appended to each sketch.

_____. THE PARAMOUNT PRETTIES. New Rochelle, N.Y.: Arlington House, 1972. 585 p.

The author discusses sixteen actresses who worked for Paramount Studios from Gloria Swanson to Shirley MacLaine. After each biographical sketch is a list of feature films each actress made with the other actors and directors involved. It is not a feminist book.

Parish, James Robert, and Stanke, Don E. THE GLAMOUR GIRLS. Introduction by Rona Barrett. New Rochelle, N.Y.: Arlington House, 1975. 751 p.

This sexist volume describes nine actresses of the 1940s and 1950s. The book includes physical statistics of each star and lists feature films in which each played.

Reed, Lynnel. BE NOT AFRAID: BIOGRAPHY OF MADAME RIDER-KELSEY. New York: Vantage, 1955. 168 p.

Corinne Rider-Kelsey (1877-1947), born in New York, was a concert singer. She studied at the Oberlin Conservatory, and often appeared with Schumann-Heink.

Rosen, Marjorie. POPCORN VENUS: WOMEN, MOVIES AND THE AMERICAN DREAM. New York: Avon Books, 1977. 244 p.

This book analyzes the images of women as portrayed in American films. It looks at the roles played by such actresses as Pickford, Garbo, Monroe, Hepburn and Fonda and how these roles reflect changing conceptions of women in society.

Seroff, Victor. THE REAL ISADORA. New York: Avon, 1971. 480 p.

This is a biography of Isadora Duncan, the dancer of the early twentieth century.

Terry, Walter. MISS RUTH: THE MORE LIVING LIFE OF RUTH ST. DENIS. New York: Dodd, Mead, 1969. xi, 206 p.

This is a biography of a great figure in modern dance.

Tunney, Kieran. TALLULAH: DARLING OF THE GODS. New York: E.P. Dutton and Co., 1973. 228 p.

This biography of Bankhead was done by one of her personal friends. It contains many intimate descriptions of her characteristics, energy, and personality.

West, Mae. GOODNESS HAD NOTHING TO DO WITH IT: THE AUTO-BIOGRAPHY OF MAE WEST. Englewood Cliffs, N.J.: Prentice-Hall, 1959. 271 p.

This is the autobiography of a flamboyant show business personality.

# Chapter 18

# WOMEN IN SPORTS

Geadelman, Patricia, et al. EQUALITY IN SPORT FOR WOMEN. Washington, D.C.: American Alliance for Health, Physical Education, and Recreation, 1977. 202 p.

> The authors deal with the law and equality for women in sports. Court precedents are examined in detail. They discuss role stereotyping in relation to sports and remedial action to bring equality.

Gerber, Ellen W., et al. THE AMERICAN WOMEN IN SPORT. Reading, Mass.: Addison-Wesley, 1974. xii, 562 p.

> The authors approach their subject historically, as to collegiate sport, Olympic competition, and sport in society. They deal with a dialectical approach, a descriptive view of the woman athlete, and the biological aspect of the woman athlete, for instance, menstruation and pregnancy.

Gibson, Althea. I ALWAYS WANTED TO BE SOMEBODY. New York: Harper and Row, 1958. 176 p.

> Gibson was women's singles champion in tennis in 1957 and 1958. She won the Wimbledon tournament both years.

Harris, Dorothy V., ed. WOMEN AND SPORT: A NATIONAL RESEARCH CONFERENCE. State College: Pennsylvania State University, 1972. 416 p.

> These are papers given in a conference on women and sport at Pennsylvania State University. The papers deal with topics such as aggression and the female athlete, femininity, achievement in sport, and the female spectator. The authors are thorough in their discussion.

Hoepner, Barbara J., ed. WOMEN'S ATHLETICS: COPING WITH CONTROVERSY. Washington, D.C.: American Association for Health, Physical Education, and Recreation, 1974. 120 p.

The editor brings together sixteen articles by experts which point up the double standard in male-dominated athletics.

King, Billie Jean. BILLIE JEAN. New York: Harper and Row, 1974. 208 p.

This is the autobiography of one of the great women tennis champions.

Klafs, Carl E., and Lyon, M. Joan. THE FEMALE ATHLETE: A COACHES GUIDE TO CONDITIONING AND TRAINING. St. Louis: C.V. Mosby, 1978. 340 p.

There is a short historical summary of attitudes and trends. The remainder of the book involves the current wisdom, including the use of drugs to win.

Lee, Mabel. MEMORIES BEYOND BLOOMERS (1924-1954). Washington, D.C.: American Alliance for Health, Physical Education and Recreation, 1978. 458 p.

A longtime professor of physical education at the University of Nebraska, Lee was active in nearly every aspect of women's sports and physical education as well as youth hostels and the Women's Army Corps in World War II.

_____. MEMORIES OF A BLOOMER GIRL (1894-1924). Washington, D.C.: American Alliance for Health, Physical Education and Recreation, 1977. 384 p.

Mabel Lee was one of the leaders of physical activity for women, from Indian clubs and Greek dance to intercollegiate sports for women. She reports on the beginning of the latter debate in the 1920s.

Lichtenstein, Grace. A LONG WAY BABY: BEHIND THE SCENES IN WOMEN'S PRO TENNIS. New York: William Morrow, 1974. 239 p.

This is the story of the changes in women's tennis and, most particularly, the record of the personalities and their problems and triumphs of the 1973 tennis season.

Oglesby, Carole A., et al. WOMEN AND SPORT: FROM MYTH TO REALITY. Philadelphia: Lea and Febiger, 1978. 256 p.

Oglesby and twelve contributors seek to prove that women can theorize about sport, hitherto a male domain. They seek to remedy the situation in which sport is symbolized and verbalized as entirely male. This is a feminist approach. The contributors go into the historical aspect as well as the implication, of civil rights legislation and ERA for women in sports.

Peterson, Hazel C. DOROTHY S. AINSWORTH: HER LIFE, PROFESSIONAL

CAREER AND CONTRIBUTIONS TO PHYSICAL EDUCATION. Moscow: University of Idaho Press, 1975. 487 p.

Ainsworth was one of the leaders in the professionalization of physical education for women.

Rudolph, Wilma. WILMA: THE STORY OF WILMA RUDOLPH. New York: Signet Books, 1977. 176 p.

This is the story of a courageous black woman who became an Olympic athlete.

Twin, Stephanie L., ed. OUT OF THE BLEACHERS: WRITINGS ON WOMEN AND SPORT. Old Westbury, N.Y.: Feminist Press, 1979. 229 p.

This work discusses women in sports from various perspectives. It has a section on the physiology of women as athletes, one on the life experiences of several contemporary women athletes and another on the structure of women's sports in the United States.

Zaharias, Babe Didrikson. THIS LIFE I'VE LED: MY AUTOBIOGRAPHY. New York: A.S. Barnes, 1955. xiii, 242 p.

Mildred "Babe" Didrikson Zaharias, a great woman athlete, participated in track in the 1932 Olympics and went on to become a champion golfer, repeatedly being voted the woman athlete of the year.

# Chapter 19

# WOMEN AND EDUCATION

Abramson, Joan. THE INVISIBLE WOMAN: DISCRIMINATION IN THE AC-ADEMIC PROFESSION. San Francisco: Jossey-Bass, 1975. 248 p.

> Abramson discusses her experience with sexism as a member of the English department at the University of Hawaii.

Angrist, Shirley S., and Almquist, Elizabeth M. CAREERS AND CONTIN-GENCIES: HOW COLLEGE WOMEN JUGGLE WITH GENDER. New York: Dunellen Press, 1975. 269 p.

> This book is based on information collected in the mid-1960s on the conflicts and choices involved in being an American educated female.

Astin, Helen, ed. SOME ACTION OF HER OWN: THE ADULT WOMAN AND HIGHER EDUCATION. Lexington, Mass.: Lexington Books, 1976. xii, 180 p.

> This is a collection of essays on continuing education for the older woman. It looks at the statistical trends and the life experiences of women returning to school.

Bernard, Jessie. ACADEMIC WOMEN. University Park: Pennsylvania State University Press, 1964. 331 p.

> The author describes the history of women in academic pursuits, their contributions as teachers and scholars.

Boas, Louise Schutz. WOMEN'S EDUCATION BEGINS: THE RISE OF WOMEN'S COLLEGES. Norton, Mass.: Wheaton College Press, 1935. Re-print. New York: Arno Press, 1971. 295 p.

> Boas traces the changing aims and curricula of early women's col-leges as they followed the altered perception of women's role.

Carnegie Commission on Higher Education. OPPORTUNITIES FOR WOMEN IN HIGHER EDUCATION. New York: McGraw-Hill, 1973. 282 p.

This is the Carnegie Commission's survey of the status of women in higher education—-students, faculty, and administrators.

Ceutra, John A. WOMEN, MEN AND THE DOCTORATE. Princeton, N.J.: Educational Testing Service, 1974. 214 p.

Ceutra surveyed the opportunities for women Ph.D.s and found significant levels of discrimination.

Chase, Mary Ellen. A GOODLY FELLOWSHIP. New York: Macmillan, 1939. 305 p.

This is the autobiography of Chase, who finished a long career in teaching as professor of English at Smith College. She relates the prejudice against women in the academic world.

Cole, Arthur C. A HUNDRED YEARS OF MOUNT HOLYOKE COLLEGE. New Haven, Conn.: Yale University Press, 1940. 426 p.

Mount Holyoke Female Seminary was founded in 1836 by Mary Lyon to provide rigorous education for young women. The seminary gradually evolved into Mount Holyoke College.

Conable, Charlotte Williams. WOMEN AT CORNELL: THE MYTH OF EQUAL EDUCATION. Ithaca, N.Y.: Cornell University Press, 1977. 211 p.

The author finds that although Cornell was the first major university to admit women, it did not, in the early years, provide equal education. She finds that the 1960s and 1970s were much better. Women in the early years were cloistered and excluded from much of the social and intellectual life at Cornell.

Cross, Barbara, ed. THE EDUCATED WOMAN IN AMERICA: SELECTED WRITINGS OF CATHARINE BEECHER, MARGARET FULLER AND M. CAREY THOMAS. New York: Columbia University, Teachers College Press, 1965. 175 p.

Cross discusses the relevance of each figure to American women's education and presents selections from their writings.

Dennis, Lawrence E., ed. EDUCATION AND A WOMAN'S LIFE. Washington, D.C.: American Council on Education, 1963. 153 p.

This book includes the proceedings of a conference on continuing education for women.

Feldman, Saul D. ESCAPE FROM THE DOLL'S HOUSE: WOMEN IN GRADUATE AND PROFESSIONAL SCHOOL EDUCATION. New York: McGraw-Hill, 1974. xv, 208 p.

This examines women in graduate schools and the trends of tradition and change in the professions.

Fitzpatrick, Blanche. WOMEN'S INFERIOR EDUCATION: AN ECONOMIC ANALYSIS. New York: Praeger Publishers, 1976. 190 p.

> This work by an economist looks at the economic forces which motivate discrimination against women in higher education.

Frankfort, Roberta. COLLEGIATE WOMEN: DOMESTICITY AND CAREER IN TURN OF THE CENTURY AMERICA. New York: New York University Press, 1977. xix, 121 p.

> This examines primarily the world of Wellesley and Bryn Mawr colleges in the 1880 to 1920 period. It includes sections, however, on Elizabeth Palmer Peabody, Martha Carey Thomas, and Alice Freeman Palmer.

Furniss, W. Todd, and Crahan, Patricia Albjerg, eds. WOMEN IN HIGHER EDUCATION. Washington, D.C.: American Council on Education, 1974. 336 p.

> This is a compilation of the preceedings of the American Council on Education's 1973 conference. The editors touch on a wide variety of issues.

Gray, Eileen. EVERYWOMAN'S GUIDE TO COLLEGE. Millbrae, Calif.: Les Femmes Press, 168 p.

> This is a practical book which advises the older woman returning to college.

Harveson, Mae Elizabeth. CATHERINE ESTHER BEECHER: PIONEER EDUCATOR. Philadelphia: University of Pennsylvania Press, 1932. Reprint. New York: Arno Press, 1969. 295 p.

> Catherine Beecher founded the Hartford Female Seminary and wrote numerous books on domestic science.

Howe, Florence, ed. WOMEN AND THE POWER TO CHANGE. New York: McGraw-Hill, 1975. xvii, 182 p.

> This includes essays by Adrienne Rich, Arlie Russel, Aleta Wallach, and Howe, the editor. The volume was sponsored by the Carnegie Commission on Higher Education. For the most part, the essays focus on women's issues in college and the possibilities of change in women's education. It has a distinctively feminist viewpoint.

Jones, Jane Louise. A PERSONNEL STUDY OF WOMEN DEANS IN COLLEGES AND UNIVERSITIES. New York: Teachers College, Bureau of Publications, 1928. 155 p.

> This book investigates the women who have risen to the position of dean in universities and colleges and how they got there.

Kendall, Elaine. "PECULIAR INSTITUTIONS": AN INFORMAL HISTORY OF THE SEVEN SISTER COLLEGES. New York: G.P. Putnam's and Sons, 1976. 272 p.

> This examines in popular fashion the beginning, growth, and development of Radcliffe College, Bryn Mawr, Smith, Barnard, Wellesley, Vassar, and Mount Holyoke.

Komarovsky, Mirra. WOMEN IN THE MODERN WORLD: THEIR EDUCATION AND THEIR DILEMMAS. Boston: Little, Brown and Co., 1953. 319 p.

> This is a sociological and psychological analysis of the issues facing education in the 1950s. It suggests the tensions women face are social in nature, rather than individual.

Lever, Janet, and Schwartz, Pepper. WOMEN AT YALE: LIBERATING A COLLEGE CAMPUS. Indianapolis, Ind.: Bobbs-Merrill, 1971. 274 p.

> This is a sociological analysis of the changes which occurred at Yale when that institution began admitting women undergraduates.

Maccia, Elizabeth Steiner, ed. WOMEN AND EDUCATION. Springfield, Ill.: Charles C Thomas, 1975. 381 p.

> This is a collection of essays on various aspects of education for women. Contributors include Florence Haven, Steve Rossi, and Wilma Scott Tobias.

Newcomer, Mabel. A CENTURY OF HIGHER EDUCATION FOR AMERICAN WOMEN. New York: Harper, 1959. 266 p.

> The author believes there has been a notable lack of progress in the education of women in recent years and, in some places, a decline of quality.

Noble, Jeanne E. THE NEGRO WOMAN: COLLEGE EDUCATION. New York: Teacher's College, Bureau of Publications, 1956. vii, 163 p.

> This surveys the opportunities for black women in higher education in the mid-twentieth century.

Radcliffe College. Committee on Graduate Education for Women. GRADUATE EDUCATION FOR WOMEN: THE RADCLIFFE PH.D. Cambridge, Mass.: Harvard University Press, 1956. 131 p.

> This report examines women as Ph.D. candidates in most fields and the impact for them and in the professions. In some respects, this book is a how-to volume, discussing who should go to graduate school and how to finance it.

Richardson, Betty. SEXISM IN HIGHER EDUCATION. New York: Seaburg Press, 1974. 221 p.

Richardson looks at many facets of discrimination against women at the university level.

Rossi, Alice S., and Calderwood, Ann. ACADEMIC WOMEN ON THE MOVE. New York: Russell Sage Foundation, 1973. xv, 560 p.

This volume consists of essays surveying women's options in entering the academic world, what women's roles in academic life currently are, and what actions are being taken towards change in the academic community.

Schmuck, Patricia Ann. SEX DIFFERENCES IN PUBLIC SCHOOL ADMINISTRATION. Arlington, Va.: National Council of Administrative Women in Education, 1975. 119 p.

Schmuck examines the discrimination against women in the field of educational administration.

Stacey, Judith, et al., eds. AND JILL CAME TUMBLING AFTER: SEXISM IN AMERICAN EDUCATION. New York: Dell, 1974. 461 p.

This is a collection of essays on schools and how they reinforce sex role stereotypes at all levels, from the nursery school to graduate school.

Steele, Marilyn. WOMEN IN VOCATIONAL EDUCATION. Flagstaff: Northern Arizona University, 1974. iv, 146 p.

This book looks at the status of women's vocational training as of 1974 and issues of sexism the findings present.

Thomas, M. Carey. THE MAKING OF A FEMINIST: EARLY JOURNALS AND LETTERS OF M. CAREY THOMAS. Edited by Marjorie Houspian Dobkin. Kent, Ohio: Kent State University Press, 1980. 312 p.

Long the president of Bryn Mawr College, Thomas insisted on rigorous education for women. This is the story of her Quaker childhood and her coming of age.

Wasserman, Elga; Lewin, Arie Y.; and Bleiweiss, Linda H., eds. WOMEN IN ACADEMIA: EVOLVING POLICIES TOWARD EQUAL OPPORTUNITY. New York: Praeger Publishers, 1975. xi, 173 p.

The editors present a volume of essays on affirmative action progress and policies as they affect academic women.

WOMEN ON CAMPUS: THE UNFINISHED LIBERATION. New Rochelle, N.Y.: Change Magazine, 1975. 256 p.

This is a group of short articles, most of which originally appeared in CHANGE magazine. They focus on the barriers for women in in education, the struggle to change them, and women who have succeeded.

Woody, Thomas. A HISTORY OF WOMEN'S EDUCATION IN THE UNITED STATES. 2 vols. New York: Science Press, 1929.

Woody describes the opportunities and restrictions on education for women, dealing with social change, academics, colleges, and professional education. This book is regarded as the standard account.

# Chapter 20

# WOMEN IN BUSINESS AND THE PROFESSIONS

Arbanel, Karin, and Siegel, Connie McClung. WOMAN'S WORK BOOK. New York: Praeger, 1975. 327 p.

> This is a practical advice book for women who seek to enter the job market.

Benedict, Ruth Fulton. AN ANTHROPOLOGIST AT WORK. New York: Atherton Press, 1966. Reprint. Westport, Conn.: Greenwood Press, 1977. 583 p.

> This is a selection of the writings of Ruth Benedict.

Bird, Caroline. BORN FEMALE: THE HIGH COST OF KEEPING WOMEN DOWN. New York: David McKay Co., 1968. xiii, 288 p.

> Bird emphasizes the economic and employment problems of women.

_____. ENTERPRISING WOMEN. New York: Mentor Books, 1976. 224 p.

> Bird provides biographies of thirty-six unusual women who succeeded in the business world.

_____. EVERYTHING A WOMAN NEEDS TO KNOW TO GET PAID WHAT SHE'S WORTH. New York: David McKay Co., 1973. ix, 304 p.

> This book tells women how to have a career and get just recompense for their efforts. It has a question and answer forward.

Cole, Doris. FROM TIPI TO SKYSCRAPER: A HISTORY OF WOMEN IN ARCHITECTURE. Boston: I Press, 1973. 136 p.

> This is the description of women's contributions to architecture and an analysis of why there have been so few women architects.

Epstein, Cynthia Fuchs. WOMAN'S PLACE. Berkeley and Los Angeles: University of California Press, 1970. 221 p.

> This is an early analysis of the discrimination professional women

face as they attempt to make careers for themselves. Epstein
found many social forces keeping women from success.

Fidell, Linda S., and DeLamater, John, eds. WOMEN IN THE PROFESSIONS:
WHAT'S ALL THE FUSS ABOUT? Beverly Hills, Calif.: Sage Publications,
1971. 144 p.

This is a discussion of job discrimination and women.

Foxworth, Jo. BOSS LADY: AN EXECUTIVE WOMAN TALKS ABOUT MAK-
ING IT. New York: Thomas Y. Crowell, 1978. x, 224 p.

Foxworth tells the story of her successful career as an advertising
executive. She aims at convincing other women that success is
possible.

Gelfman, Judith S. WOMEN IN TELEVISION NEWS. New York: Columbia
University Press, 1976. x, 186 p.

Gelfman explores what it's like for women in the television news
world.

Golde, Peggy, ed. WOMEN IN THE FIELD: ANTHROPOLOGICAL EXPERI-
ENCES. Chicago: Aldine, 1970. 343 p.

This is a collection of the experiences of twelve women anthropologists undertaking field work.

Gordon, Francine E., and Stroker, Myra H., eds. BRINGING WOMEN INTO
MANAGEMENT. New York: McGraw-Hill, 1975. 168 p.

This book is geared towards advising corporate firms on how to
recruit more women executives. It's a report of a conference held
at the Stanford Business School.

Harragan, Betty Lehan. GAMES MOTHER NEVER TAUGHT YOU: CORPORATE
GAMESMANSHIP FOR WOMEN. New York: Ranson Associates Publishing,
1977. 334 p.

This is a how-to book for women in the business world.

Harris, Barbara J. BEYOND HER SPHERE: WOMEN AND THE PROFESSIONS
IN AMERICAN HISTORY. Westport, Conn.: Greenwood Press, 1978. x,
212 p.

This book provides insight into white middle-class women and their
embrace of medicine, law, college teaching, and the clergy.

Hennig, Margaret, and Jardim, Anne. THE MANAGERIAL WOMAN. New
York: Anchor Press, 1977. xvii, 221 p.

The authors explore what motivates women in business and the fac-

tors of discrimination in the business world. They discuss how
women can break through their fear of success.

Holmstrom, Linda Lytle. THE TWO CAREER FAMILY. Cambridge, Mass.:
Schenckman, 1972. 203 p.

Holmstrom analyzes the problems of families in which both husband
and wife work, and how they cope with the demands.

Hummer, Patricia. THE DECADE OF ELUSIVE PROMISE: PROFESSIONAL
WOMEN IN THE UNITED STATES, 1920-1930. Ann Arbor, Mich.: UMI Research
Press, 1979. 157 p.

Hummer concludes that the professional and economic progress of
women in the twenties was less than formerly believed.

Johnson, Curtis S. AMERICA'S FIRST LADY BOSS. Norwalk, Conn.: Silver-
mine Publishers, 1965. xi, 164 p.

This is the biography of Margaret Swain Getchell, one of the
founders of the R.H. Macy department store. Johnson terms Getchell the first woman in America to become a top executive in a
million-dollar business.

Jongeward, Dorothy, and Scott, Dru. AFFIRMATIVE ACTION FOR WOMEN:
A PRACTICAL GUIDE. Reading, Mass.: Addison-Wesley, 1973. xvi, 334 p.

This book gives a short history of the affirmative action law and
a step-by-step procedure for women who wish to make the best of
their careers.

Kundsin, Ruth B., ed. WOMEN AND SUCCESS: THE ANATOMY OF
ACHIEVEMENT. 2d ed. New York: William Morrow, 1974. 256 p.

This volume was originally titled SUCCESSFUL WOMEN IN THE
SCIENCES. It includes sections on the life experiences of women
as architects, physicists, chemists, and so on, the family life of
professional women; women's education; and economic considerations.

Loring, Rosalind, and Wells, Theodora. BREAKTHROUGH: WOMEN INTO
MANAGEMENT. New York: Van Nostrand Reinhold, 1972. 213 p.

This is an advice book for women who wish to enter the business
world. It also speaks to those who hire women, suggesting advantages to business when they enlarge the ranks of women executives.

Lyle, Jerolyn R. WOMEN IN INDUSTRY: EMPLOYMENT PATTERNS OF
WOMEN IN CORPORATE AMERICA. Lexington, Mass.: D.C. Heath, 1973.
164 p.

This is an economic analysis of discrimination levels and employment trends for women in the corporate world. It is a technical
discussion.

Lynch, Edith M. THE EXECUTIVE SUITE--FEMININE STYLE. New York:
AMACOM, 1973. 258 p.

This is the description by a woman executive of what it is like
for women in the upper echelons of the corporate world. Lynch
also advises women on how to have a successful career.

Mead, Margaret. BLACKBERRY WINTER: MY EARLIER YEARS. New York:
William Morrow, 1972. 305 p.

This is the story of Mead's early life and the beginnings of her
career as an anthropologist and commentator on contemporary life.

_____. RUTH BENEDICT. New York: Columbia University Press, 1974.
180 p.

Mead wrote a biography of her friend and teacher Ruth Benedict,
the anthropologist.

Odlum, Hortense. A WOMAN'S PLACE: THE AUTOBIOGRAPHY OF HOR-
TENSE ODLUM. New York: Charles Scribner's Sons, 1939. 286 p.

Odlum describes her childhood in Utah and the experiences of
being transported as a young wife and mother to Manhattan. She
eventually became president of Bonwit, Teller and Company. She
took it over as a nearly defunct store and increased its business
drastically.

Pogrebin, Letty Cottin. GETTING YOURS: HOW TO MAKE THE SYSTEM
WORK FOR THE WORKING WOMAN. New York: David McKay Co., 1975.
349 p.

Pogrebin, an editor of MS. MAGAZINE, discusses how the working
woman can balance all the parts of her life and how to make a
successful career.

Potter, Jeffrey. MEN, MONEY AND MAGIC: THE STORY OF DOROTHY
SCHIFF. New York: Signet Books, 1976. 352 p.

Publisher of the NEW YORK POST for thirty-seven years, Schiff
was a highly successful business woman who wielded great power in
politics and journalism.

Reid, Doris Fielding. EDITH HAMILTON: AN INTIMATE PORTRAIT. New
York: W.W. Norton and Co., 1967. 174 p.

This is the biography of one of America's great scholars of Greek
life and literature.

Ross, Ishbel. LADIES OF THE PRESS: THE STORY OF WOMEN IN JOURNAL-ISM BY AN INSIDER. New York: Harper and Bros., 1936. Reprint. New York: Arno Press, 1974. 622 p.

This book describes the contributions and problems of many female journalists.

Sanders, Marion K. DOROTHY THOMPSON: A LEGEND IN HER TIME. Boston: Houghton Mifflin, 1973. 428 p.

This is a biography of the journalist of the 1930s and 1940s.

Schwartz, Eleanor Brantley. THE SEX BARRIER IN BUSINESS. Atlanta: Georgia State University Press, 1971. 116 p.

This is a report on a survey of business executives on their attitudes towards women as executives. It documents the existence of discrimination.

Scott, Adelin White. A PROFESSIONAL WOMAN IN A MAN'S WORLD. New York: Vantage Press, 1960. 68 p.

Scott examines the challenges of professional women in overcoming sex discrimination as it existed in the late 1950s.

Seed, Suzanne, ed. SATURDAY'S CHILD: 36 WOMEN TALK ABOUT THEIR JOBS. New York: Bantam, 1974. 159 p.

This is a collection of statements by women about their jobs. The women included had a wide variety of professions--television, sciences, government jobs, and writing.

Simcich, Tina L. SHORTCHANGED UPDATE: MINORITIES AND WOMEN IN BANKING. New York: Council on Economic Priorities, 1976. 173 p.

Simcich surveys the statistics on women employed by the major banks in the United States, as of 1976.

Stimpson, Catharine R., ed. DISCRIMINATION AGAINST WOMEN. New York: R.R. Bowker, 1973. xvii, 558 p.

Stimpson has edited a volume on the congressional hearings on equal rights in education and employment. It includes testimony by numerous witnesses and documents on women and work, law, education, professions, and government action.

Strainchamps, Ethel, ed. ROOMS WITH NO VIEW: A WOMAN'S GUIDE TO THE MAN'S WORLD OF THE MEDIA. New York: Harper and Row, 1974. xxvii, 333 p.

This volume was assembled by the Media Women's Association. In it, sixty-five women who work in publishing or television discuss their careers.

Teitz, Joyce. WHAT'S A NICE GIRL LIKE YOU DOING IN A PLACE LIKE THIS? New York: Coward, McCann and Geoghegan, 1972. 285 p.

> This is a journalistic set of articles on how women balance a career and family.

Theodore, Athena, ed. THE PROFESSIONAL WOMAN. Cambridge, Mass.: Schenkman, 1971. xi, 769 p.

> This collection of articles deals with sexism in the professions and how even "advantaged" women must face discrimination and injustice in their careers and education.

Underwood, Agness. NEWSPAPERWOMAN. New York: Harper and Brothers, 1949. 297 p.

> Underwood was a newspaper reporter, mostly for Hearst papers. In the mid-1940s she was the first woman to be a city editor on a metropolitan newspaper. She worked for the LOS ANGELES EVENING HERALD AND EXPRESS.

U.S. Department of Commerce. Office of Minority Business Enterprise. WOMEN-OWNED BUSINESSES, 1972. Washington, D.C.: 1976. 284 p.

> This government publication presents statistical information about women's ownership of industry, services, and other agencies. It consists of maps, charts, and tables arranged by regional divisions.

Williams, Marcille Gray. THE NEW EXECUTIVE WOMAN: A GUIDE TO BUSINESS SUCCESS. Radnor, Pa.: Chilton Book Co., 1977. 242 p.

> This is a how-to book for the female who has made it as an executive or who hopes to do so. She tells how to deal with male chauvinism, sex in the office, managing people, dress, and etiquette.

Winston, Sandra. THE ENTREPRENEURIAL WOMAN. New York: Newsweek Books, 1979. 239 p.

> Winston writes a how-to book for women who would like to go into business. She explores the special challenges, difficulties, and rewards for contemporary women in the corporate world.

# Chapter 21

# WOMEN IN THE LABOR FORCE

Baer, Judith A. THE CHAINS OF PROTECTION: THE JUDICIAL RESPONSE TO WOMEN'S LABOR LEGISLATION. Westport, Conn.: Greenwood Press, 1978. x, 238 p.

> The author believes that legislation that was presumed to be protective actually perpetuated male domination.

Baker, Elizabeth Faulkner. TECHNOLOGY AND WOMEN'S WORK. New York: Columbia University Press, 1964. xvi, 460 p.

> Baker describes the changing opportunities for employment of women. These range from the textile mills, clerical and secretarial to sales and professional activities. She feels that family support is no longer the monopoly of men, so housekeeping should no longer be the monopoly of women.

Baxandall, Rosalyn, et al. AMERICA'S WORKING WOMEN. New York: Random House, 1976. xxii, 408 p., ix p.

> This looks at women in U.S. history and the work they have done. It starts with Indian women, and goes on to examine women factory workers, women slaves, women in the industrial period and women in the labor movement up to 1975.

Benet, Mary Kathleen. THE SECRETARIAL GHETTO. New York: McGraw-Hill, 1972. 181 p.

> The author takes a radical view of the position of secretary. She believes secretaries are highly oppressed and must act to realign the power structures in their offices.

Cantor, Milton, and Laurie, Bruce, eds. CLASS, SEX, AND THE WOMAN WORKER. Westport, Conn.: Greenwood Press, 1977. ix, 253 p.

> This is a collection of recent scholarly articles on the history of American working women. The articles range through the rise of class consciousness among Lowell factory girls, the work of immi-

grant women, women in trade unions, and an overview. The articles center on the theme of how immigrant women handled divided allegiance caused by diverse loyalties. Some of the articles take a feminist stance. The collection grew out of a conference on the history of women at Radcliffe College in 1974.

Grosvenor, Verta Mae. THURSDAYS AND EVERY OTHER SUNDAY OFF: A DOMESTIC RAP. Garden City, N.Y.: Doubleday, 1972. 156 p.

Grosvenor describes the opporession of black women domestics. She believes white women are liberated at the expense of their black servants.

Hamburger, Robert. A STRANGER IN THE HOUSE. New York: Collier Books, 1978. New York: Macmillan, 1978. xvi, 168 p.

This is the story in words and photographs of twelve household workers.

Howe, Louise Knapp. PINK COLLAR WORKERS: INSIDE THE WORLD OF WOMEN'S WORK. New York: G.P. Putnam's Sons, 1977. 301 p.

Howe examines the statistics on women in the work force and finds women comprise the majority of beauticians, sales workers, waitresses, office workers, and homemakers. She devotes a chapter to each of these professions, and gives a descriptive account of each.

Katzman, David M. SEVEN DAYS A WEEK: WOMEN AND DOMESTIC SERVICE IN INDUSTRAILIZING AMERICA. New York: Oxford University Press, 1978. xviii, 374 p.

Katzman analyzes the relationship of employer-employee, both female. In many cases the servants were overworked by middle-class employers. Katzman sees the rejection of domestic service in the twentieth century as a rejection of the traditional woman's role.

Kenneally, James J. WOMEN AND AMERICAN TRADE UNIONS. St. Albans, Vt.: Eden Press, 1978. 250 p.

This book examines the role of women in the labor movement from the civil war to the present. It discusses the exclusion of women workers from the mainstream organizing efforts and the ways in which women organized themselves. It touches on such issues as women's suffrage, the equal rights amendment, federal protective measures, and reform organizations.

Kreps, Juanita. SEX IN THE MARKETPLACE: AMERICAN WOMEN AT WORK. Baltimore: Johns Hopkins Press, 1971. 117 p.

Written in 1971 by Kreps, who was to become the Secretary of

Commerce under President Carter, this book describes the degree of discrimination in the job market for women in the contemporary scene.

_____, ed. WOMEN AND THE AMERICAN ECONOMY: A LOOK TO THE 1980'S. Englewood Cliffs, N.J.: Prentice-Hall, 1976. 178 p.

Kreps, Secretary of Commerce under Jimmy Carter, presents a collection of essays, primarily by women economists, on the up-coming trends in business and employment for women and the so-cial changes these trends will create and reflect.

Lloyd, Cynthia B. SEX, DISCRIMINATION AND THE DIVISION OF LABOR. Columbia Studies in Economics. New York: Columbia University Press, 1975. xiv, 431 p.

This is a collection of essays. It includes sections on women in the work force, discrimination, the economics of housework and child care, government policies on women, and the economics of women's liberation.

Loeser, Herta. WOMEN, WORK AND VOLUNTEERING. Boston: Beacon Press, 1974. 254 p.

This book views volunteer work in a favorable light and believes housewives and other middle-class women can find fulfillment in unpaid labor.

Lopata, Helena Z. OCCUPATION: HOUSEWIFE. New York: Oxford University Press, 1976. 406 p.

Lopata interviewed eight hundred women in metropolitan Chicago whose principal occupation was housewife. She compares the thinking of these women with those who worked outside the home. She explores trends in the role of housewives as mother, neighbor, and community worker.

Madden, Janice Fanning. THE ECONOMICS OF SEX DISCRIMINATION. Lexington, Mass.: D.C. Heath, 1973. xiii, 140 p.

Written by a faculty member of the Wharton School of Business, this work uses classical economic theory to analyze women's role in the work force. Madden believes sex discrimination to be a complicated issue, and in the end, not altogether an economic one.

Medsger, Betty. WOMEN AT WORK: A PHOTOGRAPHIC DOCUMENTARY. New York: Sheed and Ward, 1975. xii, 212 p.

This book is a collection of photographs of women workers of all kinds--potters, models, operators, dentists, and so on. It includes short statements by some of the subjects.

Myers, Henry. WOMEN AT WORK: HOW THEY'RE RESHAPING AMERICA. Princeton, N.J.: Dow Jones Books, 1979. viii, 236 p.

> This is a series of short descriptions of women, their jobs, and the social changes they represent.

Oakley, Mary Ann. THE SOCIOLOGY OF HOUSEWORK. New York: Pantheon, 1974. 242 p.

> This is a sociological analysis of housework and housewives' attitudes towards their occupations.

_____. WOMAN'S WORK: THE HOUSEWIFE PAST AND PRESENT. New York: Pantheon, 1974. x, 275 p.

> Oakley briefly delineates the history of women as housewives and then presents four case studies of contemporary housewives.

Rainwater, Lee, et al. WORKING MAN'S WIFE: HER PERSONALITY, WORLD, AND LIFESTYLE. New York: Oceana, 1959. 256 p.

> The authors describe the problems of blue-collar women, their poor self-image, their attitude toward men, and their life in general.

Schneiderman, Rose, with Lucy Goldthwaite. ALL FOR ONE. New York: Paul Eriksson, 1967. 264 p.

> This is the story of Schneiderman and her lifelong commitment to the labor movement. She was an organizer of the International Ladies Garment Workers Union and president of the New York Women's Trade Union League.

Seiffer, Nancy. NOBODY SPEAKS FOR ME! SELF PORTRAIT OF AMERICAN WORKING CLASS WOMEN. New York: Simon and Schuster, 1976. 427 p.

> This is the story of ten lives--women who grew up working class and for the most part continue to be working class in the present.

Smuts, Robert W. WOMEN AND WORK IN AMERICA. New York: Columbia University Press, 1959. 180 p.

> Smuts deals with the kind of women who work and the kinds of work women do, their rewards, and the attitudes of both men and women.

Spradley, James P., and Mann, Brenda J. THE COCKTAIL WAITRESS: WOMAN'S WORK IN A MAN'S WORLD. New York: John Wiley and Sons, 1975. 154 p.

> This is a sociological study of bars in the United States and the special role the cocktail waitress plays. It focuses on the relations between customers and the waitresses and the sex roles they reflect.

Tetrault, Jeanne, and Thomas, Sherry. COUNTRY WOMEN: A HANDBOOK FOR THE NEW FARMER. Garden City, N.Y.: Audon Press, 1974. 383 p.

This volume gives women advice about the practicalities of farming.

Warrior, Betsey, and Leghorn, Lisa. HOUSEWORKER'S HANDBOOK. Cambridge, Mass.: Women's Center, 1975. 109 p.

This is a feminist analysis of the conditions of housework.

Wertheimer, Barbara Mayer. WE WERE THERE: THE STORY OF WORKING WOMEN IN AMERICA. New York: Pantheon Books, 1977. xx, 927 p.

The author finds that women from colonial times have worked in nearly every kind of job, usually in the face of opposition by men. Women had to struggle for occupations of choice and for equal pay for doing the job. She describes labor unions for women, culminating with the International Ladies Garment Workers Union.

Willett, Mabel Hurd. THE EMPLOYMENT OF WOMEN IN THE CLOTHING TRADES. New York: Columbia University Press, 1902. Reprint. New York: AMS Press, 1968. 206 p.

The author deals primarily with the New York scene. She emphasizes laws for better health and safety but ignores the tendency for laws to go unenforced.

# Chapter 22

# ETHNIC AND MINORITY WOMEN

Angelou, Maya. I KNOW WHY THE CAGED BIRD SINGS. New York: Random House, 1970. 281 p.

This is an autobiography of a young black woman and her experience with discrimination as a child.

ASIAN WOMEN. Berkeley, Calif.: Asian Women, 1971. 144 p.

This is a book done by Asian-American women students at the University of California at Berkeley on their experiences and history as Asian women.

Bates, Daisy. THE LONG SHADOW OF LITTLE ROCK: A MEMOIR. New York: David McKay Co., 1962. 284 p.

This is an autobiography of a black woman's participation in the civil rights movement of the late 1950s.

Baum, Charlotte, et al. THE JEWISH WOMAN IN AMERICA. New York: New American Library, 1976. 320 p.

The authors deal with the image of Jewish women and their position. Note is taken of the contribution of Jewish women in work, philanthrophy, and radical movements as well as labor organizations.

Bradford, Sarah. HARRIET TUBMAN: THE MOSES OF HER PEOPLE. 1886. Reprint. New York: Corinth Books, 1961. 149 p.

Tubman came to prominence during the Civil War by leading many slaves to freedom.

Brooks, Gwendolyn. REPORT FROM PART ONE. Detroit: Broadside, 1972. 215 p.

This is the autobiography of the contemporary black poet.

Brown, Hallie Quinn. HOMESPUN HEROINES AND OTHER WOMEN OF
DISTINCTION. Xenia, Ohio: Aldine Publishing Co., 1926. viii, 248 p.

> This is a volume of biographical sketches of black women who
> were educational, community, or religious leaders.

Browne, Martha. AUTOBIOGRAPHY OF A FEMALE SLAVE. 1857. Reprint.
Westport, Conn.: Greenwood Press, 1973. 401 p.

> This book describes the hardships of slavery in the antebellum
> South.

Cade, Toni, ed. THE BLACK WOMAN: AN ANTHOLOGY. New York:
New American Library, 1970. 256 p.

> Cade presents the writings of contemporary black women, partly
> in response to the mainstream feminist movement, which she be-
> lieves ignores the experience of black women.

Carson, Josephine. SILENT VOICES: THE SOUTHERN NEGRO WOMAN TO-
DAY. New York: Delacorte, 1969. 293 p.

> Carson interviewed a variety of black southern women on their
> problems and especially their views of the civil rights movement.

Clark, Septima, with LeGette Blythe. ECHO IN MY SOUL. New York:
E.P. Dutton, 1962. 243 p.

> This is the story of Clark's life and work in the South. It espe-
> cially describes her work in education in South Carolina and
> Tennessee during the thirties, forties, and fifties.

Coles, Robert, and Coles, Jane Hallowell. WOMEN OF CRISIS: LIVES OF
STRUGGLE AND HOPE. New York: Delacorte Press, 1978. 291 p.

> The Coleses bring together conversations with women across America--
> a migrant woman, Indian woman, Eskimo woman, and Chicana.

Cooper, Anna Julia. A VOICE FROM THE SOUTH BY A BLACK WOMAN
OF THE SOUTH. Xenia, Ohio: Aldine Printing House, 1892. 304 p.

> Cooper, who lived from 1858 until 1964, was educated at Oberlin
> College and devoted herself to creating educational opportunities
> for black people.

Copin, Fannie Jackson. REMINISCENCES OF SCHOOL LIFE AND HINTS ON
TEACHING. Philadelphia: African Methodist Episcopal Book Concern, 1913.
191 p.

> This is an autobiography of the life and work of a black teacher.

Davis, Angela. AN AUTOBIOGRAPHY. New York: Random House, 1974. x, 400 p.

>This is the story of Davis's life as a radical leader of the black and working-class struggle and what it was like to grow up black in America.

Epstein, Louis M. THE JEWISH MARRIAGE CONTRACT: A STUDY ON THE STATUS OF THE WOMAN IN JEWISH LAW. New York: Jewish Theological Seminary, 1927. Reprint. New York: Arno Press, 1973. 316 p.

>Epstein traces the development of the Jewish marriage contract and its effect on divorce, family life, and women.

Ets, Marie Hall, ROSA: THE LIFE OF AN ITALIAN IMMIGRANT. Minneapolis: University of Minnesota Press, 1970. 234 p.

>This is the story of an Italian-American woman who came to the United States in the 1880s. It details her life in Milan and Chicago and the immigrant experience.

Forten, Charlotte L. THE JOURNAL OF CHARLOTTE L. FORTEN: A FREE NEGRO ON THE SLAVE ERA. Edited by Ray Allen Billington. New York: Dryden Press, 1953. 210 p.

>Billington has edited the journals of Charlotte Forten, an upper-class black woman from Philadelphia who, during the Civil War, went South to teach and help the newly freed slaves.

Gehm, Katherine. SARAH WINNEMUCCA: MOST EXTRAORDINARY WOMAN OF THE PAIUTE NATION. Phoenix: O'Sullivan Woodside, 1975. 196 p.

>This is the biography of a Paiute woman who struggled to better the lives of her tribe in the latter half of the nineteenth century.

Guffy, Ossie. OSSIE: THE AUTOBIOGRAPHY OF A BLACK WOMAN. New York: Norton, 1971. 284 p.

>This is the story of an ordinary poor black woman and her struggle to survive.

Harley, Sharon, and Torborg-Penn, Rosalyn. THE AFRO-AMERICAN WOMAN: STRUGGLES AND IMAGES. Foreword by Dorothy Parker. Port Washington, N.Y.: Kennikat, 1978. xii, 137 p.

>This book consists of essays on the historical position of black women, ranging from their work in the women's movement to their contribution as blues singers. The second part contains essays on three black activists. Dorothy Porter lists libraries that have collections on black women.

Hedgeman, Anna Arnold. THE TRUMPET SOUNDS: A MEMOIR OF NEGRO LEADERSHIP. New York: Holt, Rinehart and Winston, 1964. 202 p.

> Hedgeman was active in black and other civic affairs from the 1920s. She worked with the YMCA and was dean of women at Howard University, Washington, D.C.

Holt, Rackman. MARY McLEOD BETHUNE. New York: Doubleday, 1964. 306 p.

> This is a biography of Bethune, an important black figure of the first half of the twentieth century.

Hunton, Addie W., and Johnson, Kathryn M. TWO COLORED WOMEN WITH THE AMERICAN EXPEDITIONARY FORCES. Brooklyn: Eagle Press, 1920. 260 p.

> This is the story of life with the black regiments overseas in World War I told by two black women who served with them.

Hurston, Zora Neale. DUST TRACKS ON A ROAD: AN AUTOBIOGRAPHY. Philadelphia: J.P. Lippincott, 1942. 294 p.

> This is the autobiography of the black writer; it is well-known and thought to be very well written.

Jacob, Henrick E. THE WORLD OF EMMA LAZARUS. New York: Schocken Books, 1949. 222 p.

> Best known for writing the inscription on the base of the Statue of Liberty, Lazarus was a champion of Jewish immigrants and wrote on Jewish themes.

Jacobs, Harriet Brent. INCIDENTS IN THE LIFE OF A SLAVE GIRL, WRITTEN BY HERSELF. Boston: 1861. 306 p.

> This is a first-person account of the life of a slave woman.

Kahn, Kathy. HILLBILLY WOMEN. New York: Avon Books, 1977. 119 p.

> Kahn has gathered the stories of nineteen women who live in the Appalachian mountains. The women speak for themselves as they tell what it is like to be poor, proud, and hillbilly.

Keckley, Elizabeth. BEHIND THE SCENES: THIRTY YEARS A SLAVE AND FOUR YEARS IN THE WHITE HOUSE. New York: G.W. Carleton, 1868. 371 p.

> This is the story of a slave who lived an atypical life.

King, Coretta. MY LIFE WITH MARTIN LUTHER KING. New York: Holt, Rinehart and Winston, 1969. 372 p.

The wife of the civil rights leader tells the personal story of her marriage to Dr. King and their efforts together in the black cause.

Kingston, Maxine Hong. THE WOMAN WARRIOR: MEMOIRS OF A GIRL-HOOD AMONG GHOSTS. New York: Random House, 1977. 243 p.

This is the autobiographical account of growing up Chinese in the United States around World War II. It is particularly interesting in the way the Chinese symbolism and mythology is described in conflict with dominant culture.

Kohut, Rebekah. MY PORTION: AN AUTOBIOGRAPHY. New York: T. Seltzer, 1925. Reprint. New York: Arno Press, 1975. 301 p.

The author, a founder of the National Council for Jewish Women, was a Jewish activist. She was the daughter of a rabbi. Gohut provides a picture of Jewish life in San Francisco in the last part of the nineteenth century.

Koltun, Elizabeth, ed. THE JEWISH WOMAN: NEW PERSPECTIVES. New York: Schocken, 1976. xx, 289 p.

This is a collection of essays, written primarily by Jewish feminists, which discuss the reconciliation of religion and politics.

Ladner, Joyce A. TOMORROW'S TOMORROW. THE BLACK WOMAN. Garden City, N.Y.: Doubleday, 1971. xxvi, 304 p.

Ladner investigates what it has been like for black females to grow up as themselves in the dominant white society. She uses a sociological and experiential approach.

Landes, Ruth. THE OJIBWA WOMAN. New York: Columbia University Press, 1938. Reprint. New York: Norton, 1971. vi, 247 p.

The author describes the manner in which women were submerged by the role stereotyping of the tribe. She goes into marriage and functions of women.

Lee, Helen Jackson. NIGGER IN THE WINDOW. New York: Doubleday, 1978. 239 p.

This is the autobiography of a black middle-class woman in New Jersey in the early and mid-twentieth century. It describes her struggle for justice and equality as a woman and a black.

Lerner, Gerda, ed. BLACK WOMEN IN WHITE AMERICA: A DOCUMENTARY HISTORY. New York: Vintage Books, 1973. xxxvi, 630 p.

Through contemporary descriptions, Lerner traces the lot of black women from slavery to the protest movements of the 1960s. Included are accounts or statements from notable black women, such as Ida B. Wells, Sojourner Truth, Fannie Barrier Williams, Shirley Chisholm, and Fannie Lou Hamer. Many lesser persons, some anonymous, also tell their story. They describe the combined problems of sexism and racism, their attitudes towards whites and males, including blacks.

Lindborg, Kristina, and Ovarda, Carlos J. FIVE MEXICAN AMERICAN, WOMEN: A CASE STUDY OF MIGRANTS IN THE MIDWEST. San Francisco: R and E Research Associates, 1977. 112 p.

The authors present the story of five Mexican-American women and analyze their lives from a sociological viewpoint. They are especially interested in the impact of the women's movement and the civil rights movement for Mexican-American migrant women.

Moody, Anne. COMING OF AGE IN MISSISSIPPI. New York: Dial Press, 1968. 348 p.

This is the story of a young black woman who grew up with the civil rights movement in the 1960s.

Mossell, N.F. THE WORK OF THE AFRO-AMERICAN WOMAN. Philadelphia: George S. Ferguson Co., 1908. 178 p.

This early twentieth-century volume was done by a black woman civic leader. It discusses black women in literature, journalism, education, and their presence at the World's Fair.

O'Connor, Ellen M., and Miner, Myrtilla. MYRTILLA MINER: A MEMOIR AND THE SCHOOL FOR COLORED GIRLS IN WASHINGTON, D.C. 1885. Reprint. New York: Arno Press, 1969. 129 p.

Against the advice of Frederick Douglass, Myrtilla Miner (1815-1864) established a school for black women in Washington, D.C. Despite odds against her, the school was a success.

Odencrantz, Louise C. ITALIAN WOMEN IN INDUSTRY. New York: Russell Sage Foundation, 1919. Reprint. New York: Arno Press, 1977. 345 p.

The author studied New York slum conditions to find out how Italian peasant women made the transition to industrial ghetto.

O'Meara, Walter. DAUGHTERS OF THE COUNTRY: THE WOMEN OF THE FUR TRADERS AND MOUNTAIN MEN. New York: Harcourt, Brace and World, 1968. 368 p.

The author analyzes the relationships of white men in the West with the native women and finds much exploitation. O'Meara used the writings of the men as sources.

Peare, Catherine O. MARY McLEOD BETHUNE. New York: Vanguard Press, 1951. 219 p.

> Peare has written the story of Bethune's life as educator, civic leader, and presidential advisor.

Reid, Inez Smith. "TOGETHER" BLACK WOMEN. New York: Emerson Hall, 1972. xiii, 383 p.

> Reid examines the political and personal beliefs of the more radical or militant black women in the early 1970s primarily middle-class women. She used questionaires to obtain her information.

Sheehan, Susan. A WELFARE MOTHER. New York: New American Library, 1975. xvi, 144 p.

> This is an in-depth study of a Puerto Rican woman who has been on welfare most of her life. In sympathetic manner, the author traces her life through various marriages, informal relationships, and the birth of four children. It is a story of the welfare system, drugs, and hopelessness for a better life-style.

Smith, Amanda. AN AUTOBIOGRAPHY OF MRS. AMANDA SMITH, THE COLORED EVANGELIST. Chicago: Meyer and Bros., 1893. xvi, 506 p.

> This is the story of the black religious figure as she preached Christianity throughout the world.

Sone, Monica. NISEI DAUGHTER. Boston: Little, Brown and Co., 1953. 238 p.

> This is the story of one woman's experience of growing up as a Japanese American in the mid-twentieth century. Of special interest is Sone's account of life in a relocation camp during World War II.

Staples, Robert. THE BLACK WOMAN IN AMERICA: SEX, MARRIAGE AND THE FAMILY. Chicago: Nelson-Hall, 1973. 269 p.

> This is a sociological study of black women's lives. The author includes sections on sexuality, prostitution, marriage, motherhood, and the women's liberation movement.

Stern, Elizabeth Gertrude. I AM A WOMAN--AND A JEW. New York: J.H. Sears and Co., 1926. Reprint. New York: Arno Press, 1969. 362 p.

> Stern provides an account of a woman caught in the clash of Jewish and American culture.

Sterne, Emma Gelders. MARY McLEOD BETHUNE. New York: Knopf, 1957. 268 p.

This is a biography of Bethune, the leader in black and other civic affairs.

Stewart, Maria. MEDITATIONS FROM THE PEN OF MRS. MARIA W. STEWART, NEGRO. Washington, D.C.: W. Lloyd Garrison and Knap, 1879. iv, 82 p.

This is the autobiography of a black educator.

Sugimoto, Etsu Inagaki. A DAUGHTER OF THE SAMURAI. New York: Doubleday, Page and Co., 1925. xv, 314 p.

This is an autobiographical account of a woman's Japanese origins and her adjustment to life in the United States in the early part of the twentieth century.

Tarry, Ellen. THE THIRD DOOR: THE AUTOBIOGRAPHY OF AN AMERICAN NEGRO WOMAN. New York: David McKay Co., 1955. ix, 304 p.

Ellen Tarry, author and journalist, was born in Alabama in 1906 of a respected black family. She had a light skin that could have enabled her to pass for white. She describes life in white America.

Terrell, John Upton, and Terrell, Donna M. INDIAN WOMEN OF THE WESTERN MORNING: THEIR LIFE IN EARLY AMERICA. New York: Dial, 1974. 214 p.

This book discusses the role of Indian women in the native culture.

Terrell, Mary Church. A COLORED WOMEN IN A WHITE WORLD. Washington, D.C.: Ransdell, 1940. 436 p.

The daughter of a slave, Terrell graduated from Oberlin College and became a teacher and the first black woman to serve on the Board of Education in the District of Columbia. She was active in the women's rights movement.

Udall, Louise. THE LIFE STORY OF HELEN SEKAQUAPTERRA AS TOLD TO LOUISE UDALL. Tuscon: University of Arizona Press, 1969. 262 p.

This is an autobiography of a Hopi woman and how she has come to terms with the white man's culture.

Wallace, Michele. BLACK MACHO AND THE MYTH OF SUPERWOMAN. New York: Dial Press, 1979. 182 p.

Wallace writes of the oppression of black women and the alienation of black women from the white middle-class women's movement. She describes the difficult role in society that black females have had to play.

Waters, Ethel. HIS EYE IS ON THE SPARROW: AN AUTOBIOGRAPHY. New York: Doubleday, 1951. 278 p.

> This is the autobiography of a remarkable black actress.

Watkins, Mel, and David, Jay. TO BE A BLACK WOMAN: PORTRAITS IN FACT AND FICTION. New York: William Morrow, 1971. 285 p.

> This is a collection of pieces on the experience of being black and female, some of them fictional, others biographical.

Wells, Ida B. CRUSADE FOR JUSTICE: THE AUTOBIOGRAPHY OF IDA B. WELLS. Edited by Alfreda Duster. Chicago: University of Chicago Press, 1970. 434 p.

> The daughter of slaves, Ida B. Wells was a journalist and lecturer. Narrowly escaping lynching because of her journalistic activities, she crusaded against lynching which was epidemic during her life time. An ally of W.E.B. DuBois, she rejected the directions of Booker T. Washington. She was a militant activist in a day when it was dangerous to be so. She also supported the suffrage movement.

# Chapter 23

# WOMEN AND CRIME

Adler, Freda. SISTERS IN CRIME: THE RISE OF THE NEW FEMALE CRIMI-NAL. New York: McGraw-Hill, 1975. 287 p.

> Adler examines the increase in crimes by women and hypothesizes that this trend is due to the changing role of women in society.

Brodsky, Annette M., ed. THE FEMALE OFFENDER. Beverly Hills, Calif.: Sage Publications, 1975. 108 p.

> This is a collection of short essays that detail the nature of crimes by women and suggest ways of coping with women criminals.

Burkhart, Kathryn Watterson. WOMEN IN PRISON. Garden City, N.Y.: Doubleday, 1973. 465 p.

> Burkhart interviewed many women inmates and in the book presents excerpts from their discussions.

Chandler, Edna Walker. WOMEN IN PRISON. Indianapolis, Ind.: Bobbs-Merrill, 1973. xiv, 144 p.

> Chandler portrays the experience of prison life for women, from entering the gate to getting parole and leaving prison.

Colebrook, Joan. THE CROSS OF LATITUDE: PORTRAITS OF FIVE DELIN-QUENTS. New York: Knopf, 1967. 340 p.

> This book describes the life of five young female delinquents, products of poverty and ghetto life.

DeRham, Edith. HOW COULD SHE DO THAT? A STUDY OF THE FEMALE CRIMINAL. New York: Clarkson N. Potter, 1969. 340 p.

> DeRham examines the lives of women who have committed serious crimes.

Giallombardo, Rose. SOCIETY OF WOMEN: A STUDY OF A WOMEN'S PRISON. New York: John Wiley and Sons, 1966. ix, 244 p.

This is the sociological analysis done in the early sixties of one particular women's prison.

Glueck, Sheldon, and Glueck, Eleanor T. FIVE HUNDRED DELINQUENT WOMEN. New York: Alfred A. Knopf, 1934. Reprint. New York: Kraus Reprint Corp., 1965. xxiv, 537 p.

This sociological study describes women by case study, deals with nativity, family, mental characteristics, their childhood, sex life, marital history, conflicts with the law, and incarceration. They deal also with their problems upon expiration of sentence and the effects of prison life.

Hanson, Kitty. REBELS IN THE STREET: THE STORY OF NEW YORK'S GIRL GANGS. Englewood Cliffs, N.J.: Prentice-Hall, 1964. 183 p.

This book describes life in a New York City girls' street gang. It is written by a social worker.

Harris, Mary B. I KNEW THEM IN PRISON. New York: Viking Press, 1936. x, 407 p.

The author describes her twenty years experience as a women's prison administrator and reformer from 1914 to 1934.

Harrison, Sara. HELLHOLE. New York: E.P. Dutton, 1967. 288 p.

This is an investigation of a women's prison in New York City.

Lampman, Henry P. THE WIRE WOMB: LIFE IN A GIRLS' PENAL INSTITU-TION. Chicago: Nelson-Hall, 1973. 181 p.

This is the story of a girls delinquent home in New Mexico, writ-ten by a staff psychologist.

Monahan, Florence. WOMEN IN CRIME. New York: Iver Washburn, 1941. xiii, 306 p.

This is an analysis of women criminals and prison by a woman active in prison administration. Monahan believes "glandular injec-tions" will solve much of the problem of women in crime.

Pollak, Otto. THE CRIMINALITY OF WOMEN. New York: A.S. Barnes and Co., 1950. xiii, 180 p.

Pollak surveys the statistics on women in crime and concludes that women are just as susceptible to a life of crime as men.

Simon, Rita James. WOMEN AND CRIME. Lexington, Mass., D.C. Heath, 1975. xvi, 126 p.

> Simon examines the extent and nature of women's involvement with crime in contemporary America. She looks at the literature on the subject and describes what crimes women commit, what treatment women receive as criminals, and how they are viewed by officials of the criminal justice system.

U.S. Department of Justice. Law Enforcement Assistance Administration. THE REPORT OF THE LEAA TASK FORCE ON WOMEN. Washington, D.C.: Government Printing Office, 1975. xiii, 55 p.

> The task force examined women in the criminal justice system and women who work in the LEAA and made recommendations for equality.

Ward, David A., and Kassebaum, Gene G. WOMEN'S PRISON--SEX AND SOCIAL STRUCTURE. Chicago: Aldine, 1965. xi, 269 p.

> The authors look at homosexual activity in women's prisons.

# Chapter 24

# VIOLENCE AGAINST WOMEN

Amir, Menachem. PATTERNS OF FORCIBLE RAPE. Chicago: University of Chicago Press, 1971. 394 p.

> This is a scholarly investigation of the background and behavior of rapists and their victims.

Brownmiller, Susan. AGAINST OUR WILL: MEN, WOMEN AND RAPE. New York: Barton Books, 1975. 541 p.

> Brownmiller analyzes rape as a power issue reflecting the different status of men and women in society and through history.

Burgess, Ann Wolbert, and Holmstrom, Lynda Lytle. RAPE: VICTIMS OF CRISES. Bowie, Md.: Robert J. Brody, 1974. 308 p.

> This book presents the story of one rape crisis intervention program started in Boston in 1972.

Chapman, Jane Roberts, and Gates, Margaret, eds. THE VICTIMIZATION OF WOMEN. Beverly Hills, Calif.: Sage Publications, 1978. 282 p.

> This volume looks at the violence against women--rape, battering, prostitution, and sexual harassment--and how women are conditioned to accept their treatment.

Connell, Noreen, and Willson, Cassandra. RAPE: THE FIRST SOURCEBOOK FOR WOMEN. New York: New American Library, 1974. 283 p.

> Written by New York radical feminists, it discusses every aspect of rape, including the legal facts and the personal experience.

Davidson, Terry. CONJUGAL CRIME: UNDERSTANDING AND CHANGING THE WIFE BEATING PATTERN. New York: Hawthorn Books, 1978. 274 p.

> This book examines the nature and extent of woman battering and the social forces that support this violence.

Goldberg, Jacob A., and Goldberg, Rosamond W. GIRLS ON CITY STREETS: A STUDY OF 1400 CASES OF RAPE. New York: American Social Hygiene Association, 1935. Reprint. New York: Arno Press, 1974. 358 p.

> This volume is based on rape in New York. It is a study conducted by the American Social Hygiene Association. Their goal was to demonstrate that mental health is a function of social injustice.

Horos, Carol. RAPE. New Canaan, Conn.: Tobey, 1974. 130 p.

> The author discusses who rapists are and how they commit their crimes. Horos gives practical advice to women on how to avoid rape.

Langley, Roger, and Levy, Richard C. WIFE BEATING: THE SILENT CRISIS. New York: E.P. Dutton, 1977. xi, 242 p.

> The authors recognize woman battering as a problem in all socio-economic groups. They discuss the phenomenon through case stories of women who have been beaten.

Lynch, W. Ware. RAPE! ONE VICTIM'S STORY. Chicago: Follett Publishing Co., 1974. 230 p.

> Lynch, in popular fashion, describes the experiences of a rape victim.

MacKinnon, Catharine A. SEXUAL HARASSMENT OF WORKING WOMEN. New Haven, Conn.: Yale University Press, 1979. xiv, 312 p.

> MacKinnon exposes the control of women at work through sexual harassment and threat by their male superiors. The author views sexual harassment of women as a pervasive social problem. MacKinnon develops an argument that even a look may be discrimination and therefore illegal.

Medea, Andra, and Thompson, Kathleen. AGAINST RAPE: A SURVIVAL MANUAL FOR WOMEN. New York: Farrar, Straus and Giroux, 1974. 154 p.

> The authors, through contact with the victims of rape, researched the experience of rape and how to cope with it.

Pekkanen, John. VICTIMS: AN ACCOUNT OF A RAPE. New York: Dial Press, 1976. viii, 287 p.

> This is a journalistic style investigation of rape. It focuses particularly on the role of the judicial system and what happens to rapists and their victims in the criminal justice machinery.

Roy, Maria, ed. BATTERED WOMEN: A PSYCHOSOCIOLOGICAL STUDY OF DOMESTIC VIOLENCE. New York: Van Nostrand Reinhold Co., 1977. xviii, 334 p.

Roy has collected a group of essays on the history of woman battering and the sociological, psychological, and legal factors of
the problem.

Russell, Diana E.H.  THE POLITICS OF RAPE:  THE VICTIM'S PERSPECTIVE.
New York:  Stein and Day, 1975.  311 p.

Russell addresses the issue of rape on several fronts--the victim,
the rapist, the issue of rape and the social and political forces
involved.

Sanford, Linda Tshirhart, and Fetter, Ann.  IN DEFENSE OF OURSELVES:  A
RAPE PREVENTION HANDBOOK FOR WOMEN.  Garden City, N.Y.: Doubleday, 1979.  xiii, 177 p.

With a feminist perspective, this book describes techniques of
self-defense for women.

Storaska, Frederic.  HOW TO SAY NO TO A RAPIST AND SURVIVE.  New
York:  Warner Books, 1975.  223 p.

This is a practical how-to book for women on how to avoid or
prevent the violence of rape.

Walker, Leonore E.  THE BATTERED WOMAN.  New York:  Harper and Row,
1979.  xviii, 270 p.

This book is done by a psychologist who views woman battering
as a sociological, psychological, and political issue.

# Chapter 25

# PROSTITUTION

Addams, Jane. A NEW CONSCIENCE AND AN ANCIENT EVIL. New York: Macmillan, 1912. Reprint. New York: Arno Press, 1972. xi, 219 p.

Addams represents the view of the Progressive era about prostitution.

Adler, Polly. A HOUSE IS NOT A HOME. New York: Rinehart and Co., 1953. 374 p.

Polly Adler was a famous keeper of a house of prostitution and associate of a variety of thugs as well as some upper-class clients. She wrote, "what I saw may shock or disgust some readers, but it was there to be seen, and it belongs on the record."

Alciem, Rachel. WASHINGTON CALL GIRL. New York: Zebra Books, 1975.

This book is the confession of a purported call girl. Its factual worth is debatable.

Bellocq, E.J. STORYVILLE PORTRAITS: PHOTOGRAPHS FROM THE NEW ORLEANS RED LIGHT DISTRICT, CIRCA, 1912. New York: Museum of Modern Art, 1970. 50 p.

Bellocq was a commercial photographer who worked in New Orleans before and after World War I. The text describes Bellocq and his work. There are thirty-three plates of photographic portraits that he did of prostitutes in New Orleans.

Brooks, Virginia. MY BATTLES WITH VICE. New York: Macaulay, 1915. 248 p.

This book deals with vice in Chicago, as viewed by a social worker.

Bullough, Vern L. THE HISTORY OF PROSTITUTION. New Hyde Park, N.Y.: University Books, 1964. 304 p.

Bullough surveys prostitution from primitive civilization to the present.

# Prostitution

Chicago. Vice Commission. THE SOCIAL EVIL IN CHICAGO: A STUDY
OF EXISTING CONDITIONS WITH RECOMMENDATIONS BY THE VICE COM-
MISSION OF CHICAGO. Chicago: Gunthorpe-Warren Printing Co., 1911.
Reprint. New York: Arno Press, 1970. 399 p.

> One of the major concerns of the Progressive era was prostitution.
> This is one of the many studies made by commissions made up of
> prominent citizens.

Gentry, Curt. THE MADAMS OF SAN FRANCISCO: AN IRREVERENT HIS-
TORY OF THE CITY BY THE GOLDEN GATE. Garden City, N.Y.: Doubleday, 1964. xii, 323 p.

> This is a popular account describing many of the madams, white
> and Asian, and their houses.

Goldman, Emma. THE TRAFFIC IN WOMEN AND OTHER ESSAYS ON FEMI-
NISM. New York: Mother Earth Publishing Co., 1917. Reprint. New York:
Times Change Press, 1970. 63 p.

> The anarchist writer gives the radical view of prostitution.

Hall, Susan. GENTLEMAN OF LEISURE: A YEAR IN THE LIFE OF A PIMP.
New York: New American Library, 1972. 213 p.

> The author by tape recorder and photograph, describes the life of
> a pimp and the bond between him and his prostitutes. From this
> comes a description of how the pimp uses the women and their
> rationalization for staying with him.

THE HISTORY OF PROSTITUTION: ITS EXTENT, CAUSES AND EFFECTS
THROUGHOUT THE WORLD. BEING AN OFFICIAL REPORT TO THE BOARD
OF ALMS-HOUSE GOVERNORS OF THE CITY OF NEW YORK. 1859. Re-
print. New York: Arno Press, 1972. 708 p.

> This report was based on interviews with two thousand women who
> responded to the question, "What was the cause of your becoming
> a prostitute?" The report was concerned with community safety,
> disease, and crime. They noted the futility of punishment.

Hollander, Xaviera. THE HAPPY HOOKER. New York: Dell, 1972. 311 p.

> These are the memoirs of a prostitute and madam which became a
> best seller.

Kneeland, George J. COMMERCIALIZED PROSTITUTION IN NEW YORK.
New York: Century Co., 1913. vii, 334 p.

> Kneeland's book is important in that it deals with the causation of
> prostitution as viewed by society in the Progressive era.

Lubove, Roy. "The Progressive and the Prostitute." THE HISTORIAN 24 (1962): 308-30.

> Lubove describes the attitude of progressive leaders toward prostitution. Generally they believed poverty was the cause. There was a considerable movement to limit prostitution as one of the reforms of the era.

Millett, Kate. THE PROSTITUTION PAPERS: "A QUARTET FOR FEMALE VOICE." New York: Ballantine Books, 1971. 149 p.

> Millett provides a radical feminist view of prostitution based on essays with four prostitutes.

Minneapolis. Vice Commission. THE PROSTITUTE AND THE SOCIAL REFORMER: COMMERCIAL VICE IN THE PROGRESSIVE ERA. Minneapolis: H.M. Hall, 1911. Reprint. New York: Arno Press, 1974. 164 p.

> This is the report of the Vice Commission of Minneapolis. The report describes prostitution in Minneapolis, the results of segregation, the incidence of venereal disease, and reports a survey of prostitutes on the reasons why they entered the oldest profession.

Pivar, David. PURITY CRUSADE: SEXUAL MORALITY, AND SOCIAL CONTROL, 1868-1900. Westport, Conn.: Greenwood Press, 1973. x, 308 p.

> The author describes the problem of prostitution and organizations such as the Society for the Promotion of Social Purity which sought to remedy the problem.

Reitman, Ben L. THE SECOND OLDEST PROFESSION; A STUDY OF THE PROSTITUTE'S "BUSINESS MANAGER." New York: Vanguard, 1931. xx, 266 p.

> Reitman describes the life-style of the pimp and his treatment of women.

Riegel, Robert E. "Changing American Attitudes Toward Prostitution." JOURNAL OF THE HISTORY OF IDEAS 29 (1968): 437-52.

> Riegel traces the attitudes of the United States toward prostitution in the Victorian era. He notes that most people were aware of prostitution of all varieties. He notes the arguments for and against the institution and relates them to nineteenth-century male attitudes toward women.

Sanger, William W. THE HISTORY OF PROSTITUTION. 1858. Reprint. New York: Eugenics Publishing, 1937. 708 p.

> In a survey in a women's prison, Sanger found that relatively few prostitutes listed seduction or economic motivation as the reason for their becoming prostitutes. He found that more commonly they

reported that they liked the life, an interesting number indicating
that the sexuality of women was more developed than Victorians
liked to admit.

Sheehy, Gail. HUSTLING: PROSTITUTION IN OUR WIDE-OPEN SOCIETY.
New York: Delacorte, 1971. xi, 273 p.

This book although badly written and designed to sell, contains
some information about prostitutes and pimps.

Stanford, Sally. THE LADY OF THE HOUSE: THE AUTOBIOGRAPHY OF
SALLY STANFORD. New York: Putnams, 1966. 255 p.

Stanford was a famous madam in the San Francisco area.

Vogliotti, Gabriel. THE GIRLS OF NEVADA. Secaucus, N.J.: Citadel
Press, 1975. 264 p.

This is the story of prostitution in a state noted for leniency toward vice.

Warren, John H., Jr. THIRTY YEARS BATTLE WITH CRIME, OR THE CRYING
SHAME OF NEW YORK, AS SEEN UNDER THE BROAD GLARE OF AN OLD
DETECTIVE'S LANTERN. 1875. Reprint. New York: Arno Press, 1970. xii,
400 p.

Nearly half of the book is devoted to prostitution in New York.
The description is Victorian.

Washburn, Charles. COME INTO MY PARLOR: A BIOGRAPHY OF THE
ARISTOCRATIC EVERLEIGH SISTERS OF CHICAGO. New York: National
Library Press, 1936. Reprint. New York: Arno Press, 1974. 225 p.

Minna and Ada Everleigh ran an elegant house of prostitution for
many years in turn-of-the-century Chicago. Their clientele repre-
sented the Chicago elite. They later moved to New York, entered
genteel marriages, and a life of philanthropy.

Winick, Charles, and Kinsie, Paul M. THE LIVELY COMMERCE: PROSTITU-
TION IN THE UNITED STATES. Chicago: Quadrangle Books, 1971. ix,
320 p.

This well-documented book presents prostitution as it existed over
the previous fifty years. The authors deal with prostitution,
madams and pimps, their methods of operation, clients, and laws concerning the traffic.

Woolston, Howard B. PROSTITUTION IN THE UNITED STATES. New York:
Century Co., 1921. Reprint. New York: Patterson Smith, 1969. 360 p.

This sociological study was the result of interviews with many
people in ten cities in the United States.

# Chapter 26

# THE PSYCHOLOGY OF WOMEN

Adams, Carole, and Kietis, Rae Laura. THE GENDER TRAP. 3 vols. London: Virago Press, 1976.

> These books were reedited for the American edition. Each deals with a specific aspect of sex role stereotyping--education and work sex and marriage, and messages and images.

Bardon, Edward J. THE SEXUAL ARENA AND WOMEN'S LIBERATION. Chicago: Nelson-Hall, 1978. viii, 249 p.

> Bardon is a psychiatrist on a college campus and has written a book describing the impact of feminism upon the sexual choices of young people.

Bardwick, Judith. PSYCHOLOGY OF WOMEN: A STUDY OF BIO-CULTURAL CONFLICTS. New York: Harper and Row, 1971. vii, 242 p.

> Bardwick articulates a new theory of the psychology of women. She particularly addresses the question of self-esteem.

_____, ed. READINGS ON THE PSYCHOLOGY OF WOMEN. New York: Harper and Row, 1972. xiii, 335 p.

> Bardwick has collected a set of academic writings on many aspects of the psychology of women.

_____, et al. FEMININE PERSONALITY AND CONFLICT. Belmont, Calif.: Brooks-Cole Publishing, 1970. 203 p.

> This book contains four scholarly essays on dimensions of the psychology of women.

Belotti, Eleva Gianni. WHAT LITTLE GIRLS ARE MADE OF: THE ROOTS OF FEMININE STEREOTYPE. New York: Schocken Books, 1967. 150 p.

> This is a popular account of the sex-role socialization process.

Bloom, Lynn Z., et al. THE NEW ASSERTIVE WOMAN. New York: Delacorte Press, 1975. 230 p.

> The authors lay out the assumptions of assertiveness training and how women can use it.

Blum, Harold P., ed. FEMALE PSYCHOLOGY: CONTEMPORARY PSYCHO-ANALYTIC VIEWS. New York: International Universities Press, 1977. 454 p.

> Blum has assembled a group of essays by current psychoanalytic thinkers on the psychology of women. Some represent revisions of Freud, but for the most part, these essays are classically Freudian.

Chesler, Phyllis. WOMEN AND MADNESS. New York: Doubleday, 1972. xxiii, 359 p.

> Chesler's classic book on women and psychiatry explores the way in which traditional therapy is harmful to women. Chesler also challenges the conventional definition of madness.

Cox, Sue, ed. FEMALE PSYCHOLOGY: THE EMERGING SELF. Chicago: Science Research Associates, 1976. x, 438 p.

> This is a textbook anthology that includes chapters on biological, cultural, and psychological issues and theories of oppression, psychotherapy, liberation, and ethnic diversity.

Franks, Violet, and Burtle, Viola, eds. WOMEN IN THERAPY: NEW PERSPECTIVE FOR A CHANGING SOCIETY. New York: Bruner-Mazel, 1974. 441 p.

> The authors dispute the Freudian concept that women are incomplete or derivative males. It is said that the woman trades freedom for security. The authors deal with cultural influences and therapy.

Hammer, Signe. DAUGHTERS & MOTHERS: MOTHERS & DAUGHTERS. New York: Time Books, 1975. Reprint. New York: Signet Books, 1976. 192 p.

> This is a psychological study of the relationships of mothers and daughters.

Horney, Karen. FEMININE PSYCHOLOGY. New York: W.W. Norton and Co., 1967. 269 p.

> Horney is the classic thinker within the psychoanalytic school who challenges Freud's model of women's nature.

Klein, Viola. THE FEMININE CHARACTER. New York: International Universities Press, 1949. 228 p.

> Klein traces the development of the idea of feminine character and shows how the fields of biology, psychology, and sociology have helped to form the concept and perpetuate it.

Lee, Patrick C., and Stewart, Robert Sussman, eds. SEX DIFFERENCES: CULTURAL AND DEVELOPMENTAL DIMENSIONS. New York: Urizen Books, 1976. 478 p.

> This volume is a group of writings on sex differences from a variety of perspectives--psychoanalytic, anthropologic, and psychological.

Maccoby, Eleanor, and Jacklin, Carol Nagy. THE PSYCHOLOGY OF SEX DIFFERENCES. Stanford, Calif.: Stanford University Press, 1974. xiii, 634 p.

> Maccoby and Jacklin extensively survey the current research on sex differences.

Mander, Anica Vesel, and Rush, Anne Kent. FEMINISM AS THERAPY. New York: Random House, 1975. 129 p.

> This is an important statement by pioneers of the women's group as personal change thinkers. It attempts to deprofessionalize therapy and to show women that a political understanding and peer support can bring about personal change.

Miller, Jean Baker. TOWARD A NEW PSYCHOLOGY OF WOMEN. Boston: Beacon Press, 1976. xi, 143 p.

> Miller's book is the primary definition of the emerging psychology of women.

_____, ed. PSYCHOANALYSIS AND WOMEN. Baltimore: Penguin Books, 1973. 415 p.

> This book is composed of sixteen essays by analysts. The authors concede that analysts have usually tried to help women adjust to their roles as wives and mothers without regard to self-fulfillment. Generally, they assume the fault lies with Freud and the implication that women see themselves as lesser persons.

Mitchell, Juliet. PSYCHOANALYSIS AND FEMINISM. New York: Pantheon Books, 1974. 456 p.

> Mitchell analyzes Freud, Deutsch, and Laing in a feminist context. She believes Freud cannot be dismissed, as his work well describes the condition of women under patriarchy. She does not believe Freud should be taken normatively, however.

Osborn, Susan M., and Harris, Gloria G. ASSERTIVENESS TRAINING FOR WOMEN. Springfield, Ill.: Charles C Thomas, 1975. ix, 204 p.

> This is a academic discussion on the theory and process of the popular assertiveness training movement.

Phelps, Stanlee, and Austin, Nancy. THE ASSERTIVE WOMAN. San Luis Obispo, Calif.: Impact, 1975. 177 p.

>The authors submit that the assertive life is better than a passive or aggressive life.

Sherman, Julia. ON THE PSYCHOLOGY OF WOMEN: A SURVEY OF EM-PIRICAL STUDIES. Springfield, Ill.: Charles C Thomas, 1971. 304 p.

>Sherman believes the reproductive cycle is connected to the psychology of women, but includes environmental factors as well.

Strouse, Jean, ed. WOMEN AND ANALYSIS: DIALOGUES ON PSYCHO-ANALYTIC VIEWS OF FEMININITY. New York: Grossman Publishers, 1974. viii, 375 p.

>This is a group of writings by well-known members of the psychoanalytic movement on women's issues. The Freudian articles are each followed by an essay with critical or dissenting viewpoints.

Tauvis, Carol, and Offir, Carole. THE LONGEST WAR: SEX DIFFERENCES IN PERSPECTIVE. New York: Harcourt Brace Jovanovich, 1977. 333 p.

>This surveys the sociological and psychological research on sex role socialization. The authors have a moderate feminist perspective.

Ulanov, Ann Belford. THE FEMININE: IN JUNGIAN PSYCHOLOGY AND CHRISTIAN THEOLOGY. Evanston, Ill.: Northwestern University Press, 1971. 347 p.

>The author believes the suppression of the feminine has been detrimental to western thought.

Unger, Rhoda Kesler, and Denmark, Florence L., eds. WOMAN: DEPENDENT OR INDEPENDENT VARIABLE. New York: Psychological Dimensions, 1975. 828 p.

>This work, which aims to define the new psychology of women, is a collection of research pieces on all aspects of women's psychology.

Weissman, Myrna M., and Paykel, Eugene S. THE DEPRESSED WOMAN: A STUDY OF SOCIAL RELATIONSHIPS. Chicago: University of Chicago Press, 1974. xx, 269 p.

>This is a scholarly investigation of the causes and treatment of depressed females. The authors suggest wide social change as the ultimate cure.

Williams, Elizabeth Friar. NOTES OF A FEMINIST THERAPIST. New York: Dell Books, 1976. 219 p.

> Williams explains what a feminist therapist is and how she works. She addresses all the conventional elements of therapy and shows how the feminist approach differs.

Williams, Juanita H. PSYCHOLOGY OF WOMEN: BEHAVIOR IN A BIO-SOCIAL CONTEXT. New York: W.W. Norton and Co., 1977. xv, 444 p.

> This book is a basic text for the psychology of women.

# Chapter 27

## SEXUALITY AND SEXUAL ORIENTATION

Abbott, Sidney, and Love, Barbara. SAPPHO WAS A RIGHT-ON WOMAN: A LIBERATED VIEW OF LESBIANISM. New York: Stein and Day, 1972. 251 p.

> This book is by two lesbian activists who discuss the historic oppression of gay women and the achievements of the growing gay movement.

Baker, Robert, and Elliston, Frederick. PHILOSOPHY AND SEX. Buffalo, N.Y.: Prometheus Books, 1975. x, 397 p.

> This is a series of philosophical statements on various aspects of sexuality--like the semantics of sex, adultery, and abortion. No one single position is represented.

Banes, Sally; Frank, Sheldon; and Horwitz, Tom. OUR NATIONAL PASSION: 200 YEARS OF SEX IN AMERICA. Chicago, Ill.: Follett Publishing Co., 1976. 230 p.

> This is an illustrated journalistic history of sexual attitudes in the United States.

Barbach, Lonnie Garfield. FOR YOURSELF: THE FULFILLMENT OF FEMALE SEXUALITY. New York: Signet Books, 1975. 191 p.

> The author is a psychologist and therapist at the human sexuality program at the University of California.

Bell, Alan P., and Weinberg, Martin S. HOMOSEXUALITIES: A STUDY OF DIVERSITY AMONG MEN AND WOMEN. New York: Simon and Schuster, 1978. 505 p.

> This is the continuation of Kinsey's work which surveys most aspects of gay life, including their sex lives, their religious and political beliefs, and their psychological health. For each area, the results are reported separately for men and women.

Benges, Ingrid. COMBAT IN THE EROGENOUS ZONE. New York: Knopf, 1973. 260 p.

This is the story of one woman's struggle with her sexuality and anger with men.

Brecher, Ruth, and Brecher, Edward. AN ANALYSIS OF HUMAN SEXUAL RESPONSE. Boston: Little, Brown and Co., 1966. 318 p.

The authors provide a popularization of William H. Masters and Virginia Johnson's HUMAN SEXUAL RESPONSE (Boston: Little Brown, 1966). They bring the medical terminology into line with the understanding of the layman.

Bry, Adelaide. THE SEXUALLY AGGRESSIVE WOMAN. New York: Signet Books, 1974. 224 p.

The author presents twenty sexually active women who discuss their amorous adventures. They range in age from eighteen to fifty-five; they are single, married, and divorced. They describe their approach and where they meet men.

Bryant, Anita. THE ANITA BRYANT STORY: THE SURVIVAL OF OUR NATION'S FAMILIES AND THE THREAT OF MILITANT HOMOSEXUALITY. Old Tappan, N.J.: Fleming H. Revell, 1977. 156 p.

Bryant, the leader of the antigay movement, tells the story of her campaign to crush gay rights.

Calderone, Mary S., ed. SEXUALITY AND HUMAN VALUES. New York: Association Press, 1974. 158 p.

This is a report of the Sex Information and Education Council of the United States (SIECUS) conference on religion and sexuality held in 1971.

Casal, Mary. THE STONE WALL: AN AUTOBIOGRAPHY. Chicago: Eyncourt Press, 1930. Reprint. New York: Arno Press, 1976. 227 p.

This is the remarkable account of a lesbian born in rural New England in 1864.

Cassiday, Jules, and Park, Angela Stewart, eds. WE'RE HERE: CONVERSATIONS WITH LESBIAN WOMEN. New York: Quartet Books, 1977. 152 p.

This is a verbatim presentation of discussions the editors had with lesbians about their lives and sexual desires.

Crew, Louie, ed. THE GAY ACADEMIC. Palm Springs, Calif.: ETC Publications, 1978. xix, 444 p.

This is a group of essays written by scholars in several academic disciplines discussing being gay.

Davis, Katharine Bement. FACTORS IN THE SEX LIFE OF TWENTY-TWO HUNDRED WOMEN. New York: Harper and Bros., 1929. Reprint. New York: Arno Press, 1972. 430 p.

This is a Freudian analysis of the sex habits of American women.

Ditzion, Sidney. MARRIAGE, MORALS AND SEX IN AMERICA: A HISTORY OF IDEAS. New York: W.W. Norton and Co., 1969. 460 p.

Ditzion finds an interaction of many social reform movements with those concerning sexual reform. He further finds that these reform movements are inextricably bound up with the feminist cause. This book should rank as the standard work on the subject. Ditzion traces these ideas from colonial times to the 1970s.

Francoeur, Robert T., and Francoeur, Anna K., eds. THE FUTURE OF SEXUAL RELATIONS. Englewood Cliffs, N.J.: Prentice-Hall, 1974. 150 p.

This is a collection of essays on sexuality and changing society by such noted authors as Marshall McLuhan and Carolyn Heilbrun.

Frederics, Diana. DIANA: A STRANGE AUTOBIOGRAPHY. New York: Dial Press, 1939. Reprint. New York: Arno Press, 1975. 284 p.

This is the autobiography of a lesbian who long sought to hide and deny her sexual preference. She attempted a marriage with a male but eventually entered into a relationship with a woman.

Friday, Nancy. FORBIDDEN FLOWERS: MORE WOMEN'S SEXUAL FANTA-SIES. New York: Pocket Books, 1975. 323 p.

This is a second collection of sexual fantasies as reported in a survey done by the author.

_____. MY SECRET GARDEN: WOMEN'S SEXUAL FANTASIES. New York: Pocket Books, 1974. 336 p.

This is a collection of women's fantasies about sex as reported in a survey done by the author.

Gittelson, Natalie. THE EROTIC LIFE OF THE AMERICAN WIFE. New York: Delacorte Press, 1972. xv, 380 p.

Thie is an account of one journalist's interviews with women across the United States on their views of love, sex, and relationships with men.

Hammond, William A. SEXUAL IMPOTENCE IN THE MALE AND FEMALE. 1887. Reprint. New York: Arno Press, 1974. 305 p.

Written by an early day psychiatrist, this work attacks a problem little discussed in the nineteenth century.

Hite, Shere. THE HITE REPORT. New York: Macmillan, 1976. xi, 438 p.

This is a popular survey on women's sexual response. Its release in 1976 gave it wide media attention. It focused particularly on women's orgasm.

Jay, Karla, and Young, Allen. OUT OF THE CLOSETS: VOICES OF GAY LIBERATION. New York: Douglas Books, 1972. 403 p.

This is one of the first publications of the gay rights movement. Most chapters are related to issues facing gay men and women; one is specifically devoted to lesbians and the women's liberation movement.

Johnston, Jill. LESBIAN NATION: THE FEMINIST SOLUTION. New York: Simon and Schuster, 1973. 279 p.

This is one of the first major works of the contemporary gay feminist movement. Johnston uses mythology, scholarship, personal experience, and political reality to indicate the need for a separate existence for women.

Katz, Jonathan. GAY AMERICAN HISTORY: LESBIANS AND GAY MEN IN THE U.S.A. New York: Thomas Y. Crowell, 1976. xiv, 690 p.

This is an extensive survey of the accomplishments of gay people, changing attitudes towards homosexuality, and the oppression experienced by women and men homosexuals in American history from 1966 to 1976.

Kinsey, Alfred Charles, et al. SEXUAL BEHAVIOR IN THE HUMAN FEMALE. Philadelphia: W.B. Saunders, 1953. xxx, 842 p.

This is a survey of sexual habits and sexuality in the female of the United States in the 1940s. Using the interview technique, Kinsey and his associates questioned eight thousand females on every conceivable sexual aspect of their lives.

_____. SEXUAL BEHAVIOR IN THE HUMAN MALE. Philadelphia: W.B. Saunders, 1948. xv, 804 p.

This is a pioneer survey of sexual habits and sexuality of the male in the United States by staff members of Indiana University. Using the interview technique, they interviewed some twelve thousand males on every aspect of sexual behavior as it existed in the period immediately after World War II.

Klaich, Dolores. WOMAN PLUS WOMAN: ATTITUDES TOWARD LESBIANISM. New York: Simon and Schuster, 1974. 287 p.

This book looks at general issues surrounding lesbianism and how gay women have been viewed in history.

Kline-Graber, Georgia, and Graber, Benjamin. WOMAN'S ORGASM: A GUIDE TO SEXUAL SATISFACTION. Indianapolis, Ind.: Bobbs-Merrill, 1975. ix, 184 p.

> This is an advice book written by sex therapists on how women may achieve greater sexual pleasure.

Kronhausen, Phyllis, and Kronhausen, Eberhard. THE SEXUALLY RESPONSIVE WOMAN. New York: Grove, 1964. 255 p.

> This book is a set of four interviews with women from varying backgrounds about their sexuality.

McLuhan, H. Marshall. THE MECHANICAL BRIDE. Boston: Beacon Press, 1951. 157 p.

> McLuhan shows how advertising and the media manipulate consumers by playing on their sexual fears.

Martin, Del, and Lyon, Phyllis. LESBIAN/WOMAN. San Francisco: Glide Publications, 1972. 283 p.

> This is a book written by participants in the lesbian liberation movement. It deals with such topics as lesbian mothers, growing up gay, self-image, and the liberation of gay women.

Masters, William H., and Johnson, Virginia. HUMAN SEXUAL RESPONSE. Boston: Little, Brown and Co., 1966. xiii, 366 p.

> This pioneer work attempted by clinical means to determine the physiological as well as psychological nature of human sexuality and response. Among other things they clinically disprove the concept of vaginal orgasm.

_____. THE PLEASURE BOND: A NEW LOOK AT SEXUALITY AND COM- MITTMENT. Boston: Little, Brown and Co., 1974. xiii, 268 p.

> Masters and Johnson explore the meaning of sex in marriage.

Money, John, ed. SEX RESEARCH: NEW DEVELOPMENTS. New York: Holt, Rinehart and Winston, 1965. xii, 260 p.

> Money believes that culture, not biology, is the determining factor in sex-role identity.

Morris, Jan. CONUNDRUM. New York: Signet Books, 1977. 208 p.

> Morris describes the problem of transsexualism from personal ex- perience. Shocking to many, transsexualism came into public focus in the last half of the twentieth century.

Myron, Nancy, and Bunch, Charlotte, eds. LESBIANISM AND THE WOMEN'S MOVEMENT. Baltimore: Diana Press, 1975. 104 p.

This is a collection of articles originally published in THE FURIES, a Washington, D.C., feminist newspaper. The articles discuss the lesbian political movement.

Nagera, Humberto. FEMALE SEXUALITY AND THE OEDIPUS COMPLEX. New York: Jason Bronson, 1975. 143 p.

This is a Freudian view of women's sexuality.

Packard, Vance. THE SEXUAL WILDERNESS: THE CONTEMPORARY UP-HEAVAL IN MALE-FEMALE RELATIONSHIPS. New York: David McKay Co., 1968. 553 p.

This is a popular discussion of changing sexual values in America based on surveys taken in the late 1960s.

Pomeroy, Wardell B. GIRLS AND SEX. New York: Delacorte, 1969. 139 p.

Pomeroy, an associate of Alfred Kinsey, provides a factual manual for young girls. He advocates masturbation as a healthy action.

Ponse, Barbara. IDENTITIES IN THE LESBIAN WORLD: THE SOCIAL CON-STRUCTION OF SELF. Westport, Conn.: Greenwood Press, 1978. xii, 228 p.

The author deals with the term lesbian and the manner in which it is used by heterosexuals as opposed to women who relate sexual-ly to other women. There is a glossary and bibliography.

Robinson, Paul. THE MODERNIZATION OF SEX: HAVELOCK ELLIS, ALFRED KINSEY, WILLIAM MASTERS AND VIRGINIA JOHNSON. New York: Harper, 1976. viii, 200 p.

Robinson deals with the anti-Victorian research promoted by four prominent shapers of sexual modernism. He takes note of the in-fluence of Freud.

Schaeffer, Leah Cahan. WOMEN AND SEX: SEXUAL EXPERIENCES AND REACTIONS OF A GROUP OF THIRTY WOMEN AS TOLD TO A FEMALE PSY-CHOTHERAPIST. New York: Pantheon Books, 1973. xiv, 269 p.

A therapist describes the sexual experiences of women as told to her in therapy.

Seaman, Barbara. FREE AND FEMALE: THE SEX LIFE OF THE CONTEMPOR-ARY WOMAN. New York: Coward, McCann and Geoghegan, 1972. 288 p.

This book is one woman's journalist's understanding of female sexu-ality based on research of the experts and general knowledge.

Sherfey, Mary Jane. THE NATURE AND EVOLUTION OF FEMALE SEXUALITY. New York: Vintage Books, 1973. 224 p.

> Sherfey argues that there is an insatiable drive in the human female which has been suppressed in the evolution of modern civilization. Sherfey was a student of Alfred Kinsey and describes his work. She rejects the Freudian concept, using the argument that the male is really derived from the female in mammalian biology. She rejects the concept of the vaginal orgasm.

Singer, June. ANDROGYNY: TOWARD A NEW THEORY OF SEXUALITY. Garden City, N.Y.: Anchor Press, 1976. viii, 375 p.

> Singer examines mythology, past and present, to find how the rigid definitions of male and female can be transcended.

Tanner, Donna M. THE LESBIAN COUPLE. Lexington, Mass.: Lexington Books, 1978. 1422 p.

> Tanner, using a sociological perspective, examines lesbian women, who they are, how they meet, their relationships, and the structural meaning of these patterns.

Tavris, Carol, and Sadd, Susan. THE REDBOOK REPORT ON FEMALE SEXUALITY. New York: Delacorte Press, 1977. xv, 186 p.

> This is a report on the REDBOOK MAGAZINE survey of one hundred thousand married women on their sexual attitudes and practices.

Van Deurs, Kady. THE NOTEBOOKS THAT EMMA GAVE ME: THE AUTOBIOGRAPHY OF A LESBIAN. Youngsville, N.Y.: Kady Van Deurs, 1978. 179 p.

> The author describes her hectic life from childhood, including long sessions of psychotherapy, by using her letters and journals.

Vida, Ginny, ed. OUR RIGHT TO LOVE: A LESBIAN RESOURCE BOOK. Englewood Cliffs, N.J.: Prentice-Hall, 1978. 318 p.

> This is a collection of articles on what it means to be a lesbian, the experience of being a gay woman, and the politics of lesbianism. It also lists organizations, publications, and other supportive services on and for the gay women's community.

Wolfe, Linda. PLAYING AROUND: WOMEN AND EXTRAMARITAL SEX. New York: William Morrow, 1975. 248 p.

> Wolfe examines the changing social view of extramarital sex.

Wolff, Charlotte. LOVE BETWEEN WOMEN. New York: St. Martin's Press, 1971. 230 p.

> This is an academic investigation of lesbianism written by a Freudian.

Wysor, Bettie. THE LESBIAN MYTH. New York: Random House, 1974. xvi, 438 p.

Wysor examines various theories of lesbianism and concludes that gay women are people like everyone else. Sections of the book are transcripts of conversations held with lesbians on issues in their lives, like sexuality, motherhood, activism, and life-style.

# Chapter 28

# ABORTION, BIRTH CONTROL, AND

# RELATED HEALTH ISSUES

Arnstein, Helene S. WHAT EVERY WOMAN NEEDS TO KNOW ABOUT ABOR-
TION. New York: Charles Scribner's Sons, 1973. 144 p.

> This book is designed for women who are in the process of deciding
> whether or not to have an abortion. It describes the process of ob-
> taining an abortion and what a woman might experience.

Boston Women's Health Book Collective. OUR BODIES, OURSELVES: A BOOK BY
AND FOR WOMEN. New York: Simon and Schuster, 1977. 383 p.

> This is the standard book on a feminist approach to health care.
> It addresses such issues as birth control, abortion, menstruation,
> sexuality, and how women feel about their bodies. It is a practi-
> cal guide.

Brody, Baruch A. ABORTION AND THE SANCTITY OF HUMAN LIFE. Cambridge: MIT Press, 1975. 162 p.

> A philosopher explicates his belief that abortion is immoral.

Bromley, Dorothy Dunbar. BIRTH CONTROL: ITS USE AND MISUSE. New
York: Harper and Brothers, 1934. 304 p.

> Bromley wrote that while birth control was still controversial, it
> had, by 1934, become respectable.

_____. CATHOLICS AND BIRTH CONTROL: CONTEMPORARY VIEWS ON
DCOTRINE. New York: Devin-Adair, 1965. 207 p.

> Bromley reflects the growing dissatisfaction of many Catholics with
> the rigid position of the Roman Catholic Church on birth control.

Callahan, Daniel. ABORTION: LAW, CHOICE AND MORALITY. New York:
Macmillan, 1970. 524 p.

> Callahan attempts to take an unbiased perspective on the abortion
> issue. He examines all facets of abortion and concludes that abor-

tion must be legally available to women while acknowledging the moral difficulties in the issue.

Carmen, Ailene, and Moody, Howard. ABORTION COUNSELING AND SO-CIAL CHANGE: FROM ILLEGAL ACT TO MEDICAL PRACTICE. Valley Forge: Judson Press, 1973. 122 p.

This book presents the story of the Clergy Consultation on Abortion and how their work has helped women obtain abortions since 1967.

Clay, Vidal S. WOMEN: MENOPAUSE AND MIDDLE AGE. Pittsburgh: KNOW, 1977. viii, 151 p.

Written by a human development specialist, this book explains the physiological and psychological facts of menopause.

Cohen, Marshall, ed. THE RIGHTS AND WRONGS OF ABORTION: A PHILOSOPHY AND PUBLIC AFFAIRS READER. Princeton, N.J.: Princeton University Press, 1974. 127 p.

This volume consists of five essays on abortion, particularly the question of the personhood of the fetus.

Delaney, Janice, et al. THE CURSE: A CULTURAL HISTORY OF MENSTRU-ATION. New York: E.P. Dutton, 1976. 276 p.

The authors document the taboos, myths, rituals, symbolism, and influence of the menstrual cycle on women.

Dennett, Mary Ware. BIRTH CONTROL LAWS: SHOULD WE KEEP THEM OR ABOLISH THEM? New York: Frederick H. Hitchcock, 1926. 309 p.

This book is a good study of the early birth control movement.

Diagram Group. WOMAN'S BODY: AN OWNER'S MANUAL. New York: Bantam Press, 1978. 441 p.

This book is a factual, concise guide for women to their own health care.

Dickinson, Robert Latou. CONTROL OF CONTRACEPTION. Baltimore: Wil-liams and Wilkins, 1931. 290 p.

Dickinson, founder of the National Committee on Maternal Health, describes the current state of medical knowledge in 1931 on the subject of contraception.

_____. TECHNIQUES OF CONCEPTION CONTROL. Baltimore: Williams and Wilkins, 1931. 56 p.

Dickinson describes the process of birth control as it was known in his time.

Dienes, C. Thomas. LAW, POLITICS, AND BIRTH CONTROL. Urbana: University of Illinois Press, 1972. vii, 374 p.

> Dienes provides an account of the attitudes of legislatures and courts toward the birth control movement, including social attitudes in the United States in the twentieth century.

Douglas, Emily Taft. MARGARET SANGER: PIONEER OF THE FUTURE. New York: Holt, Rinehart and Winston, 1970. 274 p.

> Douglas, an important woman in her own right, provides a lively account of Sanger, who fought conservative forces for the right of women to control their own biological destiny, including support of research to develop the birth control pill in the years before her death in 1966.

Dreifus, Claudia, ed. SEIZING OUR BODIES: THE POLITICS OF WOMEN'S HEALTH. New York: Random House, 1978. 321 p.

> This is a group of essays by feminists on the power and oppression of the health care system for women. The contributers include Adrienne Rich and Ellen Frankfurt.

Ebou, Martin. EVERY WOMAN'S GUIDE TO ABORTION. New York: Universe Books, 1971. 256 p.

> This book starts with the assumption that a woman has the right to choose how many children she wants. It describes how to find abortion services and what the experience may be like.

Ehrenreich, Barbara, and English, Deirdre. COMPLAINTS AND DISORDERS: THE SEXUAL POLITICS OF SICKNESS. Old Westbury: Feminist Press, 1973. 94 p.

> The authors examine the social forces which shape a woman's treatment by the medical establishment.

Frankfurt, Ellen. VAGINAL POLITICS. New York: Quadrangle Books, 1972. 250 p.

> Frankfurt has written one of the early works of the contemporary women's movement in the politics of women's health care.

Fryer, Peter. THE BIRTH CONTROLLERS. New York: Stein and Day, 1965. 420 p.

> Fryer devotes a chapter to each of several leaders in the movement, including Margaret Sanger.

Gebhard, H., et al. PREGNANCY, BIRTH, AND ABORTION. London: Heineman, 1959. Reprint. Westport, Conn.: Greenwood Press, 1976. xix, 282 p.

This is a publication of the Institute for Sex Research of Indiana University. It is based on interviews with women, black and white, widowed, divorced, and separated.

Gordon, Linda. WOMAN'S BODY, WOMAN'S RIGHT: A SOCIAL HISTORY OF BIRTH CONTROL IN AMERICA. New York: Grossman, 1976. xviii, 479 p.

In remarkable detail, Gordon traces the history of methods of birth control as well as attitudes, both male and female, towards birth control.

Gray, Madeline. MARGARET SANGER. New York: Marek Press, 1978. 494 p.

This biography of Sanger describes her work as an advocate of birth control as a key to bettering the conditions of women's lives and her personal life, relationships, and old age.

Hall, Robert E., ed. ABORTION IN A CHANGING WORLD. 2 vols. New York: Columbia University Press, 1970.

These volumes grew out of an international conference held in 1968 under the auspices of the Association for the Study of Abortion. The authorities at the conference had a wide spectrum of positions on the abortion issue.

Hardin, Garrett. MANDATORY MOTHERHOOD: THE TRUE MEANING OF "RIGHT TO LIFE." Boston: Beacon Press, 1974. viii, 136 p.

Hardin refutes the arguments of the right-to-life antiabortion movement. He argues against the notion of the fetus having the rights of a human being and for the right of a woman to control her own body.

Horos, Carol V. VAGINAL HEALTH. New Canaan, Conn.: Tobey, 1975. 174 p.

This is a practical book which tells women about self-gynecological care.

Jameson, Dee, et al. EVERY WOMAN'S GUIDE TO HYSTERECTOMY: TAKING CHARGE OF YOUR OWN BODY. Englewood Cliffs, N.J.: Prentice-Hall, 1978. 157 p.

This work advises women on how to defend their rights as they face the possibility and reality of a hysterectomy.

Kennedy, David M. BIRTH CONTROL IN AMERICA: THE CAREER OF MARGARET SANGER. New Haven, Conn.: Yale University Press, 1970. 320 p.

Kennedy describes the fight for birth control and Sanger's involvement in that struggle.

Kopp, Marie E. BIRTH CONTROL IN PRACTICE. New York: R.M. McBride and Co., 1934. Reprint. New York: Arno Press, 1972. 290 p.

Kopp provides an account of the early successes of the birth control movement and the activities of the Margaret Sanger birth clinics.

Lader, Lawrence. ABORTION. Indianapolis: Bobbs-Merrill, 1967. 212 p.

This is a proabortion treatise written by an activist in the proabortion field.

_____. ABORTION II: MAKING THE REVOLUTION. Boston: Beacon Press, 1973. xiii, 242 p.

This second volume discusses the history of the abortion struggle from 1966 to the Supreme Court decision in 1973.

_____. THE MARGARET SANGER STORY. Garden City, N.Y.: Doubleday, 1955. 352 p.

This uncritical biography of Sanger is loaded with long quotations from her work.

Lanson, Lucienne. FROM WOMAN TO WOMAN: A GYNECOLOGIST ANSWERS QUESTIONS ABOUT YOU AND YOUR BODY. New York: Knopf, 1975. 358 p.

Lanson discusses the health care information and signs of disease women most need to know.

Lee, Nancy Howell. THE SEARCH FOR AN ABORTIONIST. Chicago: University of Chicago Press, 1969. 207 p.

This is a sociological analysis of illegal abortions and how women obtained them in the mid-sixties.

Luker, Kristin. TAKING CHANCES: ABORTION AND THE DECISION NOT TO CONTRACEPT. Berkeley and Los Angeles: University of California Press, 1975. 207 p.

The author looks at the connections between contraception or lack of it and abortion.

Maddux, Hilary. MENSTRUATION. New Canaan, Conn.: Tobey, 1975. 191 p.

This is a straight-forward description of the menstrual cycle and the problems women may encounter. Also included in the book is a resource guide to women's health care facilities.

Mohr, James C. ABORTION IN AMERICA: THE ORIGINS AND EVOLUTION OF NATIONAL POLICY 1800-1900. New York: Oxford University Press, 1978. xii, 331 p.

> Mohr traces attitudes toward abortion from the tolerance of the English common law to the era of strict regulation by state statutes during the period of 1860 to 1880. The change came about because of the lobbying of physicians. Curiously, feminists of the period also opposed abortion.

Noonan, John T., Jr. CONTRACEPTION: A HISTORY OF ITS TREATMENT BY THE CATHOLIC THEOLOGIANS AND CANONISTS. Cambridge, Mass.: Harvard University Press, 1965. 561 p.

> Noonan traces the development of the Catholic position on contraception and is critical of the present rigid position.

_____, ed. THE MORALITY OF ABORTION: LEGAL AND HISTORICAL PERSPECTIVES. Cambridge, Mass.: Harvard University Press, 1970. 276 p.

> This is a collection of antiabortion essays.

Planned Parenthood of New York City. ABORTION: A WOMAN'S GUIDE. New York: Abelard-Schuman, 1973. xii, 147 p.

> This book gives the basic medical facts about abortion and birth control.

Rainwater, Lee. AND THE POOR GET CHILDREN: SEX, CONTRACEPTION, AND FAMILY PLANNING IN THE WORKING CLASS. Chicago: Quadrangle Books, 1967. 202 p.

> This volume, written just at the advent of the "pill," describes contraception as it existed at that time along with a great many case studies of sexual practices of the lower classes.

Reiternian, Carl, ed. ABORTION AND THE UNWANTED CHILD. New York: Springer Publishing Co., 1971. 181 p.

> This book done by the California Committee on Therapeutic Abortion is a proabortion work. It focuses on the need for abortion to avoid unwanted children. It portrays the hardships for the child and for the family when the child is not welcomed by the parents.

Robinson, Caroline Hadley. SEVENTY BIRTH CONTROL CLINICS. Balitmore: Williams and Wilkins, 1930. 351 p.

> Robinson describes in detail the clientele and procedures of a sample of clinics.

Robinson, Victor. PIONEERS OF BIRTH CONTROL. New York: Voluntary Parenthood League, 1919. 107 p.

> This is a brief account of the early leaders of the birth control movement.

Rock, John. THE TIME HAS COME: A CATHOLIC DOCTOR'S PROPOSAL TO END THE BATTLE OVER BIRTH CONTROL. New York: Alfred A. Knopf, 1963. 216 p.

> Rock helped to develop the "pill." He states his own faith but supports birth control.

Rollin, Betty. FIRST YOU CRY. New York: Signet Books, 1977. 240 p.

> A network correspondent, Rollin describes her experience with breast cancer. She deals with the physical ordeal, as well as the sexual and emotional factors which a woman who contracts the disease must face.

Sanger, Margaret. AN AUTOBIOGRAPHY. New York: W.W. Norton and Co., 1938. 504 p.

> This book details Sanger's life and is heavily probirth control.

_____. HAPPINESS IN MARRIAGE. New York: Brentamos, 1926. Reprint. Elmsford, N.Y.: Maxwell Reprint Co., 1969. 231 p.

> Sanger, unlike some feminists, glorified sex and insisted that a good marriage must rest on sexual fulfillment for both partners.

_____. MY FIGHT FOR BIRTH CONTROL. New York: Farrar and Rinehart, 1931. 360 p.

> This purported autobiography is said to have been ghost-written. It is essentially a polemic of the movement.

_____. THE PIVOT OF CIVILIZATION. New York: Brentano's Publishers, 1922. 284 p.

> Sanger relates birth control to eugenics, arguing that humans should be allowed to reproduce only if they were superior types.

_____. WOMEN AND THE NEW RACE. New York: Brentamos, 1920. Reprint. Elmsford, N.Y.: Maxwell Reprint Co., 1969. 234 p.

> In a vigorous polemic, Sanger argues that women in their subservience have done an injustice to themselves by bearing children they cannot take care of. She argues that this is a woman's problem but continence is not practical or desirable. Hence, birth control is the only answer. She argues that family limitation is good for the laboring man. A smaller family can live on less,

bringing down the cost of food. Sanger believed war resulted
from overpopulation; that disease, slums, and moral degradation
would disappear as family size decreased.

Sarvis, Betty, and Rodman, Hyman. THE ABORTION CONTROVERSY. New
York: Columbia University Press, 1974. 207 p.

This book, in examining the abortion issue, focuses on the history
of abortion rights and antiabortion campaigns, particularly from
1960 until the 1973 Supreme Court decision.

Schneider, Diane, and Kennedy, Florynce. ABORTION RAP. New York:
McGraw-Hill, 1971. xvi, 239 p.

This book is billed as a "brief to be presented to a people's tri-
bunal." It explains the efforts in New York to declare the abortion laws there unconstitutional.

Seaman, Barbara. THE DOCTORS' CASE AGAINST THE PILL. New York:
Wyden, 1969. 279 p.

Seaman surveys the health difficulties in the case of birth control
pills.

Steinhoff, Patricia G., and Diamond, Milton. ABORTION POLITICS: THE
HAWAII EXPERIENCE. Honolulu: University of Hawaii Press, 1977. x, 256 p.

This book details the movement in Hawaii for a nonrestrictive
abortion law. It tells how the law was changed in a very short
while, by a grassroots effort.

Sulloway, Alvah W. BIRTH CONTROL AND THE CATHOLIC DOCTRINE.
Boston: Beacon Press, 1959. 257 p.

Sulloway is critical of the Catholic position on birth control.

Tietze, Christopher, et al. ABORTION 1974-75 NEED AND SERVICES IN THE
UNITED STATES, EACH STATE AND METROPOLITAN AREA. New York: Alan
Guttmacher Institute, 1975. 128 p.

This report of the research division of Planned Parenthood presents
statistics on the availability of abortion in the U.S. and how well
the need for abortion is being met. It concludes that more services
are needed, although some difficulty exists in creating them.

Vaughan, Paul. THE PILL ON TRIAL. New York: Coward-McCann, 1970.
244 p.

This is a study of the history and social impact of oral contracep-
tives.

Walbert, David F., and Butler, Douglas, eds. ABORTION, SOCIETY AND THE LAW. Cleveland: Press of Case Western Reserve University, 1973. 393 p.

> This is a group of articles by participants in the abortion rights movement; they address contemporary issues.

Weisbord, Robert G. GENOCIDE? BIRTH CONTROL AND THE BLACK AMERICAN. Westport, Conn.: Greenwood Press, 1975. ix, 219 p.

> Many black militant males believe that the movement for birth control is a white plot to eliminate blacks. Weisbord examines this theory and the reasons for the paranoia.

Wertz, Richard W., and Wertz, Dorothy C. LYING IN: A HISTORY OF CHILDBIRTH IN AMERICA. New York: Free Press, 1977. xii, 260 p.

> The authors describe midwives in colonial America, social child-birth, the dangers of childbirth in the nineteenth century, birth in hospitals, natural childbirth, governmental regulation, and the search for the best methods.

Wood, H. Curtis, Jr., and Reuben, William S. SEX WITHOUT BABIES. New York: Lancer Press, 1971. 304 p.

> This is a popular treatment of the subject of voluntary sterilization as a method of birth control.

# Chapter 29

## MARRIED AND UNMARRIED WOMEN

Baguedor, Eve. SEPARATION: JOURNAL OF A MARRIAGE. New York: Simon and Schuster, 1972. 219 p.

This is one woman's personal account of her separation from her husband.

Bahr, Howard R., and Garrett, Gerald R. WOMEN ALONE: THE DISAFFILI-ATION OF URBAN FEMALE. Lexington, Mass.: Lexington Books, 1976. xx, 207 p.

This is a sociological study of the experience of women alone in urban areas. It covers widows primarily, but touches on single and divorced women.

Baldwin, William H. FAMILY DESERTION AND NON-SUPPORT LAWS. New York: James Kempster Printing Co., 1904. Reprint. New York: Arno Press, 1972. 136 p.

Baldwin studies the effect of desertion on lower-class families.

Bequaert, Lucia H. SINGLE WOMEN: ALONE AND TOGETHER. Boston: Beacon Press, 1976. xvi, 256 p.

This is a survey of the issues facing single women, primarily those widowed or divorced and how they cope.

Bernard, Jessie. THE SEX GAME: COMMUNICATION BETWEEN THE SEXES. New York: Atheneum, 1975. xi, 372 p.

This is a feminist, sociological examination of the relationships between men and women. Bernard conceives of the "game" as potentially cooperative, where both sexes can win.

Berson, Barbara, and Bora, Ben. SURVIVAL GUIDE FOR THE SUDDENLY SINGLE. New York: St. Martin's Press, 1974. x, 213 p.

This book is organized by theme. Each theme is addressed first from the woman's viewpoint and then from the man's viewpoint.

Bird, Caroline. THE TWO-PAYCHECK MARRIAGE: HOW WOMEN AT WORK ARE CHALLENGING LIFE IN AMERICA. New York: Rawson, Wade, 1979. 305 p.

> Bird examines the way in which working women are creating a pattern of social change.

Blake, Nelson M. THE ROAD TO RENO: A HISTORY OF DIVORCE IN THE UNITED STATES. New York: Macmillan, 1962. 340 p.

> Blake traces controversy over divorce from the beginning. He attempts to remove it from legalism and sociology. He indicates changing attitudes towards grounds. He contrasts the ease of divorce for the rich with the difficulty encountered by the poor.

Brandy, Susan. BETWEEN MARRIAGE AND DIVORCE. New York: Signet Books, 1975. 240 p.

> Brandy describes the breakup of her own marriage and the problems of emergence from divorce.

Breslin, Catherine. THE MISTRESS CONDITION. New York: E.P. Dutton, 1976. 248 p.

> The author examines the experience and conditions of women in relationships with men not sanctioned by law or church.

Caine, Lynn. WIDOW. New York: William Morrow, 1974. 222 p.

> This is an account of one upper middle-class woman's experience after the death of her lawyer husband.

Constantine, Larry L., and Constantine, Joan M. GROUP MARRIAGE: A STUDY OF CONTEMPORARY MULTILATERAL MARRIAGE. New York: Macmillan, 1973. xii, 299 p.

> This is an investigation of communal marriage.

Delora, Joann S., and Delora, Jack R., eds. INTIMATE LIFESTYLES: MARRIAGE AND ITS ALTERNATIVES. Pacific Palisades, Calif.: Goodyear Publishing Co., 1972. xv, 421 p.

> This is a collection of articles on a wide variety of topics relating to intimate relationships and changing mores.

Fleming, Jennifer Baker, and Washburn, Carolyn Kott. FOR BETTER, FOR WORSE: A FEMINIST HANDBOOK ON MARRIAGE AND OTHER OPTIONS. New York: Charles Scribner's, 1977. 406 p.

> This practical book discusses the whys and hows of marriage for women as feminists.

Goode, William J. WOMEN IN DIVORCE. New York: Free Press, 1956. xix, 381 p.

> This is a sociological survey of the adjustment process for women following divorce.

Hill, Reuben. FAMILIES UNDER STRESS. Westport, Conn.: Greenwood Press, 1949. x, 441 p.

> This volume deals with family problems created by World War II, particularly adjustments to separation and reunion. The author studies factors that caused these families to stay together or to split apart.

Hirsch, Barbara B. DIVORCE: WHAT A WOMAN NEEDS TO KNOW. Chicago: Henry Regnery Co., 1973. x, 227 p.

> This is a practical guide for women going through a divorce.

Hunt, Morton, and Hunt, Bernice. THE DIVORCE EXPERIENCE. New York: Signet Books, 1977. xiv, 305 p.

> The authors describe in readable form the problems and attitudes of newly divorced persons. They describe the psychological shock, the problems of dating, sex, children, and finances.

Jacobson, Paul. AMERICAN MARRIAGE AND DIVORCE. New York: Rinehart, 1959. xviii, 188 p.

> Jacobson provides a heavily statistical study of marriage and divorce based on census records, vital statistics of states, and local governmental agencies. He relates such factors as the economy, war, geography, the seasons, race, and religion to marriage and divorce.

Kessler, Sheila. THE AMERICAN WAY OF DIVORCE: PRESCRIPTIONS FOR CHANGE. Chicago: Nelson-Hall, 1975. 216 p.

> This is a how-to-cope book for people contemplating divorce.

Keyes, Margaret F. STAYING MARRIED. Millbrae, Calif.: Les Femmes Publishing, 1975. 157 p.

> This book is written by a psychotherapist who advises couples on how to make their marriages work.

Krantzler, Mel. CREATIVE DIVORCE: A NEW OPPORTUNITY FOR PERSONAL GROWTH. New York: M. Evans, 1973. 268 p.

> Krantzler offers techniques for the newly divorced that enable them to adjust to being single.

Lederer, William, and Jackson, Don P. THE MIRAGES OF MARRIAGE. New York: W.W. Norton and Co., 1968. 473 p.

> The authors discuss the myths surrounding the institutions of marriage.

Lewis, Alfred Allan, and Berns, Barrie. THREE OUT OF FOUR WIVES: WIDOWHOOD IN AMERICA. New York: Macmillan, 1975. 216 p.

> This is a study of widowhood based on interviews conducted with widows across the United States.

Lichtenberger, J.P. DIVORCE: A SOCIAL INTERPRETATION. New York: McGraw-Hill Book Co., 1931. Reprint. New York: Arno Press, 1972. 472 p.

> Lichtenberger provides statistics on divorce in the pre-Depression era. He deals with the effects of divorce and explores some of the myths.

Lindsey, Ben B., and Evans, Wainwright. THE COMPANIONATE MARRIAGE. New York: Boni and Liveright, 1927. Reprint. New York: Arno Press, 1974. 396 p.

> Lindsey was a judge in a juvenile court in Denver. His proposal for companionate marriage involved legalized birth control information, divorce by mutual consent, education of young people for marriage, and reform of alimony laws.

Lopata, Helena Z. WIDOWHOOD IN AN AMERICAN CITY. Cambridge, Mass.: Schenkman, 1973. 369 p.

> Lopata interviewed widows in Chicago. The focus of her inquiry was the degree of their adjustment to the status.

McBride, Angela Barron. A MARRIED FEMINIST. New York: Harper and Row, 1976. 244 p.

> McBride reports on her experience as a feminist and wife and how she synthesizes her two roles.

Montague, Louise. A NEW LIFE PLAN: A GUIDE FOR THE DIVORCED WOMAN. Garden City, N.Y.: Doubleday, 1978. 252 p.

> This is a practical book designed to help newly divorced women cope with all aspects of their lives.

Napolitane, Catherine, and Pelligrino, Victoria. LIVING AND LOVING AFTER DIVORCE. New York: Signet Books, 1977. 309 p.

> The authors are the founders of Nexus, a support network designed to help divorced women start a new life. This book is a manual on the subject.

O'Brien, Patricia. THE WOMAN ALONE. New York: Quadrangle, 1973. 285 p.

> This is the story of one reporter's experience with the single life. In leaving her family in order to investigate what it is like to be single, O'Brien encounters much discrimination against unmarried women.

O'Neill, Nena, and O'Neill, George. OPEN MARRIAGE: A NEW LIFE STYLE FOR COUPLES. New York: M. Evans and Co., 1972. 287 p.

> The authors propose a more open, independent system in which there is flexibility of roles and a sharing of responsibility. They deal with open companionship and love without jealousy. Open marriage was much discussed in the latter part of the twentieth century as a part of the feminist movement.

O'Neill, William L. DIVORCE IN THE PROGRESSIVE ERA. New Haven, Conn.: Yale University Press, 1967. xii, 295 p.

> O'Neill insists that divorce is an essential part of the family system, a "safety valve" that relieves the suffocation of the system. O'Neill notes that the divorce rate rose markedly in the late nineteenth century, setting off a controversy between moralists like Theodore Roosevelt and spokesmen for "The New Morality." The bitter controversy reached its peak about 1912 as the spokesmen for the new morality demanded sexual fulfillment as a condition of the successful marriage.

Rainwater, Lee, et al. FAMILY DESIGN: MARITAL SEXUALITY, FAMILY SIZE, AND CONTRACEPTION. Chicago: Aldine, 1965. 349 p.

> The authors compare the attitudes of middle- and lower-class couples on contraceptives, sexual attitudes, and their practices in these matters. They discuss these views in terms of the marital power structure.

Rheinstein, Max. MARRIAGE STABILITY, DIVORCE, AND THE LAW. Chicago: University of Chicago Press, 1972. 482 p.

> The author examines the social factors of divorce laws and proposes sweeping reforms in our conceptions of marriage and divorce.

Seidenberg, Robert. CORPORATE WIVES--CORPORATE CASUALITIES. New York: Amacom, 1973. 177 p.

> The author describes the difficult role women have had to play as wives in the corporate world and proposes that changes be made.

_____. MARRIAGE BETWEEN EQUALS: STUDIES FROM LIFE AND LITERATURE. New York: Anchor Press, 1973. 340 p.

> This book is a critique of traditional marriage done by a psychoanalyst.

Sheresky, Norman, and Mannes, Marya. UNCOUPLING: THE ART OF COM-
ING APART. New York: Viking Press, 1972. 208 p.

> This is a practical book which makes suggestions to couples ob-
> taining divorces on how to make it amicable and as tension-free
> as possible.

Sirjamaki, John. THE AMERICAN FAMILY IN THE TWENTIETH CENTURY.
Cambridge, Mass.: Harvard University Press, 1953. 227 p.

> Sirjamaki describes the family as a nuclear unit, separated from
> all but the closest relatives and domiciled in a separate residence.
> The isolation from the family group makes it vulnerable to dissolu-
> tion. Wives have nearly equal parity and children are endowed
> with rights.

Sklar, Anna. RUNAWAY WIVES. New York: Coward, McCann and Geoghegan, 1976. 219 p.

> The author presents the findings from her conversations with women
> around the country who have left their husbands and families for
> new lives.

Smith, James R., and Smith, Lynn G., eds. BEYOND MONOGAMY: RE-
CENT STUDIES ON SEXUAL ALTERNATIVES IN MARRIAGE. Baltimore: Johns
Hopkins University Press, 1974. 336 p.

> This is a study of how new alternatives in marriage have altered
> the traditional institution.

Spencer, Anna Garlin. THE FAMILY AND ITS MEMBERS. Philadelphia: J.B.
Lippincott Co., 1925. Reprint. Westport, Conn.: Hyperion Press, 1976.
322 p.

> The author--teacher, pacifist, and feminist--was a charter member
> of the National Council for Women and the Women's International
> League for Peace and Freedom. Spencer examines the new family
> that she saw emerging as a result of greater freedom for women as
> they achieved better education and greater economic opportunity.

Stapleton, Jean, and Bright, Richard. EQUAL MARRIAGE. Nashville, Tenn.:
Abingdon Press, 1976. 143 p.

> This short book reports on the experience of one couple and their
> guidelines for equality in marriage.

Stouffer, Samuel A., and Lazarsfeld, Paul. RESEARCH MEMORANDUM ON
THE FAMILY IN THE DEPRESSION. New York: Social Science Research
Council, 1937. Reprint. New York: Arno Press, 1975. x, 221 p.

> This volume is concerned with the problems caused by unemployment,
> the despair of fathers unable to provide for their familes, and the
> psychological problems caused for all members of the family.

Sullivan, Judy. MAMA DOESN'T LIVE HERE ANYMORE. New York: Arthur Fields, 1974. 243 p.

> This is a personal account of one woman's decision to create a new life, apart from her husband and children.

Taves, Isabella. WOMEN ALONE. New York: Funk and Wagnalls, 1968. 316 p.

> Taves attempts to show the widow and the divorcee how to achieve self-reliance.

Weiss, Robert. MARITAL SEPARATION. New York: Basic Books, 1975. 334 p.

> This is a book written by a sociologist which deals with the psychological experience of divorce. It is aimed at clinicians working in the field.

Women in Transition. WOMEN IN TRANSITION: A FEMINIST HANDBOOK ON SEPARATION AND DIVORCE. New York: Scribners, 1975. 532 p.

> This practical book describes issues facing women preparing for divorce, like emotional support, how to divorce, the children, and the new life as a single person. It presents experiences of women as they have faced these questions and what they have learned.

Yates, Martha. COPING: A SURVIVAL MANUAL FOR WOMEN ALONE. Englewood Cliffs, N.J.: Prentice-Hall, 1976. 272 p.

> Yates aims to provide single women, whether by choice, divorce, or widowhood, with information on their situations and how to cope with their difficulties.

# Chapter 30

# MOTHERHOOD

Bernard, Jessie. THE FUTURE OF MOTHERHOOD. New York: Dial Press, 1974. xiii, 426 p.

    Bernard examines motherhood as an institution in its personal and political meanings. She hypothesizes that motherhood will change a good deal in the years to come.

Boston Women's Health Book Collective. OURSELVES AND OUR CHILDREN: A BOOK BY AND FOR PARENTS. New York: Random, 1978. ix, 288 p.

    This volume looks at all facets of parenting from a feminist perspective.

Chodorow, Nancy. THE REPRODUCTION OF MOTHERING: PSYCHOANALYSIS AND THE SOCIOLOGY OF GENDER. Berkeley and Los Angeles: University of California Press, 1978. viii, 263 p.

    This is a feminist analysis of various conceptions of motherhood and the role of mothers in human development, especially the psychoanalytic conception.

Curtis, Jean. WORKING MOTHERS. Garden City, N.Y.: Doubleday, 1976. 214 p.

    This book describes the difficulties that working women and mothers face, including child care, housework and husbands.

Callahan, Sidney Cornelia, ed. THE WORKING MOTHER. New York: Macmillan, 1971. 264 p.

    Callahan has brought together a collection of essays on what it's like to be a working mother; all of them start with the assumption that mothers have a legitimate right to work.

Barber, Virginia, and Skaggs, Merrill Maguire. THE MOTHER PERSON. New York: Schocken Books, 1977. 220 p.

The authors describe the joys and frustrations a contemporary mother faces.

Fraiberg, Selma. EVERY CHILD'S BIRTHRIGHT: IN DEFENSE OF MOTHER-ING. New York: Basic Books, 1977. xiii, 162 p.

Fraiberg, the well-known researcher in child development, has written an antiday-care treatise. She believes children are best cared for at home by their mothers.

Friday, Nancy. MY MOTHER--MY SELF. New York: Delacorte Press, 1978. xviii, 425 p.

This is a popular, somewhat Freudian analysis of the mother-daughter relationship.

Goode, Ruth. A BOOK FOR GRANDMOTHERS. New York: Macmillan, 1976. xvii, 204 p.

Goode gives advice to grandmothers.

Hartley, Shirley Foster. ILLEGITIMACY. Berkeley and Los Angeles: Univer-sity of California Press, 1975. xiii, 288 p.

This is a sociological analysis of the attitudes about and conditions of children born out of wedlock.

Hope, Karol, and Young, Nancy, eds. THE MOMMA HANDBOOK FOR SIN-GLE MOTHERS. New York: Plume Books, 1976. 388 p.

Brought together by two unmarried mothers, the book contains inter-views with single mothers. It contains practical advice on welfare, divorce, raising children, education, new careers, and sharing houses with other single mothers.

Kriegsberg, Louis. MOTHERS IN POVERTY: A STUDY OF MOTHERS IN POVERTY: A STUDY OF FATHERLESS FAMILIES. Chicago: Aldine, 1970. 356 p.

Kriegsberg assembled statistics on poor women who head households alone.

McBride, Angela Barron. THE GROWTH AND DEVELOPMENT OF MOTHERS. New York: Harper and Row, 1973. xvii, 158 p.

McBride writes of the "motherhood mystique," describing the diffi-culties and the unromantic elements of the experience.

Milwaukee. County Welfare Rights Organization. WELFARE MOTHERS SPEAK OUT: WE AIN'T GONNA SHUFFLE ANYMORE. New York: W.W. Norton and Co., 1972. 190 p.

This book discusses the plight of poor women with children and their movement to take pride in themselves and to provide for their families.

Nye, Francis Ivan, and Hoffman, Lois Wladis, eds. THE EMPLOYED MOTHER IN AMERICA. Chicago: Rand McNally, 1963. Reprint. Westport, Conn.: Greenwood Press, 1976. x, 406 p.

This book explores the question of whether maternal employment causes emotional maladjustment of children and disruption of traditional marriage patterns.

Parker, Tony. IN NO MAN'S LAND: SOME UNMARRIED MOTHERS. New York: Harper and Row, 1972. 159 p.

This is the story of six different women who are mothers and not married.

Peck, Ellen, and Senderowitz, Judith, eds. PRONATALISM: THE MYTH OF MOM AND APPLIE PIE. New York: Crowell, 1974. 333 p.

This is a collection of essays, all of which take the point of view that motherhood must become an optional rather than a compulsory experience.

Radl, Shirley L. MOTHER'S DAY IS OVER. New York: Charterhouse, 1973. 238 p.

This is a discussion of the negative aspects of motherhood.

Rich, Adrienne. OF WOMAN BORN: MOTHERHOOD AS EXPERIENCE AND INSTITUTION. New York: W.W. Norton and Co., 1976. 318 p.

Rich discusses the theory of motherhood in a patriarchal society.

Roberts, Robert W., ed. THE UNWED MOTHER. New York: Harper and Row, 1966. 270 p.

This volume attempts to overview the issues of unwed mothers as defined in the early and mid-1960s.

Silverman, Anna, and Silverman, Arnold. THE CASE AGAINST HAVING CHILDREN. New York: David McKay, 1971. 212 p.

The Silvermans argue that the maternal instinct is a myth and that most people have children for the wrong reasons. They believe that marriage without children is a viable option and that other alternatives exist as well.

Vincent, Clark E. UNMARRIED MOTHERS. New York: Free Press, 1961. x, 308 p.

This looks at the 1938–58 statistics on illegitimate children in the United States and the social trends found therein.

Whelan, Elizabeth M. A BABY? . . . MAYBE: A GUIDE TO MAKING THE MOST FATEFUL DECISION OF YOUR LIFE. Indianapolis, Ind.: Bobbs-Merrill, 1975. 237 p.

This presents all sides of the issue of whether or not to have children.

Young, Leontine R. OUT OF WEDLOCK: A STUDY OF THE PROBLEMS OF THE UNMARRIED MOTHER AND HER CHILD. New York: McGraw-Hill, 1954. Reprint. Westport, Conn.: Greenwood Press, 1972. x, 261 p.

This is a sociological study of the problems of the unwed mother as they existed in the 1950s.

# Chapter 31

# CHILD-CARE PROGRAMS AND POLITICS

Auerbach, Stevanne, and Rivaldo, James A. MODEL PROGRAMS AND THEIR COMPONENTS. Child Care: A Comprehensive Guide. New York: Human Science Press, 1976. xxi, 197 p.

> This book examines the resources available for day care and what makes a day-care program successful.

_____, eds. RATIONALE FOR CHILD CARE SERVICES: PROGRAMS VS. POLITICS. Child Care: A Comprehensive Guide. New York: Human Sciences Press, 1975. xxxv, 215 p.

> This volume includes articles on many facets of day care by experts in the field. Topics include the extent of the need for day care, history of day care, the child's experience of day care, and how to create comprehensive day care.

Beer, Ethel S. WORKING MOTHERS AND THE DAY NURSERY. New York: Whiteside and Morrow, 1954. Reprint. Mystic, Conn.: Lawrence Verry, 1970. 189 p.

> This book discusses the value of a day nursery, how to run a day nursery and the responsibility of a day nursery.

Breitbart, Vicki, et al. THE DAY CARE BOOK: THE WHY, WHAT AND HOW OF COMMUNITY DAY CARE. New York: Alfred A. Knopf, 1974. 209 p.

> Breitbart examines many aspects of day care, especially the politics and the needs for day care. She includes a section on how to start a child-care center.

THE CHANGING DIMENSIONS OF DAY CARE: HIGHLIGHTS FROM CHILD WELFARE. New York: Child Welfare League of America, 1970. 62 p.

> This is a collection of short pieces surveying contemporary issues in day care, including proposals for comprehensive day-care service.

Collins, Alice H., and Watson, Eunice L. FAMILY DAY CARE: A PRACTICAL GUIDE FOR PARENTS, CAREGIVERS, AND PROFESSIONALS. Boston: Beacon Press, 1976. x, 144 p.

>   Collins and Watson describe one day-care option--day care in someone's home--in practical terms.

Committee on Standards for Day Care. CHILD WELFARE LEAGUE OF AMERI-CA: STANDARDS FOR DAY CARE SERVICE. New York: Child Welfare League of America, 1969. xi, 123 p.

>   This lists the suggested guidelines for quality day care on the contemporary scene.

Evans, E. Belle, and Saia, George E. DAY CARE FOR INFANTS: THE CASE FOR INFANT DAY CARE AND A PRACTICAL GUIDE. Boston: Beacon Press, 1972. xiv, 216 p.

>   Evans and Saia present the need for group care for children under three and how to go about creating such care.

Fein, Greta G., and Clarke-Stewart, Alison. DAY CARE IN CONTEXT. New York: John Wiley, 1973. xxi, 359 p.

>   The authors attempt to move day care from the political arena and to consider its effects on children and families and its educational possibilities.

Goad, Marcine H. EVERY PARENT'S GUIDE TO DAY CARE CENTERS. Chatsworth, Calif.: Books for Better Living, 1975. 159 p.

>   This book is intended to help parents choose what kind of child-care arrangement they would like and what to look for in a day-care center.

Greenblatt, Bernard. RESPONSIBILITY FOR CHILD CARE. San Francisco: Jossey-Bass Publishers, 1977. xvi, 317 p.

>   Greenblatt examines the social and political implications of the changing roles of family and the state in child-care arrangements. He is not a feminist, although not completely antiday-care center.

Harlow, Nora. SHARING THE CHILDREN: VILLAGE CHILD REARING WITH-IN THE CITY. New York: Harper and Row, 1975. 154 p.

>   Harlow describes the efforts of herself and a group of families on the upper west side of Manhattan to create an alternative child-care system or school.

Levitan, Sam A., and Alderman, Karen Cleary. CHILD CARE AND ABC'S TOO. Baltimore: Johns Hopkins University Press, 1975. viii, 125 p.

This is an inquiry into the current state of day care in the United States, and the possibilities for the future.

McClellan, Keith, et al. DAY CARE COST ANALYSIS: A MANUAL OF INSTRUCTIONS. Chicago: Welfare Council of Metropolitan Chicago, 1971. x, 116 p.

This is a practical book designed to help day-care centers analyze their costs of operation.

Parker, Ronald K., and Knitzer, Jane. DAY CARE AND PRESCHOOL SERVICES. Atlanta: Avatar Press, 1972. 74 p.

This pamphlet discusses the status of day care and the economic and political viability of day-care service expenses.

Prescott, Elizabeth, and Jones, Elizabeth. DAY CARE AS A CHILD REARING ENVIRONMENT. Washington, D.C.: National Association for the Education of Young Children, 1972. 65 p.

Prescott and Jones examine day care as the context in which a child grows up. They discuss the variables involved in the "environment" of day care.

Provence, Sally, et al. THE CHALLENGE OF DAY CARE. New Haven, Conn.: Yale University Press, 1977. x, 301 p.

This volume, written by day care professionals, describes the issues surrounding day care and the practical realities. It also describes the day to day experience of children in good day-care environments.

Robinson, Halbert B., et al. EARLY CHILD CARE IN THE UNITED STATES OF AMERICA. New York: Gordon and Breach, 1973. xii, 224 p.

The authors deal with changing family relationships in society. They note medical problems, welfare agencies and the increasing need for day-care centers. An extensive bibliography is appended.

Roby, Pamela, ed. CHILD CARE: WHO CARES? New York: Basic Books, 1973. xxiii, 456 p.

This is a collection of essays on day care in the United States and abroad that compares government policies and resources available for child care.

Ruderman, Florence A. CHILD CARE AND WORKING MOTHERS: A STUDY OF ARRANGEMENTS MADE FOR DAYTIME CARE OF CHILDREN. New York: Child Welfare League of America, 1968. 208 p.

This volume surveys what happens to children when their mothers work and explains community attitudes towards day-care centers.

# Child-Care Programs and Politics

Schatz, Eunice, and Flaun, Thea K., eds. INDUSTRY AND DAY CARE II: PROCEEDINGS OF THE SECOND NATIONAL CONFERENCE ON INDUSTRY AND DAY CARE. Chicago: Urban Resources Corp., 1976. 60 p.

> This publication focuses on how business can best be involved in day care.

Steinfels, Margaret O'Brien. WHO'S MINDING THE CHILDREN: THE HISTORY AND POLITICS OF DAY CARE IN AMERICA. New York: Simon and Schuster, 1973. 281 p.

> Steinfels reports on the history of child-care centers in the United States. She assesses the current day-care situation and politics involved in contemporary day care movements.

Swenson, Janet P., ed. ALTERNATIVES IN QUALITY CHILD CARE: A GUIDE FOR THINKING AND PLANNING. Washington, D.C.: Day Care and Child Development Council of America, 1972. 79 p.

> This looks at all possibilities in day care--care in the home by the family, babysitters, family day care, and day-care programs and centers.

Young, Dennis R., and Nelson, Richard R., eds. PUBLIC POLICY FOR DAY CARE OF YOUNG CHILDREN. Lexington, Mass.: Lexington Books, 1973. 115 p.

> Young and Nelson examine the politics, especially on the federal level, involved in organizing and financing day care. They propose a national day-care system with community control.

# Chapter 32

# MEN AND FEMINISM

Brenton, Myron. THE AMERICAN MALE. New York: Coward-McCann, 1966. ix, 224 p.

> Brenton describes the stereotype of maleness. He believes sex-role stereotypes are disastrous to both men and women.

DuBrin, Andrew J. THE NEW HUSBANDS AND HOW TO BECOME ONE. Chicago: Nelson-Hall, 1976. xiv, 213 p.

> DuBrin describes the changing role of men in marriage and household relationships. He gives advice to men who would like to become a "new husband."

Farrell, Warren. THE LIBERATED MAN. BEYOND MASCULINITY: FREEING MEN AND THEIR RELATIONSHIPS WITH WOMEN. New York: Random House, 1974. 384 p.

> This is one of the original works on the male liberation movement. Among other things, Farrell discusses men's consciousness raising groups.

Ferguson, Charles W. THE MALE ATTITUDE. Boston: Little, Brown and Co., 1966. xiv, 365 p.

> Ferguson studies the male ethos and ego and, among other things, what all this has done to attitudes about women as well as their position in American society. He tries to show how the unique American environment may account for the situation.

Goldberg, Herb. THE HAZARDS OF BEING MALE: SURVIVING THE MYTH OF MASCULINE PRIVILEGE. New York: Signet, 1976. 195 p.

> This book is a guide for men who wish to transcend the traditional male role.

Kouwenhoven, John A., and Thaddeus, Jamie Farrar. WHEN WOMEN LOOK AT MEN: AN ANTHOLOGY. New York: Harper and Row, 1963. xxii, 435 p.

This anthology contains short descriptions by a variety of women
of men in general, in particular, as fathers, sons, brothers, husbands, and lovers. The descriptions are not entirely flattering
to men.

Levine, James A. WHO WILL RAISE THE CHILDREN?: NEW OPTIONS FOR
FATHERS (AND MOTHERS). New York: J.B. Lippincott Co., 1976. 192 p.

Levine explores ways men can be more involved with the care of
their children. He discusses custody for divorced fathers, part-
time jobs for full-time fathers, adoptive fathers, and househusbands.

Marine, Gene. A MALE GUIDE TO WOMEN'S LIBERATION. New York:
Holt, Rinehart and Winston, 1972. 312 p.

Preferring the coinage "masculinism" to the more common "sexism,"
Marine examines the stereotype that male is normal, that male is
better. He describes sex role traditions, the principles and development of women's liberation, and tries to reassure men who
are frightened by the feminist movement.

Snodgrass, Jon, ed. A BOOK OF READINGS FOR MEN AGAINST SEXISM.
Albion, Calif.: Times Change Press, 1977. 238 p.

This radical book aims at helping men understand the oppression of
women, the roles men play, and other issues of oppression, such
as gay, class, and racial.

Wagenward, James, and Peyton, Bailey, eds. MEN: A BOOK FOR WOMEN.
New York: Avon Books, 1970. 381 p.

This is a book about men, as they are and what they would like
to be, for women. It aims to explain the male experience.

# Chapter 33

# ANTIFEMINIST WRITING SINCE 1940

Andelin, Helen B. FASCINATING WOMANHOOD. Santa Barbara, Calif.: Pacific Press, 1970. 220 p.

> Andelin, taking her direction from the alleged sexual nature of women, insists that women must recognize that God made man the master. Woman's function is to submit and support. The basis of woman's happiness is to be loved by a man.

Brown, Helen Gurley. SEX AND THE SINGLE GIRL. New York: Bernard Geis, 1962. 273 p.

> Providing the antithesis of women's liberation, Brown tells how the single girl can catch a man, presumably the dream of every woman.

Caprio, Frank S. THE SEXUALLY ADEQUATE FEMALE. New York: Citadel Press, 1953. 223 p.

> Caprio presents a Freudian view of female sexuality, notably that a woman who achieves orgasm via the clitoris is frigid. He believes that such a woman needs psychiatric help because they are antimale. This is rejected by militant feminists.

Cattell, James McKeen. ADDRESSES AND FORMAL PAPERS. 2 vols. Lancaster, Pa.: Science Press, 1947.

> A psychologist, Cattell showed statistically that only thirty-two women as compared with one thousand men achieved eminence in intellectual or artistic fields. He believed this was due to women's limited mental variability.

Decter, Midge. THE LIBERATED WOMEN AND OTHER AMERICANS. New York: Coward, McCann and Geoghegan, 1971. 256 p.

> In a volume of essays devoted to issues of the 1960s, Decter, a noted antifeminist, poses the feminist as an overindulged daughter of an affluent family. Decter believes the new feminists in confusion blame others for lack of freedom when freedom is there for

the taking. Decter says such a person is asking for the freedom
demanded by children, freedom from all difficulty.

_____. THE NEW CHASTITY AND OTHER ARGUMENTS AGAINST WOMEN'S
LIBERATION. New York: Coward, McCann and Geoghegan, 1972. 188 p.

Decter regards the women's movement as a desire on the part of
its proponents to remain little girls, free from all responsibility.
She sees a contradiction between the demand, on the one hand,
for sexual freedom and the fear, on the other, of being only a
sex object.

Deutsch, Helen. THE PSYCHOLOGY OF WOMEN. 2 vols. New York:
Grune and Stratton, 1944.

Deutsch, a disciple of Freud, believed that puberty brought a
repression of masculine characteristics and the flowering of feminine qualities such as passivity, subjectivity, sympathy for others,
intuition, and romanticism. This caused an inability to cope
with reality and made it impossible for women to be resolute.
All this was somehow connected to vaginal sexual desire and
penis envy. Motherhood should be the woman's goal.

Dingwall, Eric. THE AMERICAN WOMAN: A HISTORICAL STUDY. London:
Ducksworth, 1956. 286 p.

This is an antiwoman treatise with scholarly trappings.

Dunton, Loren. HOW TO SELL TO WOMEN. New York: McGraw-Hill,
1965. xiii, 304 p.

Dunton says women are defensive, men are objective, women are
intuitive. They think differently, so the method of selling to
women must be different. Women speak the language of feeling.
Women are subjective. Women live in fantasy. Women weep;
men fight. Women cling; men command.

Goldberg, Steven. THE INEVITABILITY OF PATRIARCHY. New York: Morrow, 1973. 318 p.

Goldberg, a sociologist, argues that patriarchy is inevitable because
of the greater drive of the male for dominance in all areas. He
seems to imply that this drive is biological.

Grossman, Edward. "In Pursuit of the American Woman." HARPER'S MAGA-
ZINE 240 (February 1970): 56-64.

Grossman believes feminists are "bitchy and spoiled" and really do
not know what they want. Because they cannot make it in the
rough world outside the home, they blame men for their shortcomings. He believes that an orgasm would reform all militant feminists.

Lederer, Wolfgang. THE FEAR OF WOMEN. New York: Grune and Stratton, 1968. viii, 360 p.

> Lederer believes men should behave aggressively toward women because this is what women really want. They do not want, he says, independence and equality, but rather only someone to protect them and restrain them from destructive behavior. If men acted more aggressively, as befits their nature, there would be no women's movement.

Lundberg, Ferdinand, and Farnham, Maryna. MODERN WOMAN: THE LAST SEX. New York: Harper, 1947. 497 p.

> This is an antifeminist statement based on concepts of psycho-analysis.

Mailer, Norman. THE PRISONER OF SEX. Boston: Little Brown and Co., 1971. 240 p.

> After several unfortunate political encounters with the women's movement, Mailer provides this volume as an antifeminist tract.

Morgan, Marabel. THE TOTAL WOMAN. Old Tappan, N.J.: F.H. Revell, 1973. 192 p.

> A woman, according to Morgan, creates a successful and romantic marriage by admiring and loving her husband and submitting to his will. She rubs his back, puts love notes in his lunch, and caters to his sexual needs. She does not belittle or dominate him. Morgan believes that if a marriage fails, it is the fault of the woman.

Peale, Ruth. THE ADVENTURE OF BEING A WIFE. Englewood Cliffs, N.J.: Prentice-Hall, 1971. 266 p.

> Peale says that God divided the human race into male and female and it is wrong to "blur the distinction." Males are aggressive and combative, with a drive to be dominant. Women should be the opposite. Feminism destroys this God-endowed arrangement. She believes feminists are lonely people who are seeking a scapegoat in male chauvinism.

Reyburn, Wallace. THE INFERIOR SEX. Englewood Cliffs, N.J.: Prentice-Hall, 1972. 235 p.

> The author states flatly that women are inferior because they have produced no great figures in any field. Of obstetrics, he says, "women have not contributed a jot to this essentially female sphere of medicine." Women are characterized by tears, giggling, getting into a tizzy, preoccupation with outward appearance. His advice to women: "Just get on with being a woman, find the contentment and reflected happiness of being secondary to men."

Rheingold, Joseph. THE FEAR OF BEING A WOMAN. New York: Grune and Stratton, 1964. xiii, 271 p.

> Rheingold, a Harvard Medical School psychiatrist, argues that biology decrees that a woman must be a wife and mother. Thus, they must grow up without fear of this role and not be subverted by "feminist doctrine." The sense of fulfillment will bring a "good life and a secure world."

Samra, Cal. THE FEMININE MISTAKE. Los Angeles, Calif.: Nash Publishing, 1971. 248 p.

> One of the founders of the Society for the Emancipation of the American Male (SEAM), Samra provides an antifeminist document heavily bolstered with biblical quotations. He believes matriarchy is the prelude to disaster. Samra appends a list of masculinist organizations.

Sebold, Hans. MOMISM: THE SILENT DISEASE OF AMERICA. Chicago: Nelson-Hall, 1976. xi, 318 p.

> Sebold hypothesizes that over-mothering is a critical issue facing the American population. He blames women for over-possessiveness as mothers.

Stassinopoulos, Arianna. THE FEMALE WOMAN. New York: Random House, 1974. ix, 175 p.

> The final sentence in book explains all: "I hope that THE FEMALE WOMAN will help to crystallize the unpopularity of Women's Lib and will encourage all those women have been sneered at by Women's Lib for far too long to hit back--to hit back with the strength and confidence of being female women."

Wylie, Philip. GENERATION OF VIPERS. New York: Rinehart, 1942. Reprint. Marietta, Ga.: Larlin Corp., 1979. xxiii, 318 p.

> Wylie believed women were vipers who sent poison through the bloodstream of manhood. Women dominate boyfriends, husband, and through "momism" demands submission of men, and destroys their sexual confidence by complaining of a lack of sexual satisfaction. He charged that women robbed men of their creativity, took their wealth, and taught girlish manners to boys. Speaking of "women in pants," he believed that feminism was "she-popery."

# ADDENDUM

Akers, Charles W. ABIGAIL ADAMS: AN AMERICAN WOMAN. Boston: Little, Brown, and Co., 1980. x, 207 p.

> This volume is a biography of Abigail Adams, a woman of courage, intellect, and character. She must rank as one of the earliest feminists in the United States. An essay on sources is appended.

Ashley, Jo Ann. HOSPITALS, PATERNALISM AND THE ROLE OF THE NURSE. New York: Teachers College Press, 1979. 283 p.

> This examines the role of nurses in the medical care system and why nurses have had little influence in that system.

Bank, Mirra. ANONYMOUS WAS A WOMAN. New York: St. Martin's Press, 1979. 128 p.

> This is a volume primarily of reproductions of American folk art done by women—quilts, needlework and so forth. The accompanying essay describes this work as real art.

Banner, Lois W. ELIZABETH CADY STANTON: A RADICAL FOR WOMEN'S RIGHTS. Boston: Little, Brown, and Co., 1979. 189 p.

> This is a short biography of Stanton and her involvement in the women's rights movement.

Barry, Kathleen. FEMALE SEXUAL SLAVERY. Englewood Cliffs, N.J.: Prentice-Hall, 1979. viii, 276 p.

> Barry presents a survey of the conditions of forced prostitution and includes in her definition of sexual slavery arrangements often sanctioned by society.

Bayh, Marvella, and Kotz, Mary Lynn. MARVELLA: A PERSONAL JOURNEY. New York: Harcourt Brace Jovanovich, 1979. 310 p.

> This is the life story of a political wife, Marvella Bayh, married

# Addendum

to Senator Birch Bayh of Indiana. Bayh tells of her childhood
and marriage and her fatal bout with breast cancer.

Berkin, Carol R., and Lovett, Clara M., eds. WOMEN, WAR, AND REVO-
LUTION. New York: Holmes and Meier, 1980. xiii, 310 p.

This volume is based on a 1978 conference at Baruch College.
The papers explore the role of women in revolution and wars in
America from the eighteenth to twentieth century.

Berman, Eleanor. RE-ENTERING: SUCCESSFUL BACK-TO-WORK STRATEGIES
FOR WOMEN SEEKING A FRESH START. New York: Crown, 1980. viii,
179 p.

This book was written out of the experience of a program at
Hunter College for housewives who wish to go back to paid work.

Brady, Katherine. FATHER'S DAYS: A TRUE STORY OF INCEST. New York:
Seaview Books, 1979. 216 p.

This is the story of the author's own personal experience of
incest.

Chesler, Phyllis. WITH CHILD: A DIARY OF MOTHERHOOD. New York:
Thomas Y. Crowell, 1979. 285 p.

This is Chesler's own story of becoming a mother, told as a feminist.

Coles, Robert, and Coles, Jane Hallowell. WOMEN OF CRISIS II: LIVES
OF WORK AND DREAMS. New York: Delacorte Press, 1980. xii, 237 p.

The sociologists present a second volume on the lives of five
women from diverse backgrounds--a Pueblo Indian, business executive,
a bank teller, a nurse, and a feminist activist.

Conway, Mimi. RISE, GONNA RISE: A PORTRAIT OF SOUTHERN TEXTILE
WORKERS. New York: Anchor Press, 1979. ix, 228 p.

This is the story of the contemporary struggle between J.P. Stevens
and the Amalgamated Clothing and Textile Workers Union. It includes the life stories of several working women.

Cott, Nancy F., and Pleck, Elizabeth H., eds. A HERITAGE OF HER OWN:
TOWARDS A NEW SOCIAL HISTORY OF AMERICAN WOMEN. New York:
Simon and Schuster, 1979. 608 p.

This is a collection of essays on the lives of women in the United
States from the seventeenth century to today. The volume includes
pieces which utilize new experimental methods of social history.
Contributors include Gerda Lerner, Eugene Genovese, Linda Gordon, Herbert Gutman, and Carroll Smith-Rosenberg.

Degler, Carl. AT ODDS: WOMEN AND THE FAMILY IN AMERICA FROM THE REVOLUTION TO THE PRESENT. New York: Oxford University Press, 1980. 527 p.

> Degler explores the relationship of women to changing family patterns. He describes their efforts in the feminist movement, their sexuality, and their protest against the family.

Deuhurst, C. Kurt; MacDowell, Betty; and MacDowell, Marsha. ARTISTS IN APRONS: FOLK ART BY AMERICAN WOMEN. New York: E.P. Dutton and Co., 1979. xviii, 202 p.

> This volume describes the art done by women in the home. It includes many illustrations of folk art as well.

Djerassi, Carl. THE POLITICS OF CONTRACEPTION. New York: W.W. Norton, 1979. 274 p.

> Written by the scientist who developed the birth control pill, this book explores the larger social issues of contraception. Djerassi is very much in favor of the continued growth in the use of oral contraceptives.

Dobash, R. Emerson, and Dobash, Russell. VIOLENCE AGAINST WIVES: A CASE AGAINST THE PATRIARCHY. New York: Free Press, 1979. xii, 339 p.

> This book examines the issue of woman battering in its largest social, political, and historical context and concludes that violence against women is acceptable in present society.

Dubbert, Joe L. A MAN'S PLACE: MASCULINITY IN TRANSITION. Englewood Cliffs, N.J.: Prentice-Hall, 1979. xi, 323 p.

> Dubbert develops the thesis that men have been trapped by a mystique of their own making. This mystique involves male power and superiority in the sexual, social, political, economic and intellectual spheres and is based on the myths of the frontier.

Dublin, Thomas. WOMEN AT WORK: THE TRANSFORMATION OF WORK AND COMMUNITY IN LOWELL, MASSACHUSETTS, 1826-1860. New York: Columbia University Press, 1975. 316 p.

> Dublin describes the lives, goals, and struggles of first the Yankee and later the Irish women who worked in the textile mills.

Dulles, Eleanor Lansing. CHANCES OF A LIFETIME: A MEMOIR. Englewood Cliffs, N.J.: Prentice-Hall, 1980. 390 p.

> This is the life story of the sister of the public figures John Foster and Allen Dulles. Eleanor Dulles was an economist and diplomat

in her own right. Her account of her life details the discrimination which befell her as a woman.

Ettorre, E.M. LESBIANS, WOMEN AND SOCIETY. Boston: Routledge and Kegan Paul, 1980. 206 p.

This book analyzes the social shifts created by the new openness of lesbians. Ettorre believes that lesbianism is not only a personal issue but a political and social movement.

Fisher, Dexter, ed. THE THIRD WOMAN: MINORITY WOMAN WRITERS IN THE UNITED STATES. Boston: Houghton-Mifflin, 1979. 608 p.

Fisher provides an anthology of literary pieces by American Indians, black women, Mexican-American women, and Asian-American women.

Fisher, Elizabeth. WOMAN'S CREATION: SEXUAL EVOLUTION AND THE SHAPING OF SOCIETY. New York: Anchor Press, 1979. 504 p.

Fisher refutes the ancient ideas of human origins and the Victorian concepts built on the biblical tales. She insists that women cannot be considered an empty vessel or a merely passive force in history.

Fleming, Jennifer Baker. STOPPING WIFE ABUSE: A GUIDE TO THE EMOTIONAL, PSYCHOLOGICAL AND LEGAL IMPLICATIONS FOR THE ABUSED WOMAN AND THOSE HELPING HER. Garden City, N.Y.: Anchor Press, 1979. xvii, 532 p.

This is a practical volume intended mostly for professionals who work with battered women. It touches on many facets of the issue.

Foner, Phillip S. WOMEN AND THE AMERICAN LABOR MOVEMENT: FROM COLONIAL TIMES TO THE EVE OF WORLD WAR I. New York: Free Press, 1979. 621 p.

The well-known labor historian documents the conditions of women workers and their contributions to the organizing movement.

Friday, Nancy. MEN IN LOVE: MEN'S SEXUAL FANTASIES--THE TRIUMPH OF LOVE OVER RAGE. New York: Delacorte, 1980. 527 p.

Friday surveys the sexual fantasies of the contemporary male and adds psychological commentary. For the most part, the book is a collection of verbal reports from men on their inner sexual fantasies.

Funt, Marilyn. ARE YOU ANYBODY? CONVERSATIONS WITH WIVES OF

CELEBRITIES. New York: Dial Press, 1979. 339 p.

> This is a collection of interviews with the wives of well-known
> contemporary figures, including Mrs. Johnny Carson, Mrs. Muham-
> mad Ali, and Mrs. Charlton Heston.

Goldberg, Herb. THE NEW MALE: FROM SELF-DESTRUCTION TO SELF-CARE.
New York: William Morrow, 1979. 319 p.

> This examines the changing definition of masculinity and how
> women's liberation enhances the male role.

Harrison, Gilbert A. TIMELESS AFFAIR: THE LIFE OF ANITA McCORMICK
BLAINE. Chicago: University of Chicago Press, 1979. 432 p.

> This is a biography of a rich Chicago woman who played an impor-
> tant role in the educational and political movements of her time
> (1866-1954).

Hedges, Elaine, and Wendt, Ingrid, eds. IN HER OWN IMAGE: WOMEN
WORKING IN THE ARTS. Old Westbury, N.Y.: Feminist Press, 1980. xxv,
308 p.

> This is a collection of essays mostly by women artists on the ex-
> perience of being a female creator. It includes sections on "House-
> hold Work and Women's Art"; "Becoming an Artist: Obstacles and
> Challenges"; "Their Own Images"; "Definitions and Discoveries";
> and "Women's Art and Social Changes."

Hill, Mary A. CHARLOTTE PERKINS GILMAN: THE MAKING OF A RADICAL
FEMINIST, 1860-1896. Philadelphia: Temple University Press, 1980. 362 p.

> Hill analyzes the thought of the leading feminist intellectual and
> writer, using her unpublished works.

Hope, Karol, and Young, Nancy. OUT OF THE FRYING PAN: A DECADE
OF CHANGE IN WOMEN'S LIVES. Garden City, N.Y.: Anchor Press,
1979. xvii, 263 p.

> The authors interviewed many women who felt they have been in-
> fluenced by the contemporary feminist movement. They describe
> how these women have changed and present the real-life women's
> culture.

Jay, Karla, and Young, Allen. THE GAY REPORT: LESBIANS AND GAY
MEN SPEAK OUT ABOUT SEXUAL EXPERIENCE AND LIFESTYLES. New York:
Summitt Books, 1979. 816 p.

> This is a fairly extensive survey of gay people's lives, attitudes,
> and experiences as shaped by their sexual orientation.

# Addendum

Katz, Esther, and Ropave, Anita. WOMEN'S EXPERIENCE IN AMERICA:
A HISTORICAL ANTHOLOGY. New Brunswick, N.J.: Transaction Books,
1980. 414 p.

> This is a collection of essays on women's role in American history.
> They show how social and domestic arrangements have been signi-
> ficant underpinnings of the total social system.

Kelley, Mary. WOMAN'S BEING, WOMAN'S PLACE: FEMALE IDENTITY
AND VOCATION IN AMERICAN HISTORY. Boston: G.K. Hall, 1979.
xiii, 372 p.

> This book consists of twenty-two essays, twenty of which were
> papers delivered at a Conference on the History of Women at St.
> Paul, Minnesota in 1977.

Lacks, Roslyn. WOMEN AND JUDAISM: MYTH, HISTORY AND STRUGGLE.
New York: Doubleday, 1980. xxii, 218 p.

> This book examines the way history has affected Jewish women,
> including the contemporary American Jewish woman.

Lagemann, Ellen Condleffe. A GENERATION OF WOMEN: EDUCATION IN
THE LIVES OF PROGRESSIVE REFORMERS. Cambridge, Mass.: Harvard University Press, 1979. viii, 207 p.

> The author looks at the lives of Grace Dodge, Maud Nathan, Lil-
> lian Wald, Leonora O'Reilly, and Rose Schneiderman, all politi-
> cally active in the late nineteenth and early twentieth century and
> analyzes how their education and ability to learn in an informal
> sense influenced their activism.

Lamson, Peggy. IN THE VANGUARD: SIX AMERICAN WOMEN IN PUBLIC
LIFE. Boston: Houghton-Mifflin Co., 1979. xiv, 233 p.

> This is Lamson's second biographical collection on women in poli-
> tics. She sketches the lives and careers of Rose Bird, Eleanor
> Holmes Norton, Elaine Noble, Elizabeth Holtzman, Juanita Kreps,
> and Millicent Fenwick.

Lash, Joseph P. HELEN AND TEACHER: THE STORY OF HELEN KELLER
AND ANNE SULLIVAN MACY. New York: Delacorte Press, 1980. xiv,
811 p.

> Lash writes a complete and controversial version of Helen Keller
> and Annie Sullivan's life together.

Lazarre, Jane. ON LOVING MEN. New York: Dial Press, 1980. 181 p.

> This work is the story of one woman's relationships with men told
> with a political and psychological perspective.

Lisle, Laurie. PORTRAIT OF AN ARTIST: A BIOGRAPHY OF GEORGIA O'KEEFE. New York: Seaview Books, 1980. x, 384 p.

This is a biography of O'Keefe, the contemporary painter. It describes her life in relation to her art.

Lopata, Helena Znaniecka. WOMEN AS WIDOWS: SUPPORT SYSTEMS. New York: Elsvier, 1979. 500 p.

Lopata provides a descriptive and theoretical study of women, both employed and unemployed, after the children are gone and the husband has died.

McHenry, Robert, ed. LIBERTY'S WOMEN. Springfield, Mass.: G. and C. Merrian Co., 1980. xi, 482 p.

This is a biographical directory of American women, from the first European woman born here, Virginia Dare, to contemporary figures.

McNally, Fiona. WOMEN FOR HIRE: A STUDY OF THE FEMALE OFFICE WORKER. New York: St. Martin's Press, 1979. 220 p.

McNally describes the problems of the women in the labor market and why clerical work usually is an occupational dead end.

McWhirter, Norris, et al., eds. GUINESS BOOK OF WOMEN'S SPORTS REC-ORDS. New York: Sterling Publishing Co., 1979. 192 p.

The editors provide statistics and records in the major sports as well as the more obscure ones. There are some photographs of outstanding female athletes.

Mazow, Julia Wolf, ed. and comp. THE WOMAN WHO LOST HER NAMES: SELECTED WRITINGS BY AMERICAN JEWISH WOMEN. New York: Harper and Row, 1980. xviii, 222 p.

This is a collection of short works and excerpts from both fiction and nonfiction on the question of being Jewish and female in the United States. Some authors included are Emma Goldman, Tillie Olson, Gracie Paley, and Andrea Dworkin.

Mirande, Alfredo, and Enriquez, Evangelina. LA CHICANA: THE MEXICAN-AMERICAN WOMAN. Chicago: University of Chicago Press, 1979. x, 238 p.

The authors extol the cultural history of Mexican-American women and their contemporary status in their own families and subculture and in the dominant Anglo world.

Morgan, Elizabeth. THE MAKING OF A WOMAN SURGEON. New York: G.P. Putnam's Sons, 1980. 368 p.

This is the story of a contemporary woman doctor and her experience in the male-dominated field of plastic surgery.

# Addendum

Munro, Eleanor. ORIGINALS: AMERICAN WOMEN ARTISTS. New York: Simon and Schuster, 1979. 528 p.

> Munro interviewed contemporary women artists. In this book, she discusses their work and the origins of their art.

Norton, Mary Beth. LIBERTY'S DAUGHTERS: THE REVOLUTIONARY EXPERIENCE OF AMERICAN WOMEN, 1750-1800. Boston: Little, Brown and Co., 1980. 384 p.

> Norton examines the changes which occurred in domestic relations in late eighteenth century America.

Nyad, Diana. OTHER SHORES. New York: Random House, 1978. 174 p.

> This is the story of the contemporary marathon swimmer.

Oakley, Ann. WOMEN CONFINED: TOWARDS A SOCIOLOGY OF CHILD-BIRTH. New York: Schocken Books, 1980. ix, 334 p.

> Oakley analyzes the experience of pregnancy and childbirth and women's feelings about their experience. She looks at the societal-medical context of childbirth and how this influences the feelings of women as they become mothers.

Oakley, Mary Ann. BECOMING A MOTHER. New York: Schocken Books, 1980. 328 p.

> Oakley examines the activity of motherhood from a scholarly and feminist viewpoint.

Pomroy, Martha. WHAT EVERY WOMAN NEEDS TO KNOW ABOUT THE LAW. Garden City, N.Y.: Doubleday, 1980. xv, 415 p.

> Pomroy, a lawyer, writes in simple fashion for the laywoman on topics like family, job, and personal and consumer laws.

Reagan, Nancy, and Libby, Bill. NANCY. New York: William Morrow and Co., 1980. 219 p.

> This is the story of Ronald Reagan's wife, printed in the year he sought the American presidency. It is a cheerful account of Mr. Reagan's character and kindness to his wife.

Rivers, Caryl; Barrett, Rosalind; and Baruch, Grace. BEYOND SUGAR AND SPICE: HOW WOMEN GROW, LEARN AND THRIVE. New York: G.P. Putnam's Sons, 1979. 333 p.

> This book examines the process of sex role, socialization, and how women could learn effectiveness, achievement, and self-affirmation. Personal experience and academic research are presented to document the possibility of a new process of socialization.

Robson, Elizabeth, and Edwards, Gwenyth. GETTING HELP: A WOMAN'S GUIDE TO THERAPY. New York: E.P. Dutton and Co., 1980. xv, 239 p.

>This book describes various kinds of psychotherapy and its alternatives. It includes a practical guide on how to choose a therapist.

Rubin, Lillian B. WOMEN OF A CERTAIN AGE: THE MIDLIFE SEARCH FOR SELF. New York: Harper and Row, 1979. 309 p.

>This is a sociological study of contemporary women between the ages of thirty-five and fifty-four who earlier gave up careers to become wives and mothers. It examines their plans for the future.

Ruth, Sheila, ed. ISSUES IN FEMINISM: A FIRST COURSE IN WOMEN'S STUDIES. Boston: Houghton-Mifflin, 1980. 704 p.

>Ruth offers an interdisciplinary treatment of the major issues and areas of women's studies and the women's movement.

Schramm, Sarah Slavin. PLOW WOMEN RATHER THAN REAPERS: AN INTELLECTUAL HISTORY OF FEMINISM IN THE UNITED STATES. Metuchen, N.J.: Scarecrow Press, 1979. ix, 441 p.

>Schramm provides an interpretive view of the current of feminist thought through the history of the United States. She believes that feminism is more tactical than ideological.

Scully, Diana. MEN WHO CONTROL WOMEN'S HEALTH: THE MISEDUCATION OF OBSTETRICIAN-GYNECOLOGISTS. Boston: Houghton-Mifflin, 1980. vii, 205 p.

>This work examines the training of physicians and the ways in which women are systematically oppressed by male doctors.

Sicherman, Barbara, and Green, Carol Hurd, eds. NOTABLE AMERICAN WOMEN: THE MODERN PERIOD. Cambridge, Mass.: Harvard University Press, 1980. 797 p.

>The editors provide biographies of 442 eminent women who died between 1951 and 1975.

Sidel, Ruth. URBAN SURVIVAL: THE WORLD OF WORKING CLASS WOMEN. Boston: Beacon Press, 1978. 180 p.

>This is the story of the lives of eight urban working women told primarily in first person.

Smith, Joan K. ELLA FLAGG YOUNG: PORTRAIT OF A LEADER. Ames: Iowa State University Research Foundation, 1979. xvi, 272 p.

>Ella Flagg Young earned a doctorate in mid-life and in 1909 was appointed superintendent of schools in Chicago, the first woman

to hold such a post. She advocated organization of teachers and was the first female president of the National Education Association.

Stearns, Peter N. BE A MAN! MALES IN MODERN SOCIETY. New York: Holmes and Meier, 1979. ix, 230 p.

Stearns focuses on how gender roles have been shaped by economic forces, changes in health, education, and attitudes toward children.

Straus, Murray A.; Gelles, Richard J.; and Steinmetz, Suzanne K. BEHIND CLOSED DOORS: VIOLENCE IN THE AMERICAN FAMILY. Garden City, N.Y.: Anchor Press, 1980. ix, 301 p.

This book surveys the degree of violence in the home, including violence against women, and concludes it is a common phenomena.

Tentler, Leslie Woodcock. WAGE-EARNING WOMEN: INDUSTRIAL WORK AND FAMILY LIFE IN THE UNITED STATES. New York: Oxford University Press, 1979. 266 p.

Tentler examines the lives of wage-earning women, unmarried daughters, independent women, and married women. Centering on large industrial cities of the East, she examines wages, working conditions, and the work community.

Wilkie, Jane. THE DIVORCED WOMAN'S HANDBOOK: AN OUTLINE FOR STARTING THE FIRST YEAR ALONE. New York: William Morrow, 1980.

This is a practical guide book for the newly divorced woman.

Wolf, Deborah Goleman. THE LESBIAN COMMUNITY. Berkeley and Los Angeles: University of California Press, 1979. ix, 196 p.

This book examines the emerging social network of gay women.

# AUTHOR INDEX

In addition to authors, this index includes all editors, compilers, and other contributors to works cited in the text. References are to page numbers and alphabetization is letter by letter.

## A

Abbott, Edith  29, 89
Abbott, Lyman  77
Abbott, Sidney  195
Abramson, Joan  149
Abzug, Bella S.  111
Adams, Abigail  39
Adams, Carole  189
Adams, Charles Francis  39
Adams, John  39
Addams, Jane  77, 185
Adler, Freda  177
Adler, Polly  185
Akers, Charles W.  235
Albertson, Chris  137
Alciem, Rachel  185
Alcott, William A.  49
Alderman, Karen Cleary  226
Alderson, Nannie T.  61
Alexander, William  39
Allen, Ruth Alice  89
Almquist, Elizabeth M.  149
Alsop, Gulielma F.  119
Altbach, Edith Hoshino  29
American Medical Association  15
American Physical Society  19
Ames, Lois  133
Ames, Mary  61
Amir, Menachem  181

Andelin, Helen B.  231
Anderson, Margaret  125
Anderson, Marian  137
Anderson, Mary  77
Andreas, Carol  107
Angelou, Maya  167
Angrist, Shirley S.  149
Anthony, Katharine  39, 61, 125
Anthony, Kathryn Susan  49
Anthony, Susan B.  61
Anticaglia, Elizabeth  29
Arbanel, Karin  155
Arling, Emanie Sachs  61
Armes, Ethel  46
Arnstein, Helene S.  203
Arofat, Ibtihay  97
Ash, Lee  1
Ashley, Jo Ann  235
Astin, Helen S.  1, 149
Astor, Mary  137
Atkinson, Ti-Grace  101
Auerbach, Stevanne  225
Austin, Nancy  192

## B

Baatz, Wilmer H.  6
Babcock, Barbara Allen  111
Baer, Helene G.  61

Baer, Judith A.  161
Baguedor, Eve  213
Bahr, Howard R.  213
Baker, Elizabeth C.  129
Baker, Elizabeth Faulkner  161
Baker, Nina Brown  119
Baker, Robert  195
Baldwin, William H.  213
Ballan, Dorothy  107
Banes, Sally  195
Bank, Mirra  235
Banner, Lois  29, 33, 235
Barbach, Lonnie Garfield  195
Barber, Virginia  221
Bardon, Edward J.  189
Bardwick, Judith  97, 189
Barker-Benfield, G.J.  49
Barlow, Marjorie Dana  1
Barnett, Avrom  89
Barrer, Myra E.  19
Barrett, Rona  142
Barrett, Rosalind  242
Barry, Kathleen  235
Barrymore, Ethel  137
Baruch, Grace  242
Bates, Daisy  167
Battis, Emery  40
Baxandall, Rosalyn  161
Baxter, Annette K.  29
Baum, Charlotte  167
Bayh, Marvella  235
Baym, Nira  125
Beadry, Ann  115
Beard, Mary Ritter  30, 78, 89
Beatty, William K.  121
Beecher, Catherine [Catharine]  62
Beeke, Gilbert Wheeler  90
Beer, Ethel S.  225
Bell, Alan P.  195
Bellocq, E.J.  185
Belotti, Eleva Gianni  189
Benedict, Ruth Fulton  155
Benet, Mary Kathleen  161
Benges, Ingrid  196
Benson, Mary Summer  40
Benston, Margaret  107
Bequaert, Lucia H.  213
Bergstrom, Len V.  9
Berkin, Carol R.  236
Berman, Eleanor  236

Bernard, Jessie  107, 149, 213, 221
Bernays, Edward L.  2
Berns, Barrie  216
Berskin, Carol Ruth  30
Berson, Barbara  213
Bianiolli, Louis  138
Billings, Victoria  101
Billington, Ray Allen  169
Binns, Archie  137
Bird, Caroline  155, 214
Birney, Catherine H.  49
Blackford, L. Minor  62
Blackwell, Alice Stone  50
Blackwell, Antoinette Louisa Brown  62
Blackwell, Elizabeth  62, 119
Blake, Nelson M.  214
Blatch, Harriet Stanton  72, 78
Bleiweiss, Linda H.  153
Bloom, Lynn Z.  190
Bloomer, D.C.  50
Blum, Harold P.  190
Blumberg, Rose  78
Blumenthal, Walter Hart  40
Blythe, LeGrette  168
Boas, Louise Schutz  149
Bogin, Ruth  56
Boles, Janet K.  111
Bolton-Smith, Robin  125
Bolzan, Emma Lydia  119
Booth, Sally Smith  40, 50
Bora, Ben  213
Boston Women's Health Book Collective  203, 221
Bosworth, Louise Marion  78
Botta, Vincenzo  125
Boutilier, Mary  114
Boyer, Paul  40
Boyle, Regis Louise  126
Bradford, Gamaliel  30
Bradford, Sarah  167
Brady, Katherine  236
Branagan, Thomas  41
Brandeis, Louis D.  78
Brandy, Susan  214
Brecher, Edward  196
Brecher, Ruth  196
Breckinridge, Sophonisba P.  90
Breitbast, Vicki S.  225

Brenton, Myron 229
Breslin, Catherine 214
Bright, Richard 218
Brodsky, Annette M. 177
Brody, Baruch A. 203
Brogger, Suzanne 101
Bromley, Dorothy Dunbar 203
Brooks, Geraldine 41
Brooks, Gladys 50
Brooks, Gwendolyn 167
Brooks, Virginia 185
Brothers, Mary Hudson 62
Brown, Alice 41, 126
Brown, Dee 62
Brown, Edward K. 126
Brown, Hallie Quinn 168
Brown, Helen Gurley 231
Browne, Martha 168
Brownlee, Mary M. 30
Brownlee, W. Elliott 30
Brownmiller, Susan 181
Bry, Adelaide 196
Bry, Doris 128
Bryant, Anita 196
Buck, Pearl S. 126
Bullard, E. John 126
Bullough, Vern 2, 30, 185
Bunch, Charlotte 107, 200
Burgess, Ann Wolbert 181
Burkhart, Kathryn Watterson 177
Burns, Edward 134
Burstall, Sara A. 62
Burtle, Viola 190
Burton, Gabrielle 101
Busbey, Katherine 78
Butler, Douglas 211
Butscher, Edward 126
Butterfield, Lyman 39
Byrd, William 41

C

Cabello-Argandona, Roberto 2
Cade, Toni 168
Caine, Lynn 214
Calderone, Mary S. 196
Calderwood, Ann 153
Calhoun, Arthur W. 30
California Mission on the Status of Women 111

Call, Hughie 63
Callahan, Daniel 203
Callahan, Sidney Cornelia 221
Cameron, Mabel Ward 19
Campbell, Barbara K. 79
Campbell, Helen 63, 127
Cantor, Aviva 2
Cantor, Milton 161
Caprio, Frank S. 231
Carden, Maren Lockwood 97
Carmen, Ailene 204
Carnegie Commission on Higher Education 149
Carr, Virginia Spencer 127
Carroll, Berenice A. 101
Carson, Josephine 168
Cary, Eve 111
Casal, Mary 196
Cassell, Joan 101
Cassiday, Jules 196
Cathell, James McKeen 231
Center for the American Woman and Politics 19
Ceutra, John A. 150
Chafe, William Henry 90, 97
Chaff, Sandra 2
Chamberlin, Hope 111
Chandler, Edna Walker 177
Chapman, Jane Roberts 181
Chase, Mary Ellen 150
Chase, Richard 63
Chavigny, Bell Gale 53
Cheney, Anne 127
Chesler, Phyllis 190, 236
Chestnut, Mary Boykin 63
Chicago, Judy 127
Chicago. Vice Commission 186
Child, Lydia Maria 50, 63
Chisholm, Shirley 112
Chittun, John W. 120
Chodorow, Nancy 221
Claflin, Tennessee 74
Clark, David Lee 42
Clark, Electa 31
Clark, Septima 168
Clarke, Adam 50
Clarke, Edward H. 63
Clarke, Mary A. 119
Clarke, Robert 119

# Author Index

Clarke-Stewart, Alison  226
Clay, Vidal S.  204
Cleaveland, Agnes Morley  63
Clement, Jesse  50
Clifford, Deborah Pickman  51
Cohen, Alden Duer  112
Cohen, Marshall  204
Cole, Arthur C.  150
Cole, Davis  155
Colebrook, Joan  177
Coles, Jane Hallowell  168, 236
Coles, Robert  168, 236
Collins, Alice H.  226
Cometti, Elizabeth  42
Committee on Standards for Day
    Care  226
Common Women Collective  3
Conable, Charlotte Williams  150
Connell, Noreen  181
Conrad, Earl  51
Conrad, Susan Phinney  51
Constantine, Larry L.  214
Conway, Mimi  236
Cook, Blanche Wiesen  80, 108
Cook, Tennessee Claflin  64
Cooke, Nicholas Francis  64
Coolidge, Mary Roberts  79
Cooper, Anna Julia  168
Cooper, James L.  31
Cooper, Sheila McIsaac  31
Copin, Fannie Jackson  168
Cott, Nancy F.  31, 51, 236
Cox, Sue  190
Crew, Louie  196
Crocker, Hannah Mather  51
Cross, Barbara  150
Crow, Martha Foote  79
Curtis, Jean  221

# D

Dall, Caroline H.  64
Daly, Mary  102
Damon, S. Foster  127
Daniel, Sadie Iola  20
Dannett, Sylvia G.L.  20, 64
Davenport, M. Marguerite  138
David, Jay  175
Davidson, Terry  181

Davis, Allen F.  79
Davis, Angela  169
Davis, Audrey B.  3
Davis, Bette  138
Davis, Harrison M.  34
Davis, Katharine Bement  197
Davis, Lenwood G.  3
Day, Dorothy  90
DeBeauvoir, Simone  102
Deckard, Barbara Sinclair  97
DeCrow, Karen  112
Dector, Midge  231-32
Degler, Carl  237
Deiss, Joseph Jay  51
DeLamater, John  156
Deland, Margaret  127
Delaney, Janice  204
Dell, Floyd  79
Delora, Jack R.  214
Denmark, Florence L.  98, 192
Dennett, Mary Ware  204
Dennis, Lawrence E.  150
Dennis, Peggy  112
DeRhain, Edith  177
Deshon, George  64
Deuhurst, C. Kurt  237
Deutsch, Helen  232
Dexter, Elisabeth Anthony  52
Dexter, Elizabeth W.  42
Diagram Group  204
Diamond, Irene  112
Diamond, Milton  210
Dickinson, Robert Latou  204
Dienes, C. Thomas  205
Dillon, Mary  64
Diner, Hasia R.  3
Dingwall, Eric  232
Dispenza, Joseph E.  31
Ditzion, Sidney  197
Dix, Dorothy  90
Dixon, Marlene  108
Djerassi, Carl  237
Dobash, R. Emerson  237
Dobash, Russell  237
Dobkin, Marjorie Houspian  153
Dollen, Charles  3
Donegan, Jane B.  120
Donovan, Frances R.  91
Douglas, Ann  65

Douglas, Emily Taft 31, 205
Dow, George Francis 42
Drake, Emma 80
Dreifus, Claudia 102, 205
Dreier, Mary E. 80
Dressler, Marie 138
Drinnon, Richard 80
Drury, Clifford Merrill 52
Dubbert, Joe L. 237
Dublin, Thomas 237
DuBois, Ellen Carol 52
DuBois, W.E. Burghardt 80
DuBrin, Andrew J. 229
Duffey, Elisa B. 65
Dulles, Eleanor Lansing 237
Dunton, Loren 232
Duster, Alfreda 175
Dworkin, Andrea 102

E

Earle, Alice Morse 42-43
Eastman, Crystal 80
Eastman, Elaine Goodale 65
Ebou, Martin 205
Edmundsen, Madeleine 112
Edwards, Anne 138
Edwards, Gwenyth 243
Eggleston, George Cary 43
Ehrenreich, Barbara 205
Eichler, Magrit 3
Eisenstein, Zillah R. 108
Eisler, Riane Tennenhaus 112
Ellet, Elizabeth F. 43, 65
Ellington, George 65
Elliott, Maud Howe 91
Elliston, Frederick 195
Emerson, R.W. 52
Engle, Paul 43
English, Deirdre 205
Enriquez, Evangelina 241
Epstein, Cynthia Fuchs 155
Epstein, Louis M. 169
Ets, Marie Hall 169
Ettore, E.M. 238
Evans, E. Belle 226
Evans, Elizabeth 43
Evans, Elizabeth Edson 65
Evans, Sara 98
Evans, Wainwright 216

F

Farnham, Eliza Woodson 52
Farnham, Maryna 233
Farrell, John C. 80
Farrell, Warren 229
Fauset, Arthur 52
Fein, Greta G. 226
Feldman, Saul D. 150
Feminist Theory Collective 3
Ferber, Edna 127
Ferguson, Charles W. 229
Fetherling, Dale 81
Fetter, Ann 183
Fidell, Linda S. 156
Field, Vena B. 43
Fields, Annie 129
Figes, Eva 108
Filene, Catherine 91
Filene, Peter Gabriel 31
Finch, Edith 81
Finley, Ruth E. 53
Firestone, Shulamith 108
Fischer, Christiane 53
Fisher, Deborah A. 11
Fisher, Dexter 238
Fisher, Elizabeth 238
Fitzgerald, Zelda 127
Fitzpatrick, Blanche 151
Fleming, Jennifer Baker 214, 238
Flexner, Eleanor 32
Flynn, Elizabeth Gurley 113
Foner, Phillip S. 84, 239
Foreman, Ann 108
Forrest, Mary 128
Forten, Charlotte L. 169
Foxworth, Jo 156
Fraiberg, Selma 222
Francoeur, Anna K. 197
Francoeur, Robert T. 197
Frank, Sheldon 195
Frankfort, Roberta 81
Frankfurt, Ellen 205
Franklin, Margaret Ladd 4
Franks, Violet 190
Frederics, Diana 197
Freedman, Carol Edry 4
Freeman, Jo 98, 102
French, Brandom 138
Friday, Nancy 197, 222, 238

# Author Index

Friedan, Betty  98, 102
Friedman, Barbara  4
Friedman, Bernard H.  81
Friedman, Jane E.  32
Friedman, Leslie J.  4
Friedman, Myra  138
Fritz, Leah  103
Frost, J. William  43
Frost, John  65
Fryer, Peter  205
Fuller, Edmund  53
Fuller, Margaret  53
Fuller, Paul  81
Funt, Marilyn  238
Furniss, W. Todd  151

## G

Gabriel, Ralph Henry  71
Garden, Mary  138
Gardner, Augustus K.  66
Garoogian, Andrew  4
Garoogian, Rhoda  4
Garret, Gerald R.  213
Gates, Margaret  181
Gattey, Charles Neilson  54
Geadelman, Patricia  145
Gebhard, H.  205
Gehm, Katherine  169
Gelb, Barbara  81
Gelfman, Judith  156
Gelles, Richard J.  244
Gentry, Curt  186
George, Carol V.R.  32
George, Margaret  44
Gerber, Ellen W.  145
Giallombardo, Rose  178
Gibson, Althea  145
Gilchrist, Beth  54
Gilman, Agnes Geneva  20
Gilman, Charlotte Perkins  82
Gilman, Gertrude Marcelle  20
Gipson, Richard McCandless  139
Githeas, Marianne  113
Gittelson, Natalie  197
Glackens, Ira  139
Glasgow, Ellen  128
Glick, Paul  91
Glimcher, Arnold B.  128
Gluck, Sherna  82
Glueck, Eleanor T.  178

Glueck, Sheldon  178
Goad, Marcine H.  226
Godbold, E. Stanley, Jr.  128
Goldberg, Herb  229, 239
Goldberg, Jacob A.  182
Goldberg, Rosamond W.  182
Goldberg, Steven  232
Golde, Peggy  156
Goldman, Emma  82, 186
Goldmark, Josephine  78
Goldstein, Leslie Freedman  113
Goldthwaite, Lucy  164
Goode, Ruth  222
Goode, William J.  215
Goodman, Ellen  98
Goodrich, Lloyd  128
Goodsell, Willystine  32
Gordon, Francine E.  156
Gordon, Linda  206
Gordon, Ruth  139
Gornick, Vivian  103
Gould, Carol C.  103
Gould, Jean  128
Goulet, Ginnie  4
Graber, Benjamin  199
Grabill, Wilson H.  32
Grady, Roy I.  120
Graham, Abbie  33, 66
Graham, Patricia Albjerg  151
Gray, Dorothy  66
Gray, Eileen  151
Gray, Madeline  206
Green, Carol Hurd  243
Green, Rena Maverick  57
Greenblatt, Bernard  226
Greenwood, Hazel  5
Greer, Germaine  103, 128
Gregory, Chester W.  91
Griffin, Susan  104
Grimes, Alan P.  83
Grimke, Sarah M.  54
Grober, Kay  65
Grossman, Edward  232
Grosvenor, Veita Mae  162
Groves, Ernest Rutherford  33
Gruberg, Martin  113
Grumman, Joan  134
Guettel, Chavnie  108
Guffy, Ossie  169
Guinoy, Louise Imogen  128
Gurko, Miriam  54, 129

# H

Haber, Barbara 5
Hageland, Ronald W. 33
Hagood, Margaret Jarman 92
Hahn, Emily 33
Hairwick, Andrea Taylor 92
Hale, Beatrice Forbes-Robinson 83
Hale, Sarah Josepha 20, 66
Hall, Florence Howe 67
Hall, Robert E. 206
Hall, Susan 186
Haller, John S. 66
Haller, Robin M. 66
Hamburger, Robert 162
Hamilton, Mary E. 92
Hammer, Signe 190
Hammond, William A. 197
Hanson, Kitty 178
Hardin, Garrett 206
Hare, Lloyd Custer Mayhew 54
Hareven, Tamara 92
Harley, Sharon 169
Harlow, Nora 226
Harper, Ida Husted 67
Harragan, Barbara J. 156
Harrington, Mildred 138
Harris, Ann Sutherland 129
Harris, Dorothy V. 145
Harris, Gloria G. 191
Harris, Mary B. 178
Harrison, Cynthia E. 5
Harrison, Gilbert A. 239
Harrison, Sara 178
Hart, John S. 129
Hartley, Shirley Foster 222
Hartman, Mary S. 33
Harveson, Mae Elizabeth 151
Hauk, Minnie 139
Haviland, Laura S. 67
Hayes, Helen 139
Hays, Elinor Rice 67
Heard, Franklin Fiske 73
Heartman, Charles F. 135
Hedgeman, Anna Arnold 170
Hedges, Elaine 239
Heilbrun, Carolyn G. 104
Hellman, Lillian 129
Hennig, Margaret 156
Henry, Alice 33, 92

Hersey, Thomas 54
Hersh, Blanche Glassman 55
Hershberger, Ruth 104
Hess, Thomas B. 129
Higham, Charles 139
Hill, Joseph Adna 83
Hill, Mary A. 239
Hill, Reuben 215
Hinding, Andrea 5
Hirsh, Barbara B. 215
Hite, Shere 198
Hoepner, Barbara J. 145
Hoffman, Lois Wladis 223
Hole, Judith 99
Hollander, Xaviera 186
Hollick, Frederick 55
Holliday, Carl 44
Holmes, Emma 67
Holmstrom, Linda Lytle 157, 181
Holt, Rackman 170
Homer, Sidney 139
Hope, Karol 222, 239
Horney, Karen 190
Horos, Carol V. 182, 206
Horwitz, Tom 195
Howe, Florence 151
Howe, Julia Ward 67
Howe, Louise Knapp 162
Howes, Durward 20
Hoyt, Nancy 129
Hughes, Marija Matich 5
Hume, Ruth Fox 120
Hummer, Patricia 157
Humphrey, Grace 34
Hunt, Bernice 215
Hunt, Morton 215
Hunton, Addie W. 170
Hurd-Mead, Kate Campbell 120
Hurston, Zora Neale 170

# I

Irwin, Inez Haynes 34, 83
Israel, Stan 6

# J

Jacklin, Carol Nugy 191
Jackson, Don P. 216
Jackson, James C. 68

# Author Index

Jacob, Henrick E. 170
Jacobs, Harriet Brent 170
Jacobs, Sue Ellen 5
Jacobson, Paul 215
James, Edward T. 20
Jameson, Dee 206
Janeway, Elizabeth 104
Jaquette, Jane 113
Jardim, Anne 156
Jastrow, Joseph 84
Jay, Karla 198, 239
Jeffrey, Julia Roy 68
Jenness, Linda 109
Jennings, Samuel K. 55
Jewett, Sarah Orne 129
Johnson, Curtis S. 157
Johnson, Kathryn M. 170
Johnson, Marilyn 113
Johnson, Virginia 199
Johnston, Jill 198
Jones, Elizabeth 227
Jones, Hettie 134
Jones, Jane Louise 151
Jones, Katharine M. 68
Jones, Mary Gwladys 44
Jones, Mary Harris 84
Jongeward, Dorothy 157
Josephson, Hannah 113
Josephson, Matthew 130

## K

Kahn, Kathy 170
Kallir, Otto 130
Kanowitz, Leo 114
Kaplan, Frances Bagley 99
Kassebaum, Gene G. 179
Katz, Esther 240
Katz, Jonathon 198
Katzman, David M. 68, 162
Kearney, Belle 68
Keats, John 130
Keckley, Elizabeth 170
Keller, Helen 84
Kelley, Florence 84
Kelley, Mary 240
Kellogg, Clara Louise 140
Kelly, Joan 6
Kelly, Rita Mae 114
Kemble, Frances A. 55

Kendall, Elaine 152
Kendall, Phebe Mitchell 120
Kenneally, James J. 162
Kennedy, David M. 206
Kennedy, Florynce 210
Kennedy, Rose Fitzgerald 114
Kessler, Sheila 215
Keyes, Margaret F. 215
Kincaid, Diane D. 114
King, Billie Jean 146
King, C. Richard 55
King, Coretta 170
King, Judith D. 6
Kingston, Maxine Hong 171
Kinsey, Alfred Charles 198
Kinsie, Paul M. 188
Kirchwey, Freda 92
Kirkpatrick, Jeane J. 114
Kisner, Arlene 74
Klafs, Carl E. 146
Klaich, Dolores 198
Klein, Herman 140
Klein, Viola 190
Kline-Graber, Georgia 199
Klotman, Phyllis Rauch 6
Knitzer, Jane 227
Kohut, Rebekah 171
Koldt, Anne 104
Koltun, Elizabeth 171
Komarovsky, Mirra 152
Knapp, Sally 120
Kneeland, George J. 186
Kopp, Marie 207
Kotz, Mary Lynn 235
Kouwenhoven, John A. 229
Kraditor, Aileen S. 34, 84
Krantzler, Mel 215
Kreinberg, Nancy 120
Kreps, Juanita 162–63
Kreuter, Gretchen 21
Krichmar, Albert 6–7
Kriegsberg, Louis 222
Kronhausen, Eberhard 199
Kronhausen, Phyllis 199
Kuhn, Annette 109
Kundsin, Ruth B. 157

## L

Lacks, Roslyn 240

Lader, Lawrence 207
Ladner, Joyce A. 171
LaFollette, Suzanne 93
Lagemann, Ellen Condleffe 240
Lakoff, Robin 104
Lamphere, Louise 35
Lampman, Henry P. 178
Lamson, Peggy 114, 240
Landes, Ruth 171
Lane, Ann J. 84
Langdon, William Chauncey 44
Langley, Roger 182
Lanson, Lucienne 207
Lasch, Christopher 77
Lash, Joseph P. 93, 114, 240
Lathan, Jean 121
Laughlin, Clara E. 85
Laurie, Bruce 161
Lawton, Mary 140
Lazarre, Jane 240
Lazarsfeld, Paul 218
Lederer, William 216
Lederer, Wolfgang 233
Lee, Helen Jackson 171
Lee, Mabel 146
Lee, Nancy Howell 207
Lee, Patrick C. 191
Leghorn, Lisa 165
Lemons, J. Stanley 93
Leonard, Eugenie Andruss 7, 44
Lerner, Gerda 7, 34, 56, 171
Leslie, Eliza 68
Lester, David 115
Lever, Janet 152
Levine, David 85
Levine, Ellen 99
Levine, James A. 230
Levine, Louis 93
Levitan, Sam A. 226
Levy, Richard C. 182
Lewin, Arie Y. 153
Lewis, Alfred Allan 216
Lewis, Edith 130
Lewis, Robert W.B. 130
Li, Christine 10
Libby, Bill 242
Lichtenberger, J.P. 216
Lichtenstein, Grace 146
Lillard, Richard G. 7
Lindbergh, Anne Morrow 93-94

Lindborg, Kristina 172
Lindsey, Ben B. 216
Lisle, Laurie 241
Litoff, Judy Barrett 121
Livermore, Mary A. 22, 69
Lloyd, Cynthia B. 163
Lobsenz, Johanna 94
Loeser, Herta 163
Logan, Mary S. 21
Long, Mary Alves 69
Lopata, Helena Znaniecka 163, 216, 241
Lopate, Carol 121
Loring, Rosalind 157
Love, Barbara 21, 195
Lovejoy, Esther Pohl 121
Lovett, Clara M. 236
Lowenberg, Bert James 56
Lubove, Roy 187
Luhan, Mabel Dodge 130
Luker, Kristin 207
Lumpkin, Katharine DuPre 56
Lundberg, Ferdinand 233
Lutz, Alma 56, 69
Lyle, Jerome R. 157
Lynch, Edith M. 158
Lynch, W. Ware 182
Lyon, M. Joan 146
Lyon, Phyllis 199

## M

McBride, Angela Barron 216, 222
McBride, Mary Margaret 140
McCall, Muhal Moses 130
McCarthy, Abigail 115
Maccia, Elizabeth Steiner 152
McClellam, Keith 227
Maccoby, Eleanor 191
McCourt, Kathleen 115
McCracken, Elizabeth 69
McCurry, Dan C. 94
MacDougall, Allan Ross 131
MacDowell, Betty 237
MacDowell, Marsha 237
McGovern, Eleanor 115
McHenry, Robert 241
McKee, Kathleen Burke 7
McKenney, Mary 7
McKenzie, Barbara 130

# Author Index

MacKinnon, Catherine A. 182
MacLean, Annie Marion 85
McLuhan, H. Marshall 199
McMichael, George L. 131
McNally, Fiona 241
McWhirter, Norris 241
Maddax, Hilary 207
Madden, Janice Fanning 163
Mailer, Norman 140, 233
Malvern, Gladys 140
Mander, Anica Vesel 191
Mandle, Joan D. 109
Mann, Brenda J. 164
Mannes, Marya 218
Manning, Caroline 94
Marat, Helen 85
Marine, Gene 230
Marks, Geoffrey 121
Marlow, H. Carleton 34
Marshall, Helen E. 56
Martin, Del 199
Martin, John 85
Martin, Prestonia 85
Martin, Sadie E. 141
Martin, Wendy 34
Martineau, Harriet 56
Mason, Elizabeth B. 8
Massey, Mary Elizabeth 69
Masters, William H. 199
Mastfield, Jacquelyn A. 121
Matthessen F.O. 131
Mauriceau, A.M. 69
Maverick, Mary A. 57
Maynard, Olga 141
Mayo, Amory D. 70
Mazow, Julia Wolf 241
Mead, Margaret 35, 99, 158
Meade, Marion 105
Medea, Andra 182
Medsger, Betty 163
Melder, Keith E. 57
Mellow, James R. 131
Meltzer, Milton 70
Meyer, Annie Nathan 70
Milinowski, Marta 141
Millay, Edna St. Vincent 131
Miller, Casey 105
Miller, Jean Baker 191
Miller, William D. 94
Millett, Kate 105, 187

Milwaukee. County Welfare Rights
    Organization 222
Miner, Myrtilla 172
Minneapolis Vice Commission 187
Mirandé, Alfredo 241
Mitchell, Juliet 191
Mohr, James C. 208
Moise, Penina 131
Monahan, Florence 178
Money, John 199
Monroe, Harriet 131
Montague, Louise 216
Moody, Anne 172
Moody, Howard 204
Moore, Grace 141
Moran, Barbara K. 103
More, Hannah 44, 57
Morgan, David 85
Morgan, Edmund S. 45
Morgan, Elizabeth 241
Morgan, Marabel 233
Morgan, Robin 99, 105
Morris, Jan 199
Moses, Anna Mary Robertson 131
Mossell, N.F. 172
Mowry, George E. 94
Muncy, Raymond Lee 70
Munro, Eleanor 242
Munsterberg, Hugo 131
Murdock, Mary Elizabeth 8
Myers, Henry 164
Myerson, Abraham 94
Myron, Nancy 107, 200

## N

Nagera, Humberto 200
Napolitane, Catherine 216
Nash, Alna 141
Nason, Elias 132
National Commission on the Obser-
    vance of International Women's
    Year 99
Necomer, Mabel 152
Negrin, Su 105
Nelson, Richard R. 228
Nevelson, Louise 132
Newland, Kathleen 105
Nies, Judith 35
Nissenbaum, Stephen 40

Nixon, Edna 45
Noble, Jeanne E. 152
Nochlin, Linda 129
Noonan, John T. 208
Norton, Mary Beth 30, 242
Noun, Louise R. 86
Nyad, Diana 242
Nye, Francis Ivan 223

## O

Oakley, Ann 242
Oakley, Mary Ann 70, 164, 242
O'Brien, Patricia 217
O'Connor, Ellen M. 172
O'Connor, Patricia 8
Odencrantz, Louise C. 172
Odlum, Hortense 158
Offir, Carole 192
Oglesby, Carole A. 146
Olsen, Tillie 132
Olson, Vicky Burgess 35
O'Meara, Walter 172
O'Neill, George 217
O'Neill, Nena 217
O'Neill, William L. 35, 217
Osborn, Susan M. 191
Osen, Lynn 121
Ovarda, Carlos J. 172
Overton, Grant 132
Ovington, Mary White 86

## P

Packard, Vance 200
Paire, Albert Bigelow 141
Palmer, Gladys L. 92
Papashuily, Helen Waite 132
Parish, James Robert 142
Park, Angela Stewart 196
Parker, Betty June 8
Parker, Dorothy 169
Parker, Franklin 8
Parker, Gail 35
Parker, Ronald K. 227
Parker, Tony 223
Paulson, Ross Evans 86
Paykel, Eugene S. 192
Peale, Ruth 233

Peare, Catherine O. 173
Peck, Ellen 223
Peck, Mary Gray 86
Peel, Robert 70-71
Pekkanen, John 182
Pelligrino, Victoria 216
Pennington, Patience 86
Penny, Virginia 71
Peratis, Kathleen Willert 111
Perkins, A.J.G. 57
Peterson, Deena 8
Peterson, Hazel C. 146
Peyton, Bailey 230
Phelps, Ann T. 8
Phelps, Stanlee 192
Pincus-Whitman, Robert 132
Pivar, David 71, 187
Planned Parenthood of New York
    City 208
Plath, Aurelia Siboken 132
Plath, Sylvia 132
Pleck, Elizabeth H. 236
Pogrebin, Letty Cottin 158
Pollak, Otto 178
Pomeroy, Wardell B. 200
Pomroy, Martha 242
Ponse, Barbara 200
Pool, Jeannie G. 9
Potter, Jeffrey 158
Powell, Chilton L. 45
Prescott, Elizabeth 227
Prestage, Jewel L. 113
Provence, Sally 227
Pruette, Lovine 95

## Q

Quaife, Milo Milton 58

## R

Rabinowitz, Clara 100
Radcliffe College, Committee on
    Graduate Education for Women
    152
Radin, Edward D. 71
Radl, Shirley L. 223
Rainwater, Lee 164, 208, 217
Rappaport, Phillip 86
Ravenel, Harriet H. 45

Rayne, Martha Louise 71
Reagan, Nancy 242
Red Collective 109
Reed, Evelyn 109, 122
Reed, Lynnel 142
Reed, Ruth 95
Reid, Doris Fielding 158
Reid, Inez Smith 173
Reitermian, Carl 208
Reitman, Ben L. 187
Reston, James, Jr. 115
Reuben, William S. 211
Reyburn, Wallace 233
Rheingold, Joseph 234
Rheinstein, Max 217
Rhoades, Kathy 115
Rich, Adrienne 105, 223
Richards, Clarice E. 71
Richards, Linda 122
Richardson, Betty 152
Richardson, Rosemary 5
Riegel, Robert E. 87, 187
Rivers, Caryl 242
Roberts, Mary M. 122
Roberts, Robert W. 223
Robinson, Caroline Hadky 208
Robinson, Halbert B. 227
Robinson, Paul 200
Robinson, Victor 122, 209
Robinson, Wilhelmina S. 21
Robson, Elizabeth 243
Roby, Pamela 227
Rock, John 209
Rodman, Hyman 210
Rogers, Agnes 95
Rogers, Anna B. 87
Rogers, William G. 132
Rollin, Betty 209
Roosevelt, Eleanor 95, 115-16
Ropave, Anita 240
Rosaldo, Michelle Zimbalest 35
Rosen, Marjorie 142
Rosenberg, Marie Barovic 9
Ross, Isabel 133
Ross, Ishbel 122, 159
Ross, Nancy 72
Ross, Susan Deller 116
Rossi, Alice 153
Rothman, Sheila 36
Rouse, Blair 128

Rowbotham, Sheila 9, 110
Roy, Maria 182
Royce, Sarah 71
Rubin, Lillian 243
Ruderman, Florence A. 227
Rudolph, Wilma 147
Ruihley, Glenn Richard 133
Rush, Anne Kent 191
Rush, Benjamin 46
Russell, Diana E.H. 183
Ruth, Sheila 243
Ryan, Mary P. 36
Ryan, Michael 57

## S

Sabrosky, Judith A. 106
Sadd, Susan 201
Safilios-Rothschild, Constantina 106
Saia, George E. 226
Salmon, Lucy Maynard 72
Samra, Cal 234
Sanders, Marion K. 116, 159
Sanford, Linda Tshirhart 183
Sanford, Mollie Dorsey 72
Sanger, Margaret 204
Sanger, William W. 187
Sarvis, Betty 210
Saxton, Martha 72
Sayre, Anne 123
Schaeffer, Leah Cahan 200
Schatz, Eunice 228
Schmuck, Patricia Ann 153
Schneider, Diane 210
Schneiderman, Rose 164
Schneir, Miriam 36
Schramm, Sarah Slavin 243
Schwartz, Eleanor Brantley 159
Schwartz, Helene E. 116
Schwartz, Pepper 152
Scott, Adelin White 159
Scott, Anne Fior 36
Scott, Dru 157
Scott, John A. 55
Scully, Diana 243
Seaman, Barbara 200, 210
Sears, Hal D. 72
Sebold, Hans 234
Secrest, Meryle 133
Seed, Suzanne 159

Seidenberg, Robert 217
Seiffer, Nancy 164
Sell, Betty H. 9
Sell, Kenneth D. 9
Senderowitz, Judith 223
Sergeant, Elizabeth Shepley 133.
Seroff, Victor 142
Sewall, May Wright 87
Sewall, Samuel 46
Sexton, Anne 133
Sexton, Linda Gray 133
Seyerstead, Per 133
Shade, William G. 32
Shaw, Anna Howard 72
Sheehan, Susan 173
Sheehy, Gail 188
Sheresky, Norman 218
Sherfey, Mary Jane 201
Sherman, Julia 192
Shew, Joel 57
Shippen, Nancy 46
Sicherman, Barbara 243
Sidel, Ruth 243
Siegel, Connie McClung 155
Silverman, Anna 223
Silverman, Arnold 223
Simcich, Tina L. 159
Simon, Rita James 179
Sinclair, Andrew 36
Singer, June 201
Sirjamaki, John 218
Skaggs, Merrill Maguire 221
Sklar, Anna 218
Sklar, Kathryn Kish 58
Smith, Amanda 173
Smith, Helena H. 61
Smith, James R. 218
Smith, Joan K. 243
Smith, Lynn G. 218
Smith, Page 37
Smuts, Robert W. 164
Snodgrass, Jon 230
Snyder, Eloise 99
Sochen, June 87
Solanas, Valerie 106
Soltow, Martha Jane 10
Sone, Monica 173
Spencer, Anna Garlin 218
Spencer, Cornelia 133
Sprodley, James P. 164
Spruill, Julia Cherry 46

Stacey, Judith 153
Stage, Sarah 123
Stanbler, Sookie 106
Stanford, Ann 46
Stanford, Sally 188
Stanke, Don E. 142
Stanton, Elizabeth Cady 87
Stanton, Theodore 72
Stanwick, Kathy 10, 113
Staples, Robert 173
Stapleton, Jean 218
Starkey, Marion 46
Starr, Louise M. 8
Stassinopoulous, Ariana 234
Stearns, Peter N. 244
Steele, Marilyn 153
Steinfels, Margaret O'Brien 228
Steinhoff, Patricia G. 210
Steinmetz, Suzanne K. 244
Stern, Elizabeth Gertrude 173
Stern, Madeleine B. 58, 73
Stern, Susan 21
Sterne, Emma Gelders 173
Stewart, Elinore Pruitt 73
Stewart, Maria 174
Stewart, Robert Sussman 191
Stimpson, Catharine R. 116, 159
Stone, Betsey 110
Storaska, Frederic 183
Stoter, Horatio Robinson 73
Stouffer, Samuel A. 218
Stowe, Harriet Beecher 62
Strainchamps, Ethel 159
Straus, Murray A. 244
Stroker, Myra H. 156
Strong, Anna Louise 95
Strouse, Jean 192
Stuhler, Barbara 21
Sugimoto, Etsu Inagaki 174
Sullivan, Judy 219
Sulloway, Alvan W. 210
Summer, William Graham 73
Sweet, Frederick A. 134
Swenson, Janet P. 228
Swift, Kate 105
Switzer, Ellen 116

## T

Taft, Jessie 87
Tanner, Donna M. 201

# Author Index

Tarbell, Ida  88
Tarry, Ellen  174
Tauvis, Carol  192
Taves, Isabella  219
Tavris, Carol  201
Teitz, Joyce  160
Tenell, Donna M.  174
Tentler, Leslie Woodcock  244
Terrell, John Upton  174
Terrell, Mary Church  174
Terry, Walter  142
Tetrault, Jeanne  165
Thaddeus, Jamie Farrar  229
Theodore, Athena  160
Thomas, Dorothy  116
Thomas, M. Carey  153
Thomas, M. Halsey  46
Thomas, Sherry  165
Thompson, Kathleen  182
Thompson, Mary Lou  106
Thorpe, Margaret Farrand  58
Tietze, Christopher  210
Timothy, Mary  116
Tingley, Donald F.  10
Tinling, Marion  41
Toklas, Alice B.  134
Tolbert, Marguerite  21
Tolchin, Martin  117
Tolchin, Susan  117
Torburg-Penn, Rosalyn  169
Trollope, Frances M.  58
Truettner, William H.  125
Truman, Margaret  37
Truth, Sojourner  58
Tunney, Kieran  142
Turner, Maryann  10
Twin, Stephanie L.  147
Tyler, Parker  134

## U

Udall, Louise  174
Ulanov, Ann Betford  192
Underwood, Agness  160
Unger, Rhoda Kesler  192
U.S. Department of Commerce, Office of Minority Business Enterprise  160
U.S. Department of Justice. Law Enforcement Assistance Administration  179

## V

Van Aben, Carol G.  121
Van Alstyne, Frances June Crosby  134
Van Deurs, Kady  201
Vaughan, Paul  210
Vernon, Hope J.  134
Vida, Ginny  201
Vincent, Clark E.  223
Vogliotti, Gabriel  188

## W

Wade, Mason  59
Wagenward, James  230
Walbert, David F.  211
Wald, Carol  37
Wald, Lillian D.  88
Walker, Leonore  183
Walker, Williston  45
Wallace, Irving  73
Wallace, Michele  174
Walsh, Correa Moylan  88
Walsh, Mary Ruth  123
Walters, Donald  74
Ward, David A.  179
Ward, Lester Frank  74
Ware, Cellestine  106
Warren, John H., Jr.  188
Warrior, Betsey  165
Wartofsky, Marx W.  103
Washburn, Carolyn Kott  214
Washburn, Charles  188
Wasserman, Elaine  153
Waters, Ethel  175
Watkins, Mel  175
Watson, Eunice L.  226
Watts, Emily Stipes  134
Weber, Gustavus A.  95
Webster, Jeannette L.  134
Weibel, Kathryn  37
Weinbaum, Batya  110
Weinberg, Martin S.  195
Weisbord, Robert G.  211
Weisbord, Vera Buch  96
Weiss, Robert  219

Weissman, Myrna M.  192
Weisstein, Naomi  110
Weitz, Shirley  38
Wells, Ida B.  175
Wells, Theodora  157
Welter, Barbara  38
Wendt, Ingrid  239
Wertheimer, Barbara Mayer  165
Wertz, Dorothy C.  211
Wertz, Richard W.  211
Wery, Mary K.  10
West, Mae  143
West, Uta  100
Westervelt, Esther Manning  11
Westin, Jeanne  96
Wharton, Anne Hollingsworth  47, 59
Wheatley, Phillis  135
Wheeler, Adade Mitchell  38
Wheeler, Helen Rippier  11
Whelan, Elizabeth M.  224
Whitney, Janet Payne  47
Wiley, Bell Irwin  74
Wilkie, Jane  244
Willard, Frances E.  22
Willett, Mabel Hurd  165
Williams, Ben Ames  63
Williams, Elizabeth Friar  193
Williams, Ellen  135
Williams, Juanita H.  193
Williams, Marcille Gray  160
Williams, Ova  11
Willson, Cassandra  181
Wilson, Dorothy Clarke  59, 123
Wilson, Margaret Gibbons  88, 243
Wilson, Robert Forrest  135
Winick, Charles  188
Winslow, Barbara  11
Winston, Sandra  160

Wolf, Deborah Coleman  244
Wolfe, Linda  201
Wolff, Charlotte  201
Wolff, Cynthia Griffin
Wolfson, Theresa  57
Wolpe, Ann Marie  109
Womanpower Project  11
Women in Transition  219
Wood, H. Curtis, Jr.  211
Woodfin, Maude H.  41
Woodhull, Victoria  74
Woody, Thomas  154
Woolston, Howard B.  188
Worthington, Marjorie  74
Wortin, Helen  100
Wortman, Marlene Stein  38
Wright, Carol D.  74
Wright, Helen  123
Wright, Louis B.  41, 47
Wylie, Philip  234

Y

Yates, Gayle Graham  106
Yates, Martha  219
Yellis, Kenneth A.  96
Yorburg, Betty  97
Yost, Edna  123
Young, Agatha  74
Young, Allen  198, 239
Young, Dennis R.  228
Young, Kimball  75
Young, Leontine R.  224
Young, Nancy  222, 239

Z

Zaharias, Babe Didrikson  147

# TITLE INDEX

This index includes all titles of books and journals cited in the text. Titles of journal articles are omitted. In some cases titles have been shortened. References are to page numbers and alphabetization is letter by letter.

## A

Abigail Adams   47
Abigail Adams: An American Woman   235
Abortion   207
Abortion: A Woman's Guide   208
Abortion: Law, Choice and Morality   203
Abortion, Society and the Law   211
Abortion and the Sanctity of Human Life   203
Abortion and the Unwanted Child   208
Abortion Controversy, The   210
Abortion Counseling and Social Change   204
Abortion in America   208, 248
Abortion in a Changing World   206
Abortion in Context   3
Abortion 1974-75 Need and Services in the United States   210
Abortion Politics   210
Abortion Rap   210
Abortion II   207
Abuse of Maternity, The   65
Academic Women   149
Academic Women on the Move   153
Account of the Proceedings on the Trial of Susan B. Anthony, An   61
Adam's Rib   104

Addresses and Formal Papers   231
Adventure of Being a Wife, The   233
Advertising the American Woman   31
Affirmative Action for Women   157
Against Rape   182
Alice Trumbull Mason   132
Almira Hart Lincoln Phelps   119
Afro-American Woman, The   169
Against Our Will   181
All for One   164
All the Happy Endings   132
Alternatives in Quality Child Care   228
Amazon Odyssey   101
American Black Women in the Arts and Social Sciences   11
American Country Girl, The   79
American Families   91
American Family in the Twentieth Century, The   218
American Feminists   87
American Heroine   79
American Labor Unions by a Member   85
American Life in Autobiography   7
American Male, The   229
American Marriage and Divorce   215
American Midwives   121
American Modern Dancers, The Pioneers   141

American Nursing  122
American Search for Women, The  34
American Sisterhood, The  34
American Woman: A Historical Study, The  232
American Woman: Her Changing Social, Economic and Political Roles, 1920-1970, The  90
American Woman: Who Was She?, The  36
American Woman in Colonial and Revolutionary Times 1565-1800, The  7
American Woman in Transition, The  88
American Woman's Home, The  62
American Women: Fifteen Hundred Biographies with over 1400 Portraits  22
American Women: Our Lives and Labor  3
American Women: Report of the President's Commission on the Status of Women and Other Publications of the Commission  99
American Women: The Feminine Side of a Masculine Society, The  33
American Women and the Labor Movement, 1825-1974  10
American Women in Sport, The  145
American Women of Science  123
America's First Lady Boss  157
America's Working Women  161
America through Women's Eyes  89
Amy Lowell: A Chronicle  127
Analysis of Human Sexual Response, An  196
And Jill Came Tumbling After  153
Androgyny  201
And the Poor Get Children  208
Angel of the Battlefield  122
Angels and Amazons  34
Anita Bryant Story, The  196
Anne Bradstreet  46
Anne Bradstreet and Her Time  127
Anne Sexton: A Self-Portrait in Letters  133
Annotated Selected Bibliography of Bibliographies on Women, An  3

Anonymous Was a Woman  235
Another Secret Diary of William Byrd of Westover 1739-1741  41
Anthropologist at Work, An  155
Archival and Manuscript Resources for the Study of Women's History  5
Are You Anybody?  238-39
Art and Life of Grandma Moses  130
Art and Sexual Politics  129
Arthur and Elizabeth Schlesinger Library on the History of Women in America: The Manuscript Inventories  1
Artists in Aprons  237
Asian Women  167
Assertiveness Training for Women  191
Assertive Woman, The  192
At Odds  237
Autobiography, An (Davis)  169
Autobiography, An (Sanger)  209
Autobiography of a Black Woman, The  169
Autobiography of a Female Slave  168
Autobiography of an American Communist, The  112
Autobiography of Mother Jones, The  84
Autobiography of Mrs. Amanda Smith  173
Azalia  138

### B

Baby? . . . Maybe, A  224
Battered Woman, The  183
Battered Women  182
Be a Man!  244
Becoming a Mother  242
Begin at Start  105
Beginnings of Sisterhood  57
Behind Closed Doors  244
Behind the Scenes  170
Bella! Ms. Abzug Goes to Washington  111
Beloved Lady  80
Be Not Afraid  142
Bessie  137
Better Half, The  36
Between Marriage and Divorce  214

Between Me and Life 133
Between Myth and Morning 104
Beyond God the Father 102
Beyond Her Sphere 156
Beyond Monogamy 218
Beyond Sugar and Spice 242
Bibliography in the History of American Women 7
Bibliography in the History of European Women 6
Bibliography of Prostitution, A 2
Bibliography on Divorce, A 6
Bibliography on the Jewish Woman 2
Bibliography on Women 3
Biblioteca Femina 10
Big Mama Rag 23
Big Star Fallin' Mama 139
Billie Jean 146
Biographical Cyclopedia of American Women, The 19
Birth Control 203
Birth Control and the Catholic Doctrine 210
Birth Control in Practice 207
Birth Control Laws 204
Birth Controllers 205
Birth Control Review 23
Bitching 105
Blackberry Winter 158
Black Family and the Black Woman, The 6
Black Macho and the Myth of Superwoman 174
Black Woman, The 168
Black Woman in America, The 173
Black Women in American Society 3
Black Women in Nineteenth Century American Life 56
Black Women in White America 171
Bloomer Girls, The 54
Bonds of Womanhood, The 51
Bonnet Brigades 69
Book for Grandmothers, A 222
Book of Abigail and John, The 39
Book of Readings for Men against Sexism, A 230
Born Female 155
Boss Lady 156
Bread and Roses 23
Breakthrough 157

Bride Goes West, A 61
Brides from Bridewell 40
Bridge for Passing, A 126
Bringing Women into Management 156
Bring Me a Unicorn 93
Brockden Brown and the Rights of Women 42
Buried Alive 138
Business of Being a Woman, The 88
By Myself 137

## C

Cannery Captives 94
Capitalist Patriarchy and the Case for Socialist Feminism 108
Career and Contributions to Physical Education 147
Careers and Contingencies 149
Careers for Women 91
Career Women of America 1776-1840 52
Carey Thomas of Bryn Mawr 81
Carrie Chapman Catt: A Biography 86
Case against Having Children, The 223
Case for Women Suffrage, The 4
Catalog of the Sophia Smith Collection 2, 8
Catherine Beecher 58
Catherine Esther Beecher 151
Catholics and Birth Control 203
Causation, Course and Treatment of Reflex Insanity in Women, The 73
Century of Higher Education for American Women, A 152
Century of Struggle 32
Chains of Protection, The 161
Challenge of Day Care, The 227
Challenging Years 78
Chances of a Lifetime 237
Changing Dimensions of Day Care, The 225
Charlotte Perkins Gilman: The Making of a Radical Feminist, 1860-1896 239
Charmed Circle 131

# Title Index

Chemist at Work, The 120
Chicana: A Comprehensive Biblio-
  graphic Study 2
La Chicana: The Mexican-American
  Woman 241
Child Care: Who Cares? 227
Child Care and ABC's Too 226
Child Care and Working Mothers 227
Child Care Issues for Parents and
  Society 4
Child Destiny 122
Child Welfare League of America 226
Chrysalis 23
Class, Sex and the Woman Worker
  161
Class and Feminism 107
Clios Consciousness Raised 33
Clout 117
Club Woman, The 23
Cocktail Waitress, The 164
College, the Market, and the Court,
  The 64
Collegiate Women 81, 151
Colonial Dames and Good Wives 42
Colonial Days and Dames 47
Colonial Women of Affairs 42
Colored Women in a White World,
  A 174
Combat in the Erogenous Zone 196
Come into My Parlor 188
Coming Nation, The 24
Coming of Age in Mississippi 172
Commercialized Prostitution in New
  York 186
Companionate Marriage 216
Complaints and Disorders 205
Concerning Women 93
Confederate Women 74
Conjugal Crime 181
Conjugal Sins against the Laws of
  Life and Health and the Effects
  upon the Father, Mother and
  Child 66
Constantia 43
Constitutional Equality 64
Constitutional Rights of Women,
  The 113
Consumption 57
Contraception 208
Contraception and Fertility in the
  Southern Appalachians 90

Control of Contraception 204
Conundrum 199
Coping 219
Corporate Wives--Corporate Casualties
  217
Country Women 24
County Women: A Handbook for the
  New Farmer 165
Courage, Fortitude, Devotedness and
  Self-Sacrifice 66
Creative Divorce 215
Criminal Abortion 73
Criminality of Women, The 178
Cross of Latitude, The 177
Crusade for Freedom 56
Crusade for Justice 175
Crusader in Crinoline 135
Crystal Eastman on Women and Revo-
  lution 80
Curious Courtship of Women's Libera-
  tion and Socialism, The 110
Curse, The 204
Curtain Going Up 140
Cyclone in Calico 119

# D

Dames and Daughters of Colonial
  Days 41
Daughter of the Samurai, A 174
Daughters and Mothers 190
Daughters of the Country 172
Daughters of the Promised Land 37
Dawns and Dusks 132
Day Care and Preschool Services
  227
Day Care as a Child Rearing Environ-
  ment 227
Day Care Book, The 225
Day Care Cost Analysis 227
Day Care for Infants 226
Day Care in Context 226
Dear-Bought Heritage, The 44
Decade of Elusive Promise, The 157
Deliver Us from Love 101
Depressed Woman, The 192
Devil in Massachusetts, The 46
Dialectic of Sex, The 108
Diana 197
Diary from Dixie, A 63

Diary of Miss Emma Holmes, The 67
Diary of Samuel Sewall, 1674-1729, The 46
Dimity Convictions 38
Directory of Woman Physicians in the U.S. 19
Discrimination against Women 159
Divorce 216
Divorce: A Selected Annotated Bibliography 7
Divorce: What a Woman Needs to Know 215
Divorced Woman's Handbook, The 244
Divorce Experience, The 215
Divorce in the Progressive Era 217
Divorce in the United States, Canada, and Great Britain 9
Doctors' Case against the Pill, The 210
"Doctors Wanted: No Women Need Apply" 123
Dolly 141
Domestic Life in New England in the Seventeenth Century 42
Domestic Manners of the Americans 58
Domestic Service 72
Dorothea L. Dix 56
Dorothy S. Ainsworth 146
Dorothy Thompson 159
Dreamers and Dealers 103
Dust Tracks on a Road 170

E

Early Child Care in the United States of America 227
Echo in My Soul 168
Economics of Sex Discrimination, The 163
Edith Hamilton 158
Edith Wharton 130
Educated Woman in America, The 150
Education and a Woman's Life 150
Education of Girls in the United States, The 62
Eleanor: The Years Alone 114
Eleanor and Franklin 93

Eleanor Roosevelt: An American Conscience 92
Elinor Wylie 129
Elizabeth Cady Stanton 70
Elizabeth Cady Stanton: A Radical for Women's Rights 235
Elizabeth Cady Stanton as Revealed in Her Letters, Diary and Reminiscences 72
Eliza Pinckney 45
Ella Flagg Young 243
Ellen Glasgow and the Woman within 128
Ellen Swallow 119
Emancipation of Angelina Grimke, The 56
Emily Dickinson 63
Eminent and Heroic Women of America, The 65
Emma Willard 69
Employed Mother in America, The 223
Employment of Women in the Clothing Trades 165
Enterprising Women 155
Entrepreneurial Woman, The 160
Erotic Life of the American Wife, The 197
Equality in Sport for Women 145
Equal Marriage 218
Equal Rights 24
Equal Rights Amendment, The 5
Equal Rights Handbook, The 112
Escape from the Doll's House 150
Essays in Feminism 103
Essays in Medical Sociology 62
Essays on Various Subjects, Principally Designed for Young Ladies 44
Every Child's Birthright 222
Everyday Life in Colonial America 47
Every Day Life in the Massachusetts Bay Colony 42
Everyday Things in American Life, 1607-1776 44
Everyone Was Brave 35
Every Parent's Guide to Day Care Centers 226
Everything a Woman Needs to Know

to Get Paid What She's Worth 155

Every Woman's Guide to Abortion 205

Everywoman's Guide to College 151

Every Woman's Guide to Hysterectomy 206

Excellency of the Female Character Vindicated, The 41

Executive Suite--Feminine Style, The 158

Exile's Daughter, The 133

## F

Factors in the Sex Life of Twenty-two Hundred Women 197

Families under Stress 215

Family and Its Members, The 218

Family Day Care 226

Family Desertion and Non-Support Laws 213

Family Design 217

Fascinating Womanhood 231

Father's Days 236

Fear of Being a Woman, The 234

Fear of Women, The 233

Feast of Words, A 135

Female Athlete, The 146

Female Complaints 123

Female Eunuch, The 103

Female Offender, The 177

Female Persuasion 58

Female Prose 129

Female Psychology 190

Female Sexuality and the Oedipus Complex 200

Female Sexual Slavery 235

Female Woman, The 234

Feminine, The 192

Feminine Character, The 190

Feminine Mistake, The 234

Feminine Mystique, The 102

Feminine Personality and Conflict 189

Feminine Psychology 190

Femininity as Alienation 108

Feminism 88

Feminism: Its Fallacies and Follies 85

Feminism: The Essential Historical Writings 36

Feminism and Marxism 107

Feminism and Materialism 109

Feminism and Socialism 109

Feminism and Suffrage 52

Feminism as Therapy 191

Feminist Studies 24

Feminization of American Culture, The 65

Fertility of American Women, The 32

Few Are Chosen 114

Films by and/or about Women, 1972 4, 20

First Lady of the Revolution 39

First White Women over the Rockies 52

First You Cry 204

Five Hundred Delinquent Women 178

Five Mexican American Women 172

Florence Kelley 78

Florine Stettheimer 134

Flower and the Nettle, The 93

Folkways 73

Following the Period of Gestation 55

For Better, for Worse 214

Forbidden Flowers 197

Foremost Women in Communications 21

Forerunner 24

For Yourself 195

Foundations of Feminism 89

Fox Girls 142

Frances Willard 64

Frances Wright 57

Free and Female 200

From a New England Woman's Diary in Dixie in 1865 61

From Parlor to Prison 82

From Rationality to Liberation 106

From Tipi to Skyscraper 155

From Woman to Woman 207

Frontier 24

Frontier Lady, A 71

Frontier Women 68

Future of Motherhood, The 221

Future of Sexual Relations 197

# G

Games Mother Never Taught You  156
Gay Academic, The  196
Gay American History  198
Gay Report, The  239
Gender Trap, The  189
Generation of Vipers  234
Generation of Women, A  240
Genocide?  Birth Control and the
 Black American  211
Gentlemen of Leisure  186
Gentle Tamers, The  62
Georgia O'Keefe  128
Gerritsen Collection of Women's
 History, The  5
Gertrude Vanderbilt Whitney  81
Getting Help  243
Getting Yours  158
Girls and Sex  200
Girls of Nevada, The  188
Girls on City Streets  182
Glamour Girls, The  142
Godfathers, The  110
Going Too Far  99
Golden Fleece  63
Golden Yesterdays  127
Good Fight, The  112
Goodly Fellowship, A  150
Goodness Had Nothing to Do with
 It  143
Grace H. Dodge  66
Graduate Education for Women  152
Grandma Moses  137
Greatest American Woman, Lucretia
 Mott, The  54
Great Women of Medicine  120
Great Women Singers of My Time  140
Grimke Sisters, The  49
Grimke Sisters from South Carolina,
 The  56
Growth and Development of Mothers,
 The  222
Group Called Women, A  101
Group Marriage  214
Guide for Catholic Young Women  64
Guiness Book of Women's Sports
 Records  241
Gyn/Ecology  102

# H

Hannah More  44
Happiness in Marriage  209
Happy Hooker, The  186
Harriet Monroe and the Poetry
 Renaissance  135
Harriet Tubman  51
Harriet Tubman:  The Moses of Her
 People  167
Harsh and Dreadful Love, A  94
Hazards of Being Male, The  229
Heart Is Like Heaven, The  61
Helen and Teacher  240
Helen Keller, Her Socialist Years
 84
Hellhole  178
Heresies  24
Heritage of Her Own, A  236
Heroines of Dixie  68
Herstory  37
High Time to Tell It  69
Hillbilly Women  170
Him/Her/Self  31
His Eye on the Sparrow  175
His Religion and Hers  82
Historical Negro Biographies  21
History of Marriage and the Family,
 A  32
History of Prostitution, The (Bullough)
 185
History of Prostitution, The (Sanger)
 187
History of Prostitution: Its Extent,
 Causes and Effects Throughout the
 World, The  186
History of the Women's Medical Col-
 lege, Philadelphia, Pa.  119
History of Woman Suffrage  87
History of Women Artists, A  131
History of Women from the Earliest
 Antiquity to the Present Time, The
 39
History of Women's Education in the
 United States  154
Hite Report, The  198
Holy Bible, Containing the Old and
 New Testament, The  50
Home Life in America  78
Home Life in Colonial Days  43

Homespun Heroines and Other Women of Distinction   168
Homosexualities   195
Horrors of the Half-Known Life, The   49
Hospitals, Paternalism and the Role of the Nurse   235
Hour of Gold, Hour of Lead   94
House Is Not a Home, A   185
Houseworker's Handbook   165
How Could She Do That?   177
How to Say No to a Rapist and Survive   183
How to Sell to Women   232
How to Win and Hold a Husband   90
How Women Can Make Money   71
Human Sexual Response   199
Hundred Years of Mount Holyoke College, A   150
Hustling   188

I

I Always Wanted to Be Somebody   145
I Am a Woman--and a Jew   173
I Am a Woman Worker   92
I Change Worlds   95
Ideas of the Woman Suffrage Movement, The   84
Identities in the Lesbian World   200
I Knew Them in Prison   178
I Know Why the Caged Bird Sings   167
Illegitimacy   222
Illegitimate Family in New York City, The   95
I'm Madly in Love with Electricity and Other Comments about Their Work by Women in Science and Engineering   120
Immigrant Woman and Her Job, The   94
Impact ERA   111
I'm Running Away from Home, But I'm Not Allowed to Cross the Street   101
Incidents in the Life of a Slave Girl   170
In Defense of Ourselves   183
Indian Women of the Western Morning   174

Industry and Day Care II   228
Inevitability of Patriarchy, The   232
Inferior Sex, The   233
In Her Own Image   239
Innocence of Joan Little, The   115
In No Man's Land   223
In the Vanguard   240
In This Our World   82
Intimate Memories   130
In Transition   97
Invisible Woman, The   149
Isn't One Wife Enough?   75
Issues in Feminism   243
Italian Women in Industry   172
It Changed My Life   98

J

Jane Addams and the Liberal Tradition   85
Jeannette Rankin   113
Jewish Marriage Contract, The   169
Jewish Woman, The   171
Jewish Woman in America, The   167
Journal of Charlotte L. Forten, The   169
Journal of a Residence on a Georgian Plantation in 1838-1839   55
Journey to Obscurity   131
Judy Garland   138
Julia Ward Howe and the Woman Suffrage Movement   67
Jury Woman   116

K

Kate   139
Kate Chopin: A Critical Biography   133
Keystone, The   25

L

Labor of Women in the Production of Cotton   89
Ladder, The   25
Ladies Bountiful   132
Ladies Garment Worker, The   25
Ladies in Revolt   33
Ladies of Seneca Falls, The   54

Ladies of the Press 159
Lady and the Vote, The 116
Lady of Godey's, The 53
Lady of the House, The 188
Lady's Friend 25
Language and Woman's Place 104
Laura Clay and the Women's Movement 81
Law, Politics and Birth Control 205
Law for a Woman, The 116
Lawyering 116
Leading Ladies 31
Legislative Handbook on Women's Issues 115
Lesbian Community, The 244
Lesbian Couple, The 201
Lesbianism and the Woman's Movement 200
Lesbian Myth, The 202
Lesbian Nation 198
Lesbians, Women and Society 238
Lesbian Tide 25
Lesbian/Woman 199
Letters 128
Letters Home 132
Letters of a Woman Homesteader 73
Letters of Edna St. Vincent Millay 131
Letters of Ellen Glasgow 128
Letters of Lydia Maria Child 63
Letters of Sarah Orne Jewett 129
Letters on the Equality of the Sexes, and the Condition of Women 54
Let Them Speak for Themselves 53
Liberated Man, The 229
"Liberated" Woman of 1914, The 79
Liberated Women and Other Americans, The 231
Liberating Women's History 101
Liberty's Daughters 242
Liberty's Women 241
Life and Labor 25
Life and Lillian Gish 141
Life and Professional Career of Emma Abbott, The 141
Life and Work of Susan B. Anthony, The 67
Life and Writings of Amelia Bloomer, The 50
Life in Prairie Land 52

Life in the Eighteenth Century 43
Life of an Italian Immigrant, The 169
Life of Emma Thursby, The 139
Life of Margaret Fuller, The 58
Life of Mary Lyon, The 54
Life Story of Helen Sekaquapteria as Told to Louise Udall, The 174
Lily Martin Spencer 125
Lively Commerce, The 188
Living and Loving after Divorce 216
Living My Life 82
Living of Charlotte Perkins Gilman, The 82
Living Wage of Women Workers, The 78
Lizzie Borden: The Untold Story 71
Lonely Hunter, The 127
Lonely Lady of San Clemente, The 115
Lonely Life, The 138
Longest War, The 192
Long Loneliness, The 90
Long Shadow of Little Rock, The 167
Long Way Baby, A 146
Looking Forward 86
Louisa May 72
Louisa May Alcott (Anthony) 125
Louisa May Alcott (Stern) 73
Louise Imogene Guiney 126
Louise Nevelson 128
Love, Sex and Sex Roles 106
Love between Women 201
Lucy Stone 50
Lying in 211

M

Madams of San Francisco, The 186
Majority Report 25
Making Do 96
Making of a Feminist, The 153
Making of a Woman Surgeon, The 241
Making of Political Women, The 114
Male and Female 35
Male Attitude, The 229
Male Guide to Women's Liberation, A 230
Mama Doesn't Live Here Anymore 219

# Title Index

Managerial Woman, The 156
Mandatory Motherhood 206
Man-Made World, The 82
Manners 66
Man's Place, A 237
Man's World, Woman's Place 104
Margaret Dreir Robins 80
Margaret Fuller: American Romantic 53
Margaret Fuller: A Psychological Biography 49
Margaret Fuller: Whetstone of Genius 59
Margaret Sanger 206
Margaret Sanger: Pioneer of the Future 205
Margaret Sanger Story, The 207
Maria Mitchell 120
Marilyn 140
Marital Separation 219
Marriage, Morals and Sex in America 197
Marriage between Equals 217
Marriage Guide, Or Natural History of Generation, The 55
Marriage Stability, Divorce and the Law 217
Married Feminist, A 216
Married Lady's Companion, The 55
Married Woman's Private Medical Companion 69
Marvella 235
Marxism and Feminism 108
Mary Baker Eddy: The Years of Discovery 70
Mary Baker Eddy: The Years of Trial 71
Mary Cassatt: Oils and Pastels 126
Mary Garden's Story 138
Mary McCarthy 130
Mary McLeod Bethune (Holt) 170
Mary McLeod Bethune (Peare) 173
Mary Ritter Beard: A Source Book 84
Mary Wollstonecraft 45
Mechanical Bride, The 199
Medical Women of America 120
Meditations from the Pen of Mrs. Maria W. Stewart, Negro 174
Memoir of Mrs. Susanna Rowson, A 132

Memoirs of an American Prima Donna 140
Memoirs of Anne C.L. Botta Written by Her Friend with Selections from Her Correspondence and from Her Writings in Prose and Poetry 125
Memoirs of Eighty Years 134
Memoirs of Jane A. Delano 119
Memoirs of Margaret Fuller Ossoli 52
Memoirs of Mary A. Maverick 57
Memories: An Autobiography 137
Memories beyond Bloomers 146
Memories of a Bloomer Girl (1894-1924) 146
Memories of a Singer 139
Men 230
Men, Money and Magic 158
Men in Love 238
Men's Studies Bibliography 8
Menstruation 207
Men Who Control Women's Health 243
Mercy Warren 41
Midstream: My Later Life 84
Midwife's Practical Directory, The 54
Millay in Greenwich Village 127
Mine Eyes Have Seen the Glory: A Biography of Julia Ward Howe 51
Mine Eyes Have Seen the Glory: The Story of a Virginia Lady, Mary Berkeley Minor Blackford 62
Minority of Members, A 111-12
Mirages of Marriage, The 216
Mirror, Mirror 37
Miss Alcott of Concord 74
Miss Leslie's Behavior Book 68
Miss Mary Cassatt 134
Miss Ruth 142
Mistress Condition 214
Model Programs and Their Components 225
Modernization of Sex, The 200
Modern Woman 233
Mollie 72
Momism 234
Momma Handbook for Single Mothers, The 222
Mom's Apple Pie 26
Morality of Abortion, The 208
Mother Jones, The Miner's Angel 81

Mother Person, The  221
Mother's Book, The  50
Mother's Day Is Over  223
Mothers in Poverty  222
Mothers of the South  92
Mothers Who Must Earn  78
Movers and Shakers  37
Mrs. E.D.E.N. Southworth, Novelist  126
Mrs. Fiske and the American Theatre  137
Ms. Magazine  26
My Battles with Vice  185
My Fight for Birth Control  209
My Life as a Political Prisoner  113
My Life with Martin Luther King  170
My Lord What a Morning  137
My Mother--My Self  222
My Own Story  138
My Portion  171
Myrtilla Miner  172
My Secret Garden  197
My Several Worlds  126
My Side  139
My Story  137
Myth America  37
My Thirty Years War  125
My Wife and I  139

N

Nancy  242
Nancy Shippen  46
Narrative of Sojourner Truth  58
Nature and Evolution of Female Sexuality, The  201
Negro American Family  80
Negro Woman, The  152
Nervous Housewife, The  94
New Assertive Woman, The  190
New Career Option for Women  8
New Chastity and Other Arguments against Women's Liberation  232
New Conscience and an Ancient Evil, A  185
New Executive Woman, The  160
New Feminism in Twentieth-Century America, The  37
New Feminist Movement, The  97
New Husbands and How to Become One, The  229

New Life Plan, A  216
New Male, The  239
Newspaperwoman  160
New Woman, The  87
New Woman, The  97
New York Women's Directory, The  11
Nigger in the Window  171
Nisei Daughter  173
Noble Deeds of American Women  50
Noble Women of the North  64
Nobody Speaks for Me!  164
No Life for a Lady  63
Notable American Women, 1607-1950  20
Notable American Women: The Modern Period  243
Notebooks That Emma Gave Me, The  201
Notes of a Feminist Therapist  193
Notes on Women Printers in Colonial America and the United States  1

O

Observations on the Rights of Women  51
Obstacle Race, The  128
Occupation: Housewife  163
Off Our Backs  26
Of Woman Born  223
Ojibwa Woman, The  171
Older Woman in Industry, The  94
Once upon a Pedestal  33
One Woman's "Situation"  44
On Lies, Secrets and Silence  105
On Loving Men  240
On My Own  115
On Reflections  139
On the Psychology of Women  192
On the Verge of Revolt  138
On Women and Power  37
Open Marriage  217
Opportunities for Women in Higher Education  149
Oral History Collection of Columbia University, The  8
Originals  242
Other Shores  242
Our American Sisters  32
Our Blood  102
Our Bodies, Our Selves  203

Our Changing Morality 92
Our Famous Women 35
Our National Passion 195
Our Right to Love 201
Our Selves and Our Children 221
Out of the Air 140
Out of the Bleachers 147
Out of the Closets 198
Out of the Frying Pan 239
Out of Wedlock 224
Oven Birds, The 35

## P

Palace of Healing 123
Paramount Pretties, The 142
Part Taken by Women in American
    History, The 21
Patriarchal Attitudes 108
Patterns of Forcible Rape 181
Pecos Pioneer, A 62
"Peculiar Institutions" 152
Peculiar Treasure, A 127
Pentimento 129
Perish the Thought 31
Personal Politics 98
Personnel Study of Women Deans in
    Colleges and Universities 151
Philosophy and Sex 195
Philosophy of Marriage in Its Social,
    Moral, and Physical Relations,
    The 57
Physician and Sexuality in Victorian
    America, The 66
Picture Catalog of the Sophia
    Smith Collection 9
Pill on Trial, The 210
Pink Collar Workers 162
Pioneer Mothers of the West 65
Pioneers of Birth Control 209
Pioneer Work in Opening the Medi-
    cal Profession to Women 119
Pivot of Civilization, The 209
Playing Around 201
Pleasure Bond, The 199
Plexus 26
Plow Women Rather than Reapers 243
Poems and Letters 135
Poems of Maria Lowell, The
Poet and Her Book, The 128

Poetry of American Women from 1632
    to 1945 134
Poet's Life, A 131
Political Economy of Women's Libera-
    tion, The 107
Political Participation of Women in
    the United States, The 10
Political Women 114
Politics of Contraception, The 237
Politics of Rape, The 183
Politics of Sexuality in Capitalism,
    The 109
Politics of the Equal Rights Amend-
    ment, The 111
Politics of Women's Liberation, The
    98
Policewoman, The 92
Popcorn Venus 142
Portrait of an Artist 241
Portrait of Marginality, A 113
Portraits of American Women 30
Practical Guide to the Women's
    Movement, A 8
Pregnancy, Birth and Abortion 205
Primers for Prudery 74
Prisoner of Sex, The 233
Prisoners of Poverty 63
Private Faces/Public Places 115
Problems of Women's Liberation 109
Professional Woman, The 160
Professional Woman in a Man's World,
    A 159
Profile of Women Holding Office
    113
Profiles of Negro Womanhood 20
Progressive Woman, The 24
Pronatalism 223
Prose Works; Narratives of a Colonial
    Virginian 41
Prostitute and the Social Reformer,
    The 187
Prostitution in the United States
    188
Prostitution Papers, The 187
Prudence Crandall 53
Psychic Factors of Civilization,
    The 74
Psychoanalysis and Feminism 191
Psychoanalysis and Women 191
Psychology of Conviction, The 84
Psychology of Sex Differences 191

Psychology of Women, The 232
Psychology of Women: A Study of Bio-Cultural Conflicts 189
Psychology of Women: Behavior in a Bio-Social Context 193
Public Policy for Day Care of Young Children 228
Puritan Ethic and Woman Suffrage, The 83
Puritan Family, The 45
Purity Crusade: Sexual Morality, and Social Control, 1868-1900 71, 187

Q

Quaker Family in Colonial America, The 43
Quest 26

R

Rachel Carson 121
Radical Feminism 104
Radical Life, A 96
Rape 182
Rape! One Victim's Story 182
Rape: The First Sourcebook for Women 181
Rape: Victims of Crisis 181
Rape Bibliography, A 9
Rationale for Child Care Services 225
Readings on the Psychology of Women 189
Real Isadora, The 142
Rebel in Paradise 80
Rebels in the Street 178
Rebirth of Feminism 99
Redbook Report on Female Sexuality, The 201
Re-Entering 236
Reign of Patti, The 140
Re-Inventing Womanhood 104
Relations of the Sexes, The 65
"Remember the Ladies": New Perspectives on Women in America 32
Remeber the Ladies: The Story of Great Women Who Helped Shape America 31

Reminiscences of Linda Richards 122
Reminiscences of School Life and Hints on Teaching 168
Report from Part One 167
Report of the LEAA Task Force on Women, The 179
Report of the Senate Vice Committee 83
Reproduction of Mothering, The 221
Research Memorandum on the Family in the Depression 218
Responsibility for Child Care 226
Restless Spirit 129
Revolutionary Feminism 109
Rights and Wrongs of Abortion, The 204
Rights of Man, The 77
Rights of Women, The 116
Rise, Gonna Rise 236
Roads They Made, The 38
Road to Reno, The 214
Roman Years of Margaret Fuller, The 51
Rooms with No View 159
Root of Bitterness 31
Roots of American Feminism, The 31
Rosalind Franklin and DNA 123
Runaway Wives 218
Ruth Benedict 158
Ruth Gibow 130

S

Saints and Sectarians 40
Salem Possessed 40
Saleslady, The 91
Salons 47
Sappho Was a Right-on Woman 195
Sarah Orne Jewett 131
Sarah Winnemucca 169
Satan in Society 64
Saturday's Child 159
Save Me the Waltz 127
Schoolma'am, The 91
Schumann-Heink 140
S.C.U.M. Manifesto 106
Search for an Abortionist, The 207
Second Oldest Profession, The 187
Second Sex, The 102
Second Twenty Years at Hull House, The 97

# Title Index

Second Wave: A Magazine of On-
going Feminism, The  26
Second Wave: A Magazine of the
New Feminism, The  26
Secretarial Ghetto, The  161
Secret Diary of William Byrd of
Westover, 1709-12, The  41
Secular and Religious Work of Penina
Moise with a Brief Sketch of Her
Life  131
Seizing Our Bodies  205
Selected Bibliography of Women's
Activities  2
Separation  213
Seven Days a Week  68, 162
Seventy Birth Control Clinics  208
Seven Women  35
Sex, Discrimination and the Division
of Labor  163
Sex and Caste in America  107
Sex and Education  67
Sex and Marriage in Utopian Com-
munities  70
Sex and the Single Girl  231
Sex Barrier in Business, The  159
Sex Differences  191
Sex Differences in Public School
Administration  153
Sex Discrimination and the Law:
Causes and Remedies  111
Sex Game, The  213
Sexes Throughout Nature, The  62
Sex in Education  63
Sex in the Marketplace  162
Sexism and Science  122
Sexism in Higher Education  152
Sexist Justice  112
Sex Radicals, The  72
Sex Research  199
Sex Roles: A Research Bibliography
1
Sex Roles: Biological, Psychologi-
cal and Social Foundations  38
Sex Roles in Law and Society  114
Sex Roles in the State House  112
Sex Role Stereotyping in the Mass
Media  4
Sexual Arena and Women's Liberation,
The  189
Sexual Barrier, The  5

Sexual Behavior in the Human Female
198
Sexual Behavior in the Human Male
198
Sexual Harassment of Working Women
182
Sexual Impotence in the Male and
Female  197
Sexuality and Human Values  196
Sexually Adequate Female, The  231
Sexually Aggressive Women, The
196
Sexually Responsive Woman, The  199
Sexual Organism and Its Healthful
Management, The  68
Sexual Politics  105
Sexual Wilderness, The  200
Sex without Babies  211
Sharing the Children  226
Shortchanged Update  159
Signs  26
Silences  132
Silent Hattie Speaks  114
Silent Voices  168
Silhouette in Diamonds  133
Single Women  213
Sisterhood Is Powerful  110
Sisterhood Is Powerful: An Anthology
of Writings from the Women's
Liberation Movement  105
Sisterhood of Man, The  105
Sisters in Crime  177
Sister Saints  35
Sister to the Sioux  65
Slaveholders Daughter, A  68
Slavery of Sex, The  55
Social Evil in Chicago, The  186
Social History of the American Family,
A  30
Social History of the United States
10
Socialism and the Fight for Women's
Rights  109
Socialist Woman, The  27
Social Life in the Early Republic  59
Social Thought of June Addams, The
77
Society in America  56
Society of Women  178

Sociology of Housework, The 164
Sojourner 27
Sojourner Truth 52
Some Action of Her Own 149
Some Ethical Gains through Legislation 84
So Short a Time 81
South Carolina's Distinguished Women of Laurens County 21
Southern Lady from Pedestal to Politics, 1830-1930, The 36
Southern Women in the Recent Educational Movement in the South 70
Spearheads for Reform 79
Spirit of Houston, The 99
Staying Married 215
Staying on Alone 134
Stone Wall 196
Stopping Wife Abuse 238
Story of a Pioneer, The 72
Story of My Life, The 69
Story of the Woman's Party, The 83
Storyville Portraits 185
Stranger and Traveler 59
Stranger in the House, A 162
Strictures on the Modern System of Female Education 57
Strong Minded Women 86
Study of Women, The 99
Subject Collections 1
Subordinate Sex, The 30
Suffragist and Democrats 85
Survival Guide for the Suddenly Single 213
Susan B. Anthony: Her Personal History and Her Era 61
Susan B. Anthony: Rebel Crusader, Humanitarian 69
Sweeper in the Sky 123
Sylvia Plath: Method and Madness 126
Sylvia Plath: The Woman and the Work 126

T

Taking Chances 207
Tallulah 142
Techniques of Conception Control 204

Technology and Women's Work 161
Tenderfoot Bride, A 71
Tenements of Chicago, 1908-1935, The 89
Teresa Carreno, "By the Grace of God" 141
Terrible Siren, The 61
Think and Act 71
Thinking Like a Woman 103
Third Door, The 174
Third Woman, The 238
Thirty Years Battle with Crime 188
This I Remember 115
This Life I've Led 147
This Was My Newport 91
Thorn of a Rose, The 133
Those Extraordinary Blackwells 67
Thoughts on Female Education 46
Three Out of Four Wives 216
Three Wise Virgins 50
Through the Flower 127
Thursdays and Every Other Sunday Off 162
Time Has Come, The 209
Timeless Affair 239
Times to Remember 114
To Be a Black Woman 175
To Be a Woman in America, 1850-1930 29
"Together" Black Women 173
Tomorrow's Tomorrow 171
Tongue of Flame 70
Total Woman, The 233
Toward a New Psychology of Women 191
Toward a Recognition of Androgeny 104
Trade Union Women, The 92
Traffic in Women and Other Essays on Feminism, The 186
Trumpet Sounds, The 170
Tuning in to the Movement 10
Turning Points 98
Twelve American Women 29
Twenties, The 94
Twenty Seventh Wife, The 73
Twenty Years at Hull House with Autobiographical Notes 77
Two Career Family, The 157
Two Colored Women with the American Expeditionary Forces 170

Two-Paycheck Marriage, The  214

U

Unbought and Unbossed  112
Unfinished Woman, An  129
Unmarried Mothers  223
Unwed Mother, The  223
Up from the Pedestal  34
Uphill  115
Urban Survival  243

V

Vaginal Health  206
Vaginal Politics  205
Vanguard, The  27
Various Diseases  70
Victimization of Women, The  181
Victims  182
Victorian Lady on the Texas Frontier  55
Violence against Wives  237
Virginians at Home  45
Vivien Leigh  138
Voice from the South by a Black Woman of the South, A  168
Voices of the New Feminism  106

W

Wage-Earning Women  85
Wage-Earning Women: Industrial Work and Family Life in the United States  244
Walls Came Tumbling Down, The  86
Washington Call Girl  185
Weathering the Storm  42
Welfare Mother, A  173
Welfare Mothers Speak Out  222
We're Here  196
Westward the Women  72
We the Women  73
We Were There  165
What a Young Wife Ought to Know  80
What Can a Woman Do  71
What Every Woman Needs to Know about Abortion  203
What Every Woman Needs to Know about the Law  242

What Is Remembered  134
What Little Girls Are Made of  189
What's a Nice Girl Like You Doing in a Place Like This?  160
What Women Should Know  65
What Women Want: An Interpretation of the Feminist Movement  83
What Women Want: The Ideas of the Movement  83
When Sherman Came  68
When Women Look at Men  229
White Caps  122
Who Discriminates against Women?  98
Who's Minding the Children  228
Who's Who among Black Americans  21
Who's Who in Illinois  20
Who's Who of American Women  22
Who's Who of the Colored Race  22
Who Will Raise the Children?  230
Why American Marriages Fail  87
Why Women Are So  79
Widow  214
Widowhood in an American City  216
Wife Beating  182
Willa Cather: A Critical Biography  126
Willa Cather: A Memoir  133
Willa Cather: Living  130
Wilma  147
Windows on Henry Street  88
Wire Womb, The  178
With Child  236
Woman, Culture and Society  35
Woman: Dependent or Independent Variable  192
Woman Alone, The  217
Woman and Nature  104
Woman and the Law  111
Woman as Writer  134
Woman at Work  77
Woman Citizen, The  93
Woman Hating  102
Womanhood in America  36
Womahood Media  11
Woman Movement from the Point of View of Social Consciousness, The  87
Woman Plus Woman  198

Woman Patriot, The 27
Woman Power 106
Woman Question in American History, The 38
Woman Rebel 27
Woman Rice Planter, A 86
Woman's Being, Woman's Place 240
Woman's Body 204
Woman's Body, Woman's Right 206
Womansbook, The 101
Woman's Column 27
Woman's Consciousness, Man's World 110
Woman's Creation 238
Woman's Life and Work in the Southern Colonies 46
Woman's Life in Colonial Days 44
Woman's Life Work, A 67
Woman's Orgasm 199
Woman's Place 155
Woman's Place: The Autobiography of Hortense Odlum, A 158
Woman's Proper Place 36
Woman's Record, or, Sketches of All Distinguished Women from Creation to A.D. 1854 20
Woman's Story of Pioneer Illinois, A 58
Woman's Work 70
Woman's Work Book 155
Woman's Work in America 70
Woman's Work in Municipalities 78
Woman Warrior, The 171
Woman Who Lost Her Names, The 241
Woman Who Waits, The 91
Women: A Bibliography on Their Education and Careers 1
Women: A Feminist Perspective 102
Women: A Journal of Liberation 27
Women: A Select Bibliography of Books 6
Women: A Selected Bibliography 8
Women, Men and the Doctorate 150
Women: Menopause and Middle Age 204
Women, War and Revolution 236
Women, Work and Volunteering 163
Women, World War and Permanent Peace 87

Women Alone 219
Women Alone: The Disaffiliation of Urban Females 213
Women and American Trade Unions 162
Women and Analysis 192
Women and Crime 177
Women and Education 152
Women and Equality: Changing Patterns in American Culture 90, 97
Women and Judaism 240
Women and Leisure 95
Women and Madness 190
Women and Men Midwives 120
Women and Philosophy 103
Women and Sex 200
Women and Social Change in America 106
Women and Society 9
Women and Sport: A National Research Conference 145
Women and Sport: From Myth to Reality 146
Women and Success 157
Women and Support Networks 108
Women and the American Economy 163
Women and the American Labor Movement 239
Women and the Crisis, The 74
Women and the "Equal Rights Amendment" 116
Women and the Labor Movement 33, 92
Women and the Law 114
Women and the Myth, The 53
Women and the New Race 209
Women and the Power to Change 151
Women and the Public Interest 107
Women and the Scientific Professions 121
Women and Urban Society 3
Women and Womanhood in America 33
Women and Work in America 164
Women Are Here to Stay 95
Women Artists 1550-1950 129
Women as a Force in History 30
Women as Widows 241

# Title Index

Women As World Builders 79
Women at Cornell 150
Women at Work: A Photographic Documentary 163
Women at Work: The Transformation of Work and Community 237
Women at Yale 152
Women Builders 20
Women Camp Followers of the American Revolution 40
Women Composers 21
Women Confined 243
Women Doctors of the World 121
Women Doctors Today 120
Women for Hire 241
Women in Academia 153
Women in a Changing World 100
Women in America 29
Women in America: A Guide to Books, 1963-1975 5
Women in American History (Haber) 5
Women in American History (Humphrey) 34
Women in American History, The 34
Women in American Politics 113
Women in Class Struggle 108
Women in Crime 178
Women in Defense Work during World War II 91
Women in Divorce 215
Women in Eighteenth Century America 40
Women in Gainful Occupations 1870 to 1920 83
Women in Higher Education 151
Women in Industry 78
Women in Industry: A Study of American Economic History 29
Women in Industry: Employment Patterns of Women in Corporate America 157
Women in Mathematics 121
Women in Medicine 121
Women in Medicine: A Bibliography of the Literature on Women Physicians 2
Women in Modern America 29
Women in Music History 9
Women in Perspective 6
Women in Physics 19
Women in Politics 113

Women in Prison 177
Women in Public Office 19
Women in Sexist Society 103
Women in Television News 156
Women in the American Economy 30
Women in the American Revolution 43
Women in the Field 156
Women in the Modern World 152
Women in the Professions 156
Women in Therapy 190
Women in the Twentieth Century 90
Women in Transition 219
Women in U.S. History 3
Women in Vocational Education 153
Women in White 121
Women Lawyers in the United States 116
Women of a Certain Age 243
Women of America, The 69
Women of America: A History 30
Women of Courage from Revolutionary Times to the Present 37
Women of Crisis: Lives of Struggle and Hope 168
Women of Crisis II 236
Women of Minnesota 21
Women of New York, The 65
Women of '76, The 40, 50
Women of the American Revolution, The 43
Women of the Nineteenth Century 53
Women of the South 128
Women of the West 66
Women of Watergate, The 112
Women on Campus 153
Women-Owned Businesses 160
Women's Athletics 145
Women's Bureau, The 95
Women's Education--A World View 8
Women's Education Begins 149
Women's Experience in America 240
Women's Fate 102
Women's Fiction 125
Women's Garment Workers, The 93
Women's Higher and Continuing Education 11
Women's Inferior Education 151
Women's Liberation: Black Women, Working Women, Revolutionary Feminism 11

Women's Liberation: Blueprint for the Future 106
Women's Liberation and Revolution 9
Women's Liberation and the Socialist Revolution 110
Women's Movement, The 97
Women's Movement in the Seventies, The 6
Women's Movement Media 5
Women's Organizations and Leaders, 1975-1976 19
Women's Prison--Sex and Social Structure 179
Women's Rights Movement in the United States 1848-1970, The 7
Women's Studies: A Guide to Reference Sources 7
Women's Studies Newsletter 28
Women's Suffrage and Prohibition 86
Women State Legislators 117
Women Studies Abstracts 11, 28
Women's Who's Who of America 22
Women's Work and Women's Studies 1973-1974 4
Women's Yellow Pages 4
Women Wage Earners 63

Women Who Make Our Novels, The 132
Woodhull and Clafin's Weekly 74
Words and Women 105
Work-a-Day Girl 85
Working-Class Women and Grass-Roots Politics 115
Working Girls of Boston, The 74
Working Man's Wife 164
Working Mother, The 221
Working Mothers 221
Working Mothers and the Day Nursery 225
Work of the Afro-American Woman, The 172
World of Emma Lazaras, The 170
Wree-View, The 28

Y

Yankee Diva 139
Years Alone, The 95
You Might as Well Live 130
Young Husband, The 49
Young Lady's Own Book, The 59
Young Wife, The 49
You're Only Human Once 141

# SUBJECT INDEX

Alphabetization is letter by letter.   References are to page numbers.   Refer to
the table of contents for main areas of the text.

## A

Abbott, Edith   16
Abbott, Emma   141
Abbott, Grace   16
Abolitionist movement   15
Abortion   64, 65, 73, 99, 203-11
    antifeminist and   66
    bibliography on   3
Abortion Rights Association   16
Adams, Abigail   30, 39, 47, 235
Adams, John   39, 47
Addams, Jane   14, 15, 29, 35, 77,
    79, 80, 85, 108
Adkinson, Florence W.   27
Ainsworth, Dorothy S.   146
Akron, University of   15
Alcott, Louisa May   15, 30, 72, 73,
    74, 125
Aldis, Mary   16
Alschuler, Rose   15
Amalgamated Clothing and Textile
    Workers   236
American Academy of Arts and
    Sciences   120
American Antislavery Society   14
American Association of University
    Women   14, 16
American Civil Liberties Union   111,
    116
American Council on Education   151

American Jewish Historical Society   15
American Medical Women's Associa-
    tion   15
American Peace Society   14
American Psychological Association   98
Anderson, Margaret   125
Anderson, Marian   37, 137
Anderson, Mary   77
Anthony, Susan B.   14, 15, 29, 31,
    33, 35, 37, 61, 69, 86, 87
Antifeminism   231-34
Army Nurse Corps   119
Asian-American women   167, 171, 173,
    174
Association for the Advancement of
    Women   123
Association for Voluntary Sterilization
    16
Association of Junior Leagues of
    America   16
Association of Southern Women for
    the Prevention of Lynching   17
Astor, Mary   137
Atlanta University   17
Atwood, Margaret   134
Austin, Mary   16

## B

Bacall, Lauren   137
Bailey, Hannah J.   15

Baldwin, Evelyn Briggs 14
Bancroft Library (University of California) 16
Bara, Theda 142
Bankhead, Tallulah 142
Barnard College 152
Barney, Natalie 133
Barrymore, Ethel 137
Barton, Clara 14, 70, 127
Bayh, Marvella 235
Beach, Sylvia 133
Beard, Mary Ritter 16, 84
Beecher, Catherine [Catharine] 33, 35, 58, 150, 151
Beecher, Henry Ward 58
Benedict, Ruth 15, 158
Benson, Naomi Achenbach 17
Berkshire Conference of Women Historians 33
Bernard, Jessie 121
Bethune, Mary McLeod 170, 173-74
Bettelheim, Bruno 121
Bickerdyke, Mary Ann 119
Bird, Rose 240
Birth control 36, 54, 64, 69-70, 80, 83, 203-11
   antifeminists and 66
   of low-income families during the Depression 90
   social issues and 237
Blackford, Mary Berkeley Minor 62
Blackstone, William 114
Black Woman Oral History Project 14
Blackwell, Alice Stone 27
Blackwell, Anna 14
Blackwell, Ellen 14
Blackwell, Emily 13, 122
Blackwell, Elizabeth 13, 67, 119, 122
Blackwell, Henry 14, 27
Black women 3, 6, 11, 14, 20, 21, 22, 51, 52-53, 56, 58, 62, 69, 167-75
Blaine, Anita McCormick 16
Blatch, Harriet Stanton 16, 24, 78
Blodgett, Katharine Burr 123
Bloomer, Amelia 33, 50, 54, 58
Blossom, Frederick A. 23
Bogart, Humphrey 137
Borden, Lizzie 71
Botta, Anne C.L. 125
Boyce, Neith 87

Bradstreet, Anne 34, 46, 127
Brooks, Romaine 133
Broun, Heywood 130
Brown, Antoinette 14, 67
Brown, Brockden 42
Bryant, Louise 81
Bryn Mawr College 81, 151, 152
Buck, Pearl S. 126, 133
Bullard, Laura Curtis 35
Burns, Lucy 83
Butler, Jessie Haver 82
Byrd, William 41

C

California, University of 195
California, University of, at Los Angeles 16
California Committee on Therapeutic Abortion 208
Cannon, Annie Jump 123
Caraway, Hattie 114
Careers. See Women in the Labor Force
Carreno, Teresa 141
Carson, Rachel 29, 121
Cassatt, Mary 126, 133, 134
Cather, Willa 16, 66, 126, 130, 133
Catholic Church on birth control 203, 208, 210
Catholic Worker's Movement 90, 94
Catt, Carrie Chapman 14, 16, 66, 86
Chandler, Elizabeth 16
Chase, Mary Ellen 150
Chavigny, William Henry 53
Chestnut, Mary Boykin 74
Chicago, Judy 127
Chicago, University of 16
Chicago Art Institute 133
Chicago Historical Society 16
Chicago Women in Broadcasting 16
Chicago Women's Trade Union League 77-78
Child, Lydia Maria 35, 51, 58, 61-62, 63, 70
Child care 4, 99, 225-28
Chisholm, Shirley 172
Chopin, Kate 133
Christian Science Church 14, 70, 71

Claflin, Tenn. 64, 74
Claremont Graduate School 17
Clarke, E.H. 67
Clay, Annie 81
Clay, Cassius M. 81
Clay, Laura 81
Clay, Mary B. 81
Clay, Virginia Turnstall 74
Clergy Consultation on Abortion 204
Coleman, Anne Raney 55
Colorado, University of, Library 17
Communist party 112
Conference for Women in Public Life
   (1972) 117
Congressional Union 83
Connecticut College Library 15
Constantia. See Sargent, Judith
   Murray
Contraception. See Birth control
Coolidge, Mary Roberts 16
Cornell, Katharine 140
Cornell University 15, 150
Craft, Ellen 56
Crandall, Prudence 53
Crime. See Female crime
Crosby, Fanny 134

**D**

Daniel, Margaret Truman 16
Dare, Virginia 241
Darwin, Charles 62
Daughters of Bilitis 25
Daughters of the American Revolution
   16, 17
Davis, Angela 116, 169
Davis, Bette 138
Davis, Varina Howell 74
Day, Dorothy 35, 90, 94
de Ford, Miriam Allen 82
Deland, Margaret 127
Delano, Jane Arminda 119
Dell, Floyd 87
Deutsch, Helen 191
Dewson, Mary Williams 15
Dickinson, Anna Elizabeth 14
Dickinson, Emily 15, 30
Didion, Joan 134
Divorce 6, 7, 9, 70, 87, 213-19
Dix, Dorothea L. 29, 50, 56
Dodge, Grace H. 66, 240

Douglas, Helen Gahagan 16
Dressler, Marie 138
Du Bois, W.E.B. 175
Duke University 17
Dulles, Allen 238
Dulles, Eleanor Lansing 237
Dulles, John Foster 238
Duncan, Isadora 79, 142
Dworkin, Andrea 241

**E**

Eastman, Crystal 80, 87, 108
Eastman, Elaine Goodale 65
Eastman, Max 80, 87
Eddy, Mary Baker 14, 70
Eells, Myra Fairbanks 52
Eisenhower, Julie Nixon 112
Ella Strong Denison Library (Scryps
   College) 17
Emerson, Ralph Waldo 53
Equality League for Self-Supporting
   Women 78
Equal Rights Amendment 5, 111, 112,
   116, 117
Erikson, Erik 121
Essex Institute 15
Everleigh, Ada 188
Everleigh, Minna 188

**F**

Farnham, Eliza Woodson 52
Farr, Wanda K. 123
Female crime 40, 71, 177-79
Feminist thought 101-6
Fenwick, Millicent 240
Ferber, Edna 127
Fiske, Minnie Maddern 137
Fitzgerald, F. Scott 127
Fitzgerald, Zelda 127
Flynn, Elizabeth Gurley 113
Fonda, Jane 142
Forten, Charlotte. See Grimke,
   Charlotte Forten
Franklin, Aretha 140
Franklin, Rosalind 122
Franklin D. Roosevelt Library 15
Freedmans Bureau 61
Freidan, Betty 13
Fremont, Jessie Benton 16

# Subject Index

French, Alice  16, 131
Freud, Sigmund  108, 110, 191
Fritchie, Barbara  34
Fuller, Margaret  15, 29, 30, 31, 38,
      45, 51, 52, 53, 58, 59, 150
Furies, the  107

## G

Gale, Zona  16, 24
Garden, Mary  138
Garland, Judy  138
General Federation of Women's Clubs
      23
Geneva College  122
Gerstenberg, Alice  16
Getchell, Margaret Swain  157
Gibow, Ruth  130
Gibson, Althea  145
Gilbreth, Lillian Moller  123
Gilman, Charlotte Perkins  16, 24,
      31, 35, 79, 82, 239
Gish, Lillian  141
Glasgow, Ellen  17, 128
Glaspell, Susan  87
GODEY'S LADY'S BOOK  53
Godwin, William  42
Goldman, Emma  79, 89, 82-83,
      108, 241
Gordon, Ruth  139
Graham, Katharine  112
Graham, Martha  141
Gratz, Rebecca  14, 15
Gray, Mary Augusta Dix  52
Greenwood, Grace  58
Grimke, Angelina  16, 35, 49, 56
Grimke, Charlotte Forten  56, 168
Grimke, Sarah  16, 31, 35, 49, 56
Guiney, Louise Imogen  126, 128

## H

Hale, Sarah Josepha  53
Hall, William B.  61
Hamer, Fannie Lou  172
Hamilton, Alice  14, 123
Hamilton, Edith  14, 158
Hamilton, Florence Jaffray  14
Harland, Hester  16
Harper, Ida Husted  14
Harry S. Truman Library  16

Hartford Female Seminary  151
Hauk, Minnie  139
Haviland, Laura S.  67
Hawaii, University of  149
Hayes, Helen  139
Health of Women  57, 206, 209
Heilbrun, Carolyn  197
Hellman, Lillian  129
Henry, Alice  25
Henry E. Huntington Library  16
Henry Street Settlement House  15, 88
Hentz, Caroline Lee Whiting  17
Hepburn, Katharine  139, 142
Herstein, Lillian  16
Hickok, Lorena  15
Hispanic-American women  2, 172, 173
Hubbard, Bela  16
Hull House  15, 29, 77, 78, 80, 89
Hutchinson, Anne  29, 31, 33, 34, 40
Hyman, Libbie Henrietta  123
Hockley, E. Azalia  138
Holiday, Billie  140
Holmes, Emma  67
Holtzman, Elizabeth  112, 240
Homer, Louise Dilworth Beatty  139
Hoover, Lou Henry  16
Houthton Library (Harvard)  15
Howard University  170
Howe, Julia Ward  14, 15, 34, 51,
      67, 70

## I

Illinois, University of,--Circle Campus
      15
Illinois Women's Political Caucus  16
Indian women  168, 169, 171, 174
Indigent Widows and Single Women's
      Society  15
Italian-American women  169, 172
International Ladies Garment Workers
      164
International Woman's Congress (1900)
      87

## J

James, Ada L.  16
Jewett, Sarah Orne  15, 35, 129, 131
Jewish women  2, 15, 167, 169, 170,
      171, 173

Jackson, Mahalia 140
Jacobi, Mary Putnam 119
John F. Kennedy Library 15
Johnson, Jemima 34
Johnson, Virginia 196
Jones, Beverly W. 61
Jones, Mary Harris 35, 37, 81, 84
Joplin, Janis 138
Jordan, Barbara 112
Junkin, Margaret 17

K

Kelley, Florence 78
Keller, Helen 84, 240
Kellogg, Clara Louise 140
Kemble, Frances A. 55
Kennedy, John F. 99
Kennedy, Rose 114
Kettler, Ernestine Hara 82
King, Billie Jean 146
King, Grace Elizabeth 17
King, Martin Luther 170-71
Kinsey, Alfred 195, 198, 200, 201
Kohut, Rebecca 171
Kreps, Juanita 240

L

La Follette, Suzanne 31
Laing, R.D. 191
Lazarus, Emma 15, 170
League of Women Voters 14, 17, 86, 93
Lee, Jarene 56
Lee, Mabel 146
Leigh, Vivian 138
Lesbianism 25, 26, 105, 133, 179, 195, 196, 197, 198, 199, 200, 201, 202, 238, 239, 244
LIBERATOR (periodical) 80
Library of Congress 14
Lindbergh, Anne Morrow 93, 94
Little, Joan 115
Livermore, Mary Rich 15, 34, 69, 70
Lockwood, Belva 15
London Anti-Slavery Convention (1840) 87
Louisiana State University 17
Lowell, Amy 15, 127, 133

Lowell, James Russell 53, 134
Lowell, Maria White 134
Luhan, Mabel Dodge 130, 133
Lutz, Alma 15
Lyon, Mary 30, 54, 150

M

McBride, Mary Margaret 140
McCarthy, Abigail 115
McCarthy, Eugene 115
McCarthy, Mary 130, 134
McClure, William 51
McCord, Louisa 58
McCormick, Edith Rockefeller 133
McCormick, Nancy (Nettie) Fowler 16
McCullers, Carson 127
McGovern, Eleanor 115
McGovern, George 115
MacLaine, Shirley 142
McLuhan, Marshall 197
Madison, Dolley 17, 34, 37
Marriage 44, 45, 46, 49, 50, 54, 57, 79, 213-19
Marriott Library (University of Utah) 17
Marsh, Edwin T. 61
Marx, Karl 108, 110
Mason, Alice Trumbull 132
Massachusetts Institute of Technology 119
Masters, William H. 196
Masturbation 64
Mather, Cotton 51
Maverick, Mary A. 57
May, Catharine Dean Barnes 17
Mead, Margaret 29, 123, 158
Media Women's Association 159
Men 8, 229-30, 237, 239
Menopause 204
Menstruation 69, 204, 207
Methodist Church 72
Metropolitan Museum of Art 42
Midwest Women's Historical Collection 15
Mill, John Stewart 31
Millay, Edna St. Vincent 127, 128, 129, 131
Miller, Harriet Mann 14
Miner, Myrtilla 14, 172

# Subject Index

Minnesota, University of 16
Minnesota Historical Society 16
Minnesota League of Women Voters
16
Minnesota Woman Suffrage Association
16
Mississippi Department of Archives
and History 17
Mitchell, Maria 15, 120, 123
Mitchell, Martha 112
Moise, Penina 131
MONTHLY REVIEW 107
Monroe, Harriet 16, 131, 133, 135
Monroe, Marilyn 140, 142
Moore, Grace 141
More, Hannah 44
Mormons and women 35, 70, 73-74,
75
Moses, Anna Mary Robertson 130,
131
Mosher, Eliza 16
Moskowitz, Belle 15
Motherhood 221-24, 242
Mott, Lucretia Coffin 15, 34, 54
Mount Holyoke College 54, 150, 152
MS/MAGAZINE 103
Murray, Mary Lindley 34

## N

Nashoba Community 70
Nathan, Maud 240
National American Women's Suffrage
Association 86
National Archives for Black Women's
History 15
National Association for the Advance-
ment of Colored People 86
National Association of Social Workers
16
National Black Feminist Organization
16
National Committee on Maternal
Health 204
National Consumers League 93
National Council for Jewish Women
171
National Council of Catholic Women
116
National Council of Negro Women 15

National Organization of Women 14,
34, 97, 218
National Woman's party 14
National Women's Studies Association
28
National Women's Trade Union League
80
Nestor, Agnes 16
Nevelson, Louise 128, 132
Nexus 216
Newberry Library 16
New York Infirmary 119
New York Public Library 15
NEW YORK TIMES MAGAZINE 103
New York Women's Trade Union
League 164
Nixon, Patricia 115
Noble, Elaine 240
Nordica, Lillian 139, 140
Norris, Kathleen 15
North Carolina, University of 17
Northwestern University Library 16
Norton, Eleanor Holmes 240

## O

Oberlin College 95, 110, 168, 174
O'Connor, Flannery 134
Odlum, Hortense 158
Ohio Historical Society 15
O'Keefe, Georgia 128, 241
Olson, Tillie 132, 241
Oneida Colony 70
Oregon, University of, Library 17
O'Reilly, Leonora 240
Otis, James 39
Ovington, Mary White 86
Owen, Robert Dale 57

## P

Paley, Gracie 241
Palmer, Alice Freeman 81, 151
Palmer, Bertha Honore 133
Parker, Dorothy 130
Parton, Dolly 141
Patti, Adeline 140
Paul, Alice 16, 83
Peabody, Elizabeth Palmer 14, 50,
81, 151

Peabody, Mary 14
Peabody, Sophia 14
Pennington, Mary Engle 123
Pennsylvania Historical Society 15
Phelps, Almira Hart Lincoln 119
Philleo, Prudence Crandall 15
Pickford, Mary 142
Picon, Molly 15
Pinckney, Eliza 45
Pinkham, Lydia 123
Pitcher, Milly 34
Plath, Sylvia 126, 132
Princeton University 15
Pringle, Elizabeth Allston 86
Prostitution 64, 83, 86-87, 103,
    181, 185-88
    bibliographies on 1, 2
    on the frontier 62
    as a means for survival 85
Pryor, Sara 16
Psychology of women 189-93

Q

Quakers 43

R

Radcliffe College 152
Rainey, Ma 140
Rank, Ida 87
Rankin, Jeanette 16, 17, 113
Rape 9, 181, 182, 183
Rappite Community 70
Reagan, Nancy 242
Red Cross 119
Reed, John 81
Richards, Ellen H. 123
Richards, Linda 122
Rider-Kelsey, Corinne 142
Ripley, Sarah Alden 30
Robins, Margaret Dreier 25, 80
Rodman, Henrietta 87
Roosevelt, Anna Eleanor 15
Roosevelt, Eleanor 15, 20, 31, 93,
    95, 99, 114, 115, 116
Roosevelt, Franklin 93
Ross, Betsy 34
Rowson, Susanna 132
Royce, Josiah 72
Royce, Sarah 72

Rudolph, Wilma 147
Rutgers University 117

S

Sabin, Florence Reva 123
Sacajawea 66
St. Denis, Ruth 29, 142
Sanford, Mollie Dorsey 72
Sanger, Margaret 14, 23, 27, 29,
    31, 205, 206, 207, 209
Saperstein, Esther 16
Sargent, Judith Murray 43
Schiff, Dorothy 158
Schlesinger Library 1, 13-14
Schneiderman, Rose 164, 240
Schumann-Heink, Ernestine 140
Sedgewick, Catherine Maria 50
Seibert, Florence B. 123
Sekaquapteria, Helen 174
Seneca Falls Convention 32, 35, 54,
    87
Senter, Laura Ellsworth 82
Sewall, Samuel 46
Sex Information and Education Council
    196
Sexism 40, 101, 103, 104, 105, 122,
    152, 153, 160
Sex roles 28, 31, 38, 104, 106, 189
    advertising and media stereotyping
        of 4, 31
    bibliography on 1
    Margaret Mead on 35
    stereotyping of 189
    of women in the late Victorian era
        96
Sexton, Anne 133
Sexual harassment 182
Sexuality of women 36, 39, 45, 49,
    57, 64, 65, 67, 68, 72, 74, 85,
    103, 104, 195-202
Shinn, Millicent W. 16
Shippen, Nancy 46
Shaw, Anna Howard 72
Shawn, Ted 141
Signourney, Lydia Hunt 35
Sloane, Deborah 112
Smith, Alfred E. 15
Smith, Bessie 137, 140
Smith, Gerrit 15
Smith, Margaret Chase 16, 37

# Subject Index

Smith, Maurine 16
Smith, Sarah White 52
Smith College 150, 152
Socialist-feminism 107-10
Socialist Worker's party 109
Society for Cutting Up Men 106
Society for the Emancipation of the American Male 234
Sophia Smith Library 2, 9, 14
Southworth, Emma D.E.N. 126
Spalding, Eliza Hart 52
Spanish-American women 2
Spencer, Anna Garland 15
Spencer, Cornelia Phillips 17
Spencer, Herbert 62
Spencer, Lilly Martin 125
Stanford, Sally 188
Stanford Business School 156
Stanford University Library 16
Stanton, Elizabeth Cady 14, 15, 33, 35, 51, 70, 72, 87, 235
Starr, Ella Gates 14
State Historical Society of Wisconsin 16
Stein, Gertrude 16, 131, 134
Stettheimer, Florine 134
Stevenson, Adlai 95
Stewart, Elinore Pruitt 73
Stewart, Maria W. 174
Stiebling, Hazel K. 123
Stone, Lucy 14, 15, 27, 50, 67, 87
Stowe, Harriet Beecher 30, 34, 35, 58, 135
Strong, Anna Louise 17, 35, 95
Suffrage 4, 27, 52, 57, 69, 72, 81, 82, 83, 85, 86, 237
Sullivan, Annie 240
Swain, Clara 123
Swallow, Ellen 119
Swanson, Gloria 142
Swarthmore College Library 15
Swisshelm, Jane 58
SYNTHESIS 108
Syracuse University Library 15

## T

Tarbell, Ida 14
Tarry, Ellen 174
Terrell, Mary Church 174
Thanet, Octave. See French, Alice

Thomas, M. Carey 81, 150, 151,
Thompson, Dorothy 158
Thurber, James 130
Thursby, Emma 139
Thygeson, Sylvie 82
Tietjens, Eunice 16
Tillson, Christiana Holmes 58
Toklas, Alice B. 16, 134
Tracy, Spencer 138
Transsexualism 199
Trollope, Anthony 58
Trollope, Frances M. 58
Troy Female Seminary 69
Truman, Bess Wallace 16
Truth, Sojourner 15, 56, 58, 172
Tubman, Harriet 35, 51, 56
Tulane University 17

## U

Underwood, Agness 160
United Daughters of the Confederacy 17, 25

## V

Van Valkenberg, Ellen 16
Vassar College 15, 119, 123, 152
VILLAGE VOICE, THE 103
Virginia, University of 17
Visiting Nurses Association 16

## W

Wald, Lillian D. 15, 88, 108, 240
Walker, Mary Richardson 52
Warhol, Andy 106
Warren, Mercy Otis 29, 39, 41
Washington, Booker T. 175
Washington, Martha 34, 49
Washington, University of 17
Washington State University 17
Watergate 112
Waters, Ethel 175
Weisbord, Vera Buch 96
Welch, Raquel 142
Wellesley College 81, 151, 152
Wells, Ida B. 172, 175
Welty, Eudora 134
West, Mae 143

Western Reserve Historical Society 15
Western Reserve College 123
Wharton, Edith 130, 135
Wharton School of Business 163
Wheatley, Phillis 135
Whitman, Narcissa Prentiss 52
Whitney, Gertrude Vanderbilt 81
Wife battering 181, 182, 183, 237, 238, 244
Wiggins, Kate Douglas 16
Wilcox, Ella Wheeler 16
Willard, Emma Hart 29, 69
Willard, Frances 30, 64, 70
Williams, Fannie Barrier 172
Wisconsin Women's Suffrage Association 16
Witchcraft 40, 46
Wollstonecraft, Mary 31, 33, 44, 45
Woman's Medical College 119
Women
  and the arts 125-35
  bibliographies of 1-11
  biographical directories of 19-22
  in business 155-60
  in colonial America 7, 39-47
  and education 1, 8, 11, 149-54
  in Europe 6
  general history of 23-28
  in Illinois 20
  in Jacksonian America 49-59
  in the labor force 1, 3, 4, 10, 28, 29, 30, 52, 68, 71, 72, 73, 79, 83, 91, 92, 93, 94, 161-65
  manuscript collections of 13-17
  in medicine 2, 14, 19, 119-24
  in Minnesota 21
  in performing arts 9, 21, 137-43
  in politics 10, 19, 111-17
  in the professions 155-60
  in the Progressive era 77-88
  in science 19, 119-24
  in South Carolina 21
  in sports 145-47
  in Victorian America 61-75
Women's Bureau, Department of Labor 95
Women's Christian Temperance Union 17, 64, 68
Women's Dental Association 15
Women's Equity Action League 14
Women's International League for Peace and Freedom 15, 17, 218
Women's Joint Congressional Committee 93
Women's party 84
Women's Peace party 16
Women's Republican Patriotic League 17
Women's studies 7
Women's Trade Union League 14, 93
Woodhull, Victoria 15, 61, 64, 74
Woollcott, Alexander 130
World Health Organization 122
Wright, Frances 33, 57, 70
Wyatt, Edith 16
Wylie, Elinor 129

Y

Yale University, women students at 152
Young, Ann Eliza Webb 73
Young, Brigham 73
Young, Ella Flagg 243
Young Womens Christian Association 170
Youth Against Fascism and War 107
Young Womens Christian Association 66, 85

Z

Zaharias, Mildred Didrikson 147